*Business and Banking*

A volume in the series

*Cornell Studies in Political Economy*

EDITED BY PETER J. KATZENSTEIN

A full list of titles in the series appears at the end of the book.

# Business and Banking

## POLITICAL CHANGE AND ECONOMIC INTEGRATION IN WESTERN EUROPE

### PAULETTE KURZER

CORNELL UNIVERSITY PRESS

*Ithaca and London*

First published 1993 by Cornell University Press.

International Standard Book Number 0-8014-2798-3
Library of Congress Catalog Card Number 92-56780
Printed in the United States of America
*Librarians: Library of Congress cataloging information*
*appears on the last page of the book.*

⊗ The paper in this book meets the minimum requirements
of the American National Standard for Information Sciences—
Permanence of Paper for Printed Library Materials, ANSI Z39.48-1984.

# Contents

# Tables

# *Preface*

In this book I address several questions that go to the heart of the political economy debate, a debate that centers on variations in political and social institutions and their implications for economic policy-making. The book focuses on the fate of tripartite distributive arrangements between business, labor, and government in the 1980s in four small European democracies—Austria, Sweden, Belgium, and the Netherlands. I selected these four countries because they raise the following questions: Why did consensual labor-business exchanges end at least a decade earlier in Belgium and the Netherlands than in Austria and Sweden? Why have cracks begun to appear in the Swedish model and in Austria's social partnership? Do Keynesian demand management and tripartite deliberations still have a future in Europe? This book provides an answer to these questions.

Each of the four countries legislated numerous entitlement programs, instituted redistributive incomes policies to narrow pay differences among different groups of skilled and unskilled employees, and fostered consensual tripartite exchanges between labor, business, and government. These arrangements were explicitly founded on a three-way exchange in which labor agreed to no-strike provisions, employers agreed to share the fruits of increased productivity with labor, and governments pledged to maintain full employment and to guarantee an equitable distribution of economic growth.

By the early 1980s in Belgium and the Netherlands economywide bargaining had fallen apart; company-level negotiations deliberately promoted greater wage differentials; and many entitlement programs were under attack. Center-right governments spoke of removing market rigidities and of bolstering corporate profits. At the same time, similar social arrangements in Sweden and Austria did not experience equally drastic transformations.

I attribute ideological, political, and policy changes in the Netherlands and Belgium indirectly to changes in the international economy. The altered structure of the international economy offers business and finance many new opportunities to invest in financial techniques and instruments abroad and at home. The results have been a shift away from productive investments and the de-coupling of growth from investments. In addition, as business and finance became more mobile, their power resources increased, and those of labor decreased. Although each of the four countries constructed a variant of class compromise, the greater mobility of capital and deepening financial integration corroded social concertation, the system by which labor participated in and influenced national policy, in Belgium and the Netherlands first. Austria and Sweden were able to withstand the external pressures of financial integration and capital mobility despite the fact that they too are small trade-dependent European nations.

How do we explain these differences? To solve the puzzle, I explore the connections of each country to the international political economy, focusing on these variables: the historic and present preferences of business and finance, central bank independence, and foreign economic policy. My main contention is that because of a mixture of business and finance preferences, administrative rulings, and protectionist foreign economic policies, Austria and Sweden experienced delay in the augmentation of the power resources of capital. I emphasize *delay* because similar social arrangements in the two countries are moving parallel to those in Belgium and the Netherlands. In contrast to Belgium and the Netherlands, however, Austria and Sweden entertained qualitatively different links to global markets and the international economy until the late 1980s. Because of the greater domestic orientation of banks and business and nonmembership in the European Community, their government had a far greater capacity to implement policies that fostered tripartite exchanges and to steer economic adjustments than the governments of Belgium and the Netherlands had.

In this book I criticize the major theories on class compromises for not giving sufficient attention to the growing trend toward transnationalization. Because of international interdependence, governments have lost the ability to carve out national economic strategies and to sustain social accords. Labor unions might be ready to concede dozens of points, but companies and employers are unlikely to base their corporate strategies and investments on falling labor costs and the promise of harmonious labor relations. Given these conditions, tripartite deliberations and central wage bargaining are bound to fall apart. They

cannot be reconstituted regardless of the means or willpower mar-
shaled by left-wing governments or the leaders of trade union confederations.

In Chapter 1, which provides a theoretical introduction to the book,
I elaborate these points. In Chapter 2, I summarize the main features
of tripartite arrangements in the four countries and explain how business and banking related to social concertation in the 1960s. In the
second part of the book I begin with a discussion of the economic
changes wrought by the turmoil in world trade and monetary relations
after 1974. I also cover the reaction of the political establishment in
each of the four countries to economic stagnation and discuss the shift
in thinking and policy action in Belgium and the Netherlands. In
Chapters 4 and 5, I analyze the growing attraction of global diversification for business and its impact on tripartite arrangements. These two
chapters are slightly different from the others, for I have paired Austria with Belgium and Sweden with the Netherlands to take into consideration the different evolution of business structures in the four countries. Holding companies dominate Austria's and Belgium's business
communities, whereas transnational firms characterize those in
Sweden and the Netherlands.

In Chapter 6, I compare the relations between the financial community, central bank independence, and tripartite institutions in Belgium
and the Netherlands. In Chapter 7, I explore the same set of variables
in Austria and Sweden and underscore the importance of central banks
as political institutions with different policy agendas.

In the third part, I investigate how membership in the European
Community has reinforced the outward identification of business and
finance in the Low Countries (I do not include Luxembourg in this
study) and has therefore indirectly contributed to the collapse of social
concertation. In Chapter 8, I review the debates on European Community membership and the decisions in Austria and Sweden not to join.
In Chapter 9, I weigh the impact of regional integration and, in particular, the influence of the European Monetary System on the decision-
making process of central banks and on the internationalization of
business.

During the years this book was in progress I have incurred many
debts to many individuals. Most of the field work for this comparative
study was completed in the summers of 1987, 1988, and 1989. I thank
trade unionists, central bankers, and business leaders for their time in
helping me understand the politics of their countries. In the United
States, more people than I can possibly mention have spent time and
effort answering my questions and supplying me with materials. I sin-

gle out those people who have read either a substantial part or the entire manuscript: Christopher Allen, Peter Hall, Liesbet Hooghe, Renate Matsson, Reinhard Neck, Anton Pelinka, Jonas Pontusson, Herman Schwartz, and Steven Wolinetz. I also join the list of scholars who have acknowledged the invaluable editorial and analytical skills of Peter Katzenstein. His comments and suggestions have greatly sharpened my thinking on the topic and have made this a better book. I am also indebted to Miriam Avins for her excellent editing and for improving the readability of the book.

I received financial support from various sources. A grant from the Bicentennial Swedish-American Foundation permitted me to visit Sweden. Eduard Hochreiter of the Austrian central bank arranged for my extended stay in Vienna. My thanks also to the Babson College Board of Research, which generously underwrote two trips to Europe and kindly supplied additional research funds at a later stage. Victoria Delbona and Beverly Balconi did a marvelous job typing the revisions. Earlier versions of parts of the argument were published as "Unemployment in Open Economies: The Impact of Trade, Finance, and European Integration," in *Comparative Political Studies* 24 (1991), and "Internationalization of Business and Domestic Class Compromises," in *West European Politics* 4 (1991).

Most of all, I am grateful to my husband, David Spiro, without whose love and faith this book never would have been completed.

PAULETTE KURZER

*Somerville, Massachusetts*

# Abbreviations

| | |
|---|---|
| BWK | Austrian Federal Chamber of Commerce (Bundeswirtschaftskammer) |
| CVP/PSC | Social Christian Party (Christelijke Volkspartij/Parti Social Chrétien) |
| DNB | Central Bank of the Netherlands (De Nederlandsche Bank) |
| FEB/VBO | Federation of Belgian Enterprises (Fédération des Entreprises Belges/Verbond van Belgische Ondernemingen) |
| LO | Swedish Trade Union Confederation (Landorganisationen i Sverige) |
| NBB/BNB | National Bank of Belgium (Nationale Bank van België/Banque Nationale de Belgique) |
| OeNB | National Bank of Austria (Oesterreichische Nationalbank) |
| ÖIAG | Austrian Corporation for Industrial Administration (Österreichischen Industrieverwaltungs Aktiengesellschaft) |
| ÖVP | Austrian People's Party (Österreichische Volkspartei) |
| PvdA | Dutch Labor Party (Partij van de Arbeid) |
| SAP | Swedish Social Democratic Party (Socialdemokratiska Arbetareparti) |
| SAF | Swedish Federation of Employers (Svenska Arbetsgivareföreningen) |
| SPÖ | Austrian Socialist Party (Sozialistische Partei Österreich) |
| VF | Swedish Association of Engineering Companies (Verkstadsföreningen) |
| VNO | Association of Dutch Enterprises (Vereniging Nederlandse Ondernemingen) |

PART I

# INTRODUCTION

CHAPTER ONE

# *The Theoretical Framework*

The British Labour party's fourth consecutive defeat, in the general election of April 1992, prompts many to observe that contemporary politics in Britain and other European countries have at least one thing in common: everywhere the Left is in trouble. In Austria, Belgium, and the Netherlands, three of the four countries I study in this book, social democratic parties are again or still in power, but they simply follow the cues and programs of right-wing or conservative parties and have no alternatives to proposals to shrink the public sector, privatize social services, and deregulate labor markets. Although social democrats had ruled Sweden for all but six years since the 1930s, the party has been out of power since it lost the 1991 election.

The repeated disappointments in elections and in the governing performances of European social democratic parties have been explained in many ways. Hypotheses range from the view, at one extreme, that the failures are the result of paralysis within the parties to the view, at the other extreme, that they are the consequence of systemic alterations in the socioeconomic environment of advanced capitalist states.[1] Some of the more popular explanations focus on technological innovations in the workplace and the disappearance of blue-collar jobs

---

[1] For a review of the debate on the decline of the Left, consult Thomas A. Koelble, "Social Democracy between Structure and Choice," *Comparative Politics* 24 (1992): 359–72. See also Adam Przeworski and John Sprague, *Paper Stones: The History of Electoral Socialism* (Chicago: University of Chicago Press, 1986); and Frances Fox Piven, "The Decline of Labor Parties: An Overview," in *Labor Parties in Postindustrial Societies*, ed. Frances Fox Piven (New York: Oxford University Press, 1992), 1–19. For a more optimistic evaluation, cf. Wolfgang Merkel, "After the Golden Age: Is Social Democracy Doomed to Decline?" in *The Crisis of Socialism in Europe*, ed. Christiane Lemke and Gary Marks (Durham, N.C.: Duke University Press, 1992), 136–70.

*3*

in the 1970s. De-industrialization and the reshaping of the workplace, scholars claim, undermine internal labor cohesion and erode the organizational strength of trade union federations. Because staunch trade unionists are also steady social democratic voters, the loss of union members and growing schisms between different categories of workers cripple labor parties.[2] Interorganizational conflicts caused by growing diversity of workplace experiences and market position also obstruct economywide wage bargaining and national deliberations that could result in central accords.

A second approach traces the fall of leftist parties to the crisis of Keynesianism or demand management in the 1970s. Public-sector expansion was a powerful mechanism for counteracting downward business cycles. Leftist parties used budget financing to stimulate investments and maintain full employment in periods of international recessions and decline of industrial output. The disappearance of market steering capabilities, which are crucial for realizing campaign pledges, for "humanizing" capitalism, and for supplying material welfare, erodes the popularity of social democratic parties.[3] In addition, many concerns of younger voters focus on nontraditional issues related to the quality of life. The ideological discourse of socialist and social democratic parties are ill-suited for dealing with the protest movements that have risen because of mounting concern about environmental degradation, bureaucratic inertia, and urban decay.[4] Elites from the Left have no response to demands for greater market efficiency and less administrative centralization. Nor are they able to carry on as before; they confront a large philosophical void.

I examine the troubles of the Left in Europe from a slightly different perspective. I highlight the importance of financial and monetary integration for understanding how the balance of power between labor and capital has shifted in favor of the latter. Business occupies a privileged position in capitalist societies by virtue of its control over economic resources and influence over political and social institutions. In addition to capital's normal privileges as the ultimate arbiter of a country's future economic prosperity, capital has become more mobile and transnational in the past decade. This mobility allows business and finance

[2] See, for example, Miriam Golden and Jonas Pontusson, eds., *Bargaining for Change: Union Politics in North America and Europe* (Ithaca: Cornell University Press, 1992).

[3] Fritz W. Scharpf, *Crisis and Choice in European Social Democracy* (Ithaca: Cornell University Press, 1991); Richard Rose and Guy Peters, *Can Government Go Bankrupt?* (New York: Basic Books, 1978).

[4] Russell Dalton and Manfred Kuechler, eds., *Challenging the Political Order: New Social and Political Movements in Western Democracies* (Oxford: Polity Press, 1990); and Herbert Kitschelt, "The Socialist Discourse and Party Strategy in West European Democracies," in *Crisis of Socialism in Europe*, ed. Lemke and Marks, 191–227.

*4*

to move with ease across borders into different money-making ventures and away from arrangements considered inflexible and outdated.

Social arrangements like tripartism corroded first in Belgium and the Netherlands but lasted through the 1980s in Austria and Sweden. The thesis of this book is that the mobility and structure of business, the internationalization of finance, and world market integration vary among these countries and that labor in Belgium and the Netherlands faced a more powerful adversary because of the greater mobility of capital. Ultimately, I attribute the greater sensitivity of Belgium and the Netherlands to trends in global markets to the position of the financial sector relative to other economic institutions and state agencies. Financial communities with numerous international networks supply the primary force for removing financial and capital flow barriers and strongly advocate further financial integration and greater trade liberalization. Belgium and the Netherlands have such financial institutions, but Sweden and Austria do not possess strongly international-oriented financial communities.

The disintegration of business-labor pacts has undermined working-class solidarity and class voting while the economic policy instruments of social democratic governments based on centralized wage bargaining or incomes policies lost their effectiveness and credibility. Social arrangements served many goals, among them that of instilling allegiance among workers to a leftist party and that of bridging the conflicting demands of labor and business. The delegitimation of class compromises in the eyes of employers and the public is one of the causes for the electoral and ideological decline of the Left.

The future of social democracy hangs on its ability to adapt to a new socioeconomic environment. For the Left, a new historical mission would reinvigorate its appeal to voters. But the quest for a new mission cannot succeed unless the Left comes to terms with the economic changes of the past decade. These revolutionary changes involve the liberalization of trade and finance and the emergence of new financial instruments, markets, and techniques. The importance for the Left and labor movements is that these structural changes frame the interests of capital, a framework that no longer concurs with the interests of labor or left-wing governments. Maximization of profits implies a different logic today than two decades ago. Productive investments that generate jobs and general economic prosperity are among the many forms of investments available to firms. Investments in production, however, are far more risky than investments in financial instruments, currencies, stocks, options, and bonds. Financial investments are liquid, mobile, and convertible. Their distinctive advantages for investors fostered enormous expansion of financial activities. The growth of financial and capital flows and the existence of multiple combinations of financial investments challenge not only the fundamental assumptions of organized labor but also the national jurisdiction of governments.

Although the process of globalization can be said to have begun at the time of Lenin (at the beginning of the twentieth century), the transnational nature of capital has reached its apex in the last quarter of this century. For Lenin, in *Imperialism: The Highest Stage of Capitalism* (1917), finance capital, which consisted of an amalgamation of banking capital and industry, created trusts, cartels, syndicates, and other arrangements to partition the world into spheres of influence. According to Lenin, the predicament for the Left was that national conflicts among imperialist states, which were a result of their race to claim different parts of the world, pitted colony against colony and worker against worker. International socialism fell apart under the pressure of nationalism. The international aggression that culminated in World War I destroyed the transnational working-class movement. After World War II, socialist leaders discredited the idea of resurrecting a similar movement. Trade union movements retained strong national orientations, and national political rivalries between social democratic and communist parties, both of which could claim to be the legitimate heirs of socialism, impeded transnational cooperation further.

Yet the true age of globalism occurs during the latter part of the twentieth century. Evidence of a veritable explosion of capital movements is found everywhere. Toward the end of the 1980s, short-term international financial transactions averaged about $650 billion per day—$500 million a minute—equal to forty times the amount of world trade per day.[5] The structural changes in the international economy have led to liberalization reforms even in noncapitalist countries, in part because traditional modes of government intervention are no longer effective or feasible. The loss of policy autonomy can be dated to the collapse of the Bretton Woods regime and the shift to floating exchange rates after 1973, coupled with the sudden rise in energy prices that same year, which generated fluctuating exchange rates and currency volatility. This placed new demands on countries to stabilize prices and government spending in order to counteract pressures on the exchange rate and to avoid depreciations. Policy instruments of governments which were effective during the era of price stability and fixed exchange rates were inappropriate or unproductive after 1973.

The altered monetary environment burdened small and large countries alike after 1974. Financial integration challenged the entrenched

---

[5] Jeffrey A. Frieden, "Invested Interests: The Politics of National Economic Policies in a World of Global Finance," *International Organization* 45 (1991): 428.

convictions of policy officials and the workings of domestic institutions in all European countries. For example, in an account of French policy-making, Michael Loriaux shows that inflation and instability after 1974 deprived state officials of their principal means of achieving internal monetary equilibrium. To regain control over monetary policy and to be able to stabilize currency fluctuations, the French authorities liberalized their financial institutions in 1984 and did away with the system of selective credit restrictions. After 1984, when policymakers recognized that national sovereignty was curbed in a system of capital mobility and fluctuating exchange rates, the French establishment reversed itself and called for a European central bank and fixed exchange rates.[6]

Social arrangements like consensual tripartism have not escaped unharmed. Strains on the system of social concertation are particularly apparent in the effort to arrive at tripartite accords. Governments are often obliged to assist in the formulation and implementation of social arrangements, although many independent budgetary measures that were formerly useful to foster intraclass cooperation are no longer available or practical.

Low interest rates stimulate production and investments and add jobs, but in a world of integrated financial markets and high capital mobility, independent interest rate setting is virtually out of the question. Governments that seek to stimulate capital investments by lowering interest rates have to face the unpleasant fact that a rate below rates in neighboring countries prompts a run on the currency, creating inflationary expectations and, eventually, rising interest rates. Low interest rates are only effective if corporations expect a strong consumer recovery or favorable export opportunities, in which case lowering interest rates is superfluous, since business would have increased productive investments in any event. In a similar vein, fiscal stimulation, financed through the sale of government bonds (at interest rates fixed by international markets), induces large inflows of capital which appreciate the exchange rate and raise the price of exports. Subsequently, domestic production falters as imports are cheapened by the exchange rate appreciation while demand for exports shrink.

The growth of financial activities and the availability of many different kinds of financial instruments are major stumbling blocks for governments that desire to induce an increase in production or investments or a change in prices. State officials cannot affect the relation between the expected rate of return on financial assets and capital

---

[6] Michael Loriaux, *France after Hegemony: International Change and Financial Reform* (Ithaca: Cornell University Press, 1991).

7

investments. Yet corporations invest in machinery and production only if they believe that the average rate of profit for potential capital investments exceeds the return on financial assets. Since financial assets yield faster returns and offer more flexible investments, the pace of capital accumulation may not expand even if the government formulates seemingly appropriate policies.[7]

There are ways in which the autonomy of government policy might conceivably be protected from the confines that arise from the mobility of capital. A country can issue capital and exchange rate controls in order to detach domestic capital markets from international ones. The installation of various controls, however, does not effectively arrest capital and financial outflows; many new financial instruments are specifically designed to circumvent government regulations. For example, in the early 1980s, before France had removed its capital controls, newly elected president François Mitterrand enacted an ambitious package of reforms that raised family allowances, housing allocations, pension payments, and the minimum wage. His administration also reduced the workweek, lowered the retirement age to fifty-five, and legislated other measures to combat unemployment. Keynesian reflation caused public expenditures to rise precipitously, which resulted in higher inflation and depressed investments. The financial community, expressing its lack of confidence in the course of government policies, moved funds abroad, and large capital outflows forced the government to devalue the currency three times between October 1981 and March 1983. By early 1984, austerity measures replaced reflationary fiscal policies, and President Mitterrand abandoned most of his campaign pledges.[8]

If large countries such as France were forced to cope with the altered conditions of the international political economy, countries with small open economies like Austria or Belgium were certainly unable to avoid the constraints imposed by financial interpenetration. This generalization requires one major caveat: the detrimental influence of international financial penetration has only begun to undermine the social arrangements in Austria and Sweden in the 1990s.

This last point will be examined by taking a closer look at two schools of thought which dominate the debate on the foundations of class

[7] James R. Crotty, "The Limits of Keynesian Macroeconomic Policy in the Age of the Global Marketplace," in *Instability and Change in the World Economy*, ed. Arthur MacEwan and William K. Tabb (New York: Monthly Review Press, 1989), 82–100. Robert Pringle, "Financial Markets versus Governments," in *Financial Openness and National Autonomy*, ed. Tariq Banuri and Juliet B. Schor (Oxford: Clarendon Press, 1992), 89–109.

[8] Loriaux, *France after Hegemony*, 214–20; Peter Hall, *Governing the Economy: The Politics of State Intervention in Britain and France* (New York: Oxford University Press, 1986), 193–201.

compromises and on the distinctiveness of policy-making in small states. The first paradigm is the power resource model, which has shaped our thinking on why advanced industrialized states display striking variations in social spending patterns, economic performance, level of industrial conflicts, and the existence or not of corporatist interest representation. The second paradigm, which I call the small-state argument and which complements the first, holds that collective action and domestic institutions in small states acquire unique features to cope with their sensitivity to external shocks. Neither theory is able to explain the difference in timing of the trials in social concertation in Belgium and the Netherlands, on the one hand, and in Sweden and Austria, on the other. Both approaches fail to draw attention to the power resources of capital, whose influence is augmented because of its international alliances and connections, and both neglect to incorporate in their theoretical frameworks the existing constraints on the policy-making capacities of national governments.

## The Power Resource Model

An elegant formulation of the power resource model is presented by Adam Przeworski and Michael Wallerstein.[9] They address two interrelated questions: Why do business and labor form class compromises? And why are these arrangements fundamentally unstable?

Class compromises are only likely to emerge if workers are reasonably certain that their future wages will increase as a consequence of their employers' current profits. Workers will agree to capital accumulation by their employers as long as they are promised an improvement in their own welfare at some future period. Indeed, in the post-war period in Europe, it was normal to link wage rates to productivity gains either explicitly or informally. In return, leaders of the trade

---

[9] Adam Przeworski and Michael Wallerstein, "The Structure of Class Conflict in Democratic Capitalist Societies," *American Political Science Review* 76 (1982): 215–38; Peter Lange, "Unions, Workers, and Wage Regulation: The Rational Bases of Consent," in *Order and Conflict in Contemporary Capitalism*, ed. John Goldthorpe (Oxford: Clarendon Press, 1984); and Kerry Schott, *Policy, Power and Order: The Persistence of Economic Problems in Capitalist Economies* (New Haven, Conn.: Yale University Press, 1984); Alex Hicks and Duane Swank, "Welfare Expansion Revisited: Policy Routines and Their Mediation by Party, Class, and Crisis, 1957–1982," *European Journal of Political Research* 17 (1989): 401–30; Peter Lange and Geoffrey Garrett, "The Politics of Growth: Strategic Interaction and Economic Performance in the Advanced Industrialized Countries," *Journal of Politics* 47 (1985): 792–812; David R. Cameron, "Social Democracy, Corporatism, Labor Quiescence, and the Representation of Economic Interest in Advanced Capitalist Society," in *Order and Conflict*, ed. Goldthorpe, 143–79; Walter Korpi and Michael Shalev, "Strikes, Industrial Relations and Class Conflict in Capitalist Societies," *British Journal of Sociology* 30 (1979): 164–87.

union confederation would agree to settle disputes amicably and accept the appropriation of profits by capitalists.

Business must also perceive an advantage in the political regulation of class conflict. Recurrent industrial unrest or sustained strikes convince business to seek an accommodation with workers as long as business itself has created the necessary organizational structures to enter into central bargaining and to implement agreements. Although a united business community might consider defeating a militant labor movement through lockouts or juridical persecution, business generally prefers to avoid a lengthy contest with an equally unified working class. When workers are not strongly united, business does not need political mechanisms to resolve wage or industrial issues. If business is not united and workers are, then labor need not seek an accommodation with capital and can rely on its allies or organizational strength to obtain concessions.

Class compromise theorists such as Przeworski and Wallerstein realize that class compromises are fundamentally unstable. Labor and business constantly reassess their opportunities and gains to take into account new information and changing expectations. Either labor or business may have second thoughts about continuing to support class compromises.

Governments, particularly those with strong ties to the trade union movement, have taken responsibility for ensuring the stability of class compromises. The presence of a leftist government makes business more inclined to cooperate in order to avert open confrontations during a period when state agencies are controlled by politicians sympathetic to the working class.[10]

In the 1960s, in many countries, governments allayed some of labor's concerns about whether a political exchange would last by offering to narrow income inequalities and to reduce job insecurity. Workers knew that, even if business exploited the withheld wages for purposes other than reinvestments, they could still expect to see material improvements in the future. Full employment promises would be met by governments that rapidly expanded public services and hired large numbers of public employees. Left-wing governments were especially efficient in translating public spending into new jobs.[11]

---

[10] Walter Korpi, *The Democratic Class Struggle* (Boston: Routledge and Kegan Paul, 1983); and M. G. Schmidt, "The Welfare State and the Economy in Periods of Economic Crisis: A Study of Twenty-three OECD Nations," *European Journal of Political Research* 11 (1983): 1–26.

[11] Thomas R. Cusack, Ton Notermans, and Martin Rein, "Political-Economic Aspects of Public Employment," *European Journal of Political Research* 17 (1989): 471–500; Manfred G. Schmidt, "The Role of the Parties in Shaping Macroeconomic Policy," in *The Impact of Parties: Politics and Policies in Democratic Capitalist States*, ed. Francis G. Castles (Beverly Hills, Calif.: Sage, 1982), 97–126.

For Przeworski and Wallerstein, the structural conditions of capitalist organization of production define the range or form of possible class compromises. The appropriation of profits by capitalists is a necessary but insufficient condition for an improvement of the material welfare of workers. A class compromise is therefore only feasible if workers are reasonably certain that future wages will increase as a consequence of current profits.[12]

This idealized construction of class compromise no longer works once the concept of capital mobility and financial integration is introduced. Because political trade-offs depend on the expectations of workers that current sacrifices yield higher earnings and more jobs later, the high mobility of capital heightens the sense of insecurity among workers. Labor now uses a different scale to weigh the importance of immediate gains against expected gains. It makes more sense to demand the maximum in the present because business is not bound morally or economically to the concessions of labor. The management boards of transnational corporations whose headquarters are located in their parent countries consider many different factors in deciding where to invest. Workers in a multinationalized economy can be certain that globalized firms invest wherever the conditions are most auspicious and that wage moderation by itself does not constitute an irresistibly tempting incentive. In today's international political economy, the decision to press ahead with foreign direct investments is informed by such intangibles as proximity to import markets to cut off local competition, savings on transport and storage, and the ability to participate in cross-national ventures. None of these considerations is related to wage costs. Cognizant of their predicament, workers become more reluctant to concede anything if capital does not meet its part of the bargain.

In fact, capitalists with international links do not need consensual deliberations to obtain concessions from workers or governments, which are conveniently divided into separate national collectives. Competition among national labor movements and governments ensures that international capital can play off one against the other to obtain the concessions it wants. If labor were united on a global level, it could prevent transnational capital from looking for the best deal. However, the international reach of labor lags far behind that of business and finance. Business, in the meantime, is unlikely to permit a resumption of class compromises since it can obtain concessions from labor and governments without reciprocating. International capital does not even have to accept consensual tripartitism to bribe workers to repudiate strikes as a means of settling disputes. Transnational corporations have a broad financial base, and in the event of a strike or threat of a strike at

---

[12] Przeworski and Wallerstein, "The Structure of Class Conflict," 217.

one of their subsidiaries, the firm may still be able to continue to meet its market commitments and maintain cash flows, thereby minimizing the costs of a shutdown.[13]

Financial penetration, the second major change in the economic environment, also raises questions about the theoretical premises of the power resource model. For labor, the abundance of financial investment opportunities uncouples the link between growth and jobs. Industrial firms, not just banks and other financial institutions, are likely to exploit financial innovations and techniques because of widespread liberalization of capital flows and the existence of thriving offshore banking centers. Financial profits are better, more predictable, and quicker than long-term investments in capital goods, physical plants, or human resources, whose ultimate payoff may not be seen until five years later. Financial investors (e.g., banks, institutional investors, and nonbank financial corporations) can, moreover, destroy any government initiative on behalf of tripartite arrangements by moving out of a country, putting pressure on the currency, and depleting the foreign exchange reserves of the central bank.

In the past, governments could spend lavishly on public programs to reconcile the conflicting demands of labor and business. However, such expansionary programs produce expectations among financial asset holders that future inflation rates will drift above the rates of the country's main trading partners. This perception triggers capital outflows and foreign currency speculation. If the outflow continues unabated, governments must reverse their policies to arrest further outflows.

In short, the most persistent dilemma for labor is that increased mobility of capital has also increased the power resources of capital. The effect of this mobility is that managers and owners of financial assets and transnational corporations are favored, and labor is hurt.[14] The greatest hurdle for leftist governments is that they cannot come to the aid of their allies in the labor movement because expansionary government programs and inducement packages for business trigger unwanted and uncontrollable capital outflows.

### Small State Argument

Are labor movements and their political parties in small countries more capable of solving the problems associated with financial integra-

---

[13] Ron Bain, *Comparative Industrial Relations* (New York: St. Martin's, 1985), 188–89. For further information on the impact of transnational corporations on labor arrangements, see International Labour Organization (ILO), *Employment Effects of Multinational Enterprises in Industrial Countries* (Geneva: ILO, 1981).

[14] Industries or sectors specifically tied to the national market and unable to enter into new fields or production areas are also victims. Frieden, "Invested Interests," 425–51.

tion and business globalization? There is a school of thought that claims that domestic institutions in small countries are adept at coping with the repercussions of international crises and changes. Because consensual tripartism is regularly found in small countries, which are more vulnerable to external fluctuations, scholars who study small states conclude that social concertation in these countries is better acclimated to uncertainties and international pressures.[15]

According to the small-state argument, the economic size of small open economies forces them to concentrate on foreign trade and to specialize in a narrow range of export goods. This focus makes them vulnerable to economic fluctuations and exogenous shocks. The solution to this problem is for the government to create a large public sector, which functions as a buffer between the domestic market and the international political economy. Because the perception of vulnerability is deeply engrained in the minds of government officials and organized interest groups, society is prepared to make the necessary adjustments to minimize its exposure to unpredictable fluctuations in world markets. The shared anxiety about vulnerability to external economic shocks prompts a search for intraclass collaboration and legitimizes the notion of social protection. Because class compromises come about to avoid mutual risks, they are also more stable.

Scholars such as Cameron, Ingham, and Stephens argue that small states are organized for consensual practices as a result of their institutional development. The argument holds that foreign trade and export orientation predetermine a simple industrial structure and a corresponding early concentration of industry. Such economic centralization facilitates the rise of unified employer associations and a unified trade union federation. The centralization of employer associations and trade union federations provides the structural precondition for social concertation; economywide bargaining could not exist without organizational centralization. An important outgrowth of a wide degree of unionization is that the working class strongly identifies with social democratic parties; a stable cohort of voters regularly delivers electoral victories. Unity in the industrial arena and an electoral majority in the

[15] James Fulcher, "On the Explanation of Industrial Relations Diversity: Labor Movements, Employers, and the State in Britain and Sweden," *British Journal of Industrial Relations* 26 (1988): 246–64; David Cameron, "The Expansion of the Public Economy," *American Political Science Review* 72 (1978): 1243–61; Geoffrey Ingham, *Strikes and Industrial Conflict in Britain and Scandinavia* (London: Macmillan, 1974); Simon Kuznets, "Economic Growth of Small Nations," in *Economic Consequences of the Size of Nations*, ed. E. A. G. Robinson (New York: St. Martin's, 1963), 14–21; Peter Katzenstein, *Small States in World Markets* (Ithaca: Cornell University Press, 1985); S. N. Eisenstadt, "Reflections on Center-Periphery Relations and Small European States," in *Small States in Comparative Perspective*, ed. R. Alapuro (Oslo: Norwegian University Press, 1985); John D. Stephens, *The Transition from Capitalism to Socialism* (London: Macmillan, 1979), 120–22, 129–30.

political arena prompt capital to seek tripartite distributive arrangements to avoid labor conflict and to spur governments to provide elabo
rate social welfare programs.[16]

Cooperation across class divisions is facilitated by recurrent cycles of
economic deterioration that government, business, and labor ascribe to
the nation's exposure to international developments. Decline in demand for exports or decline in foreign investments immediately shows
in the order books and employment levels of domestic firms. Such
economic deterioration also aggravates underlying industrial tensions
and results in heightened class conflict. After the Great Depression of
the 1930s, labor and business in many European countries struck a
historic compromise to prevent another economic and social crisis in
the future.[17]

Nevertheless, looking back to the social compromises of the 1930s
and the postwar period, it appears that different orientations of business produce striking variations in the ways in which governments in
small states have formulated compensatory mechanisms to cope with
economic vulnerability. Peter Katzenstein divides business communities
according to their degree of internationalization and distinguishes between industrial adjustment policies that emphasize free-market–style
accommodation and those that stress interventionist market steering
mechanisms.[18] In countries where international business dominates,
social partnerships emphasize global adaptation and ascribe a positive
role to the free interplay of market forces. By comparison, in countries
where business is more domestic-oriented, public intervention and restructuring of market processes stress more interventionist forms of
adaptation. Industrial policy in such countries is built around a system
of supporting domestic business against foreign corporations. Public
resources finance the costs of industrial restructuring and adjustments,
while state policies are also highly visible in the areas of regional development, manpower programs, and economic planning.[19] Belgium and
the Netherlands are examples of countries in which international business leads and governments shun aggressive market intervention. Aus-

[16] Cameron, "Expansion of the Public Economy." Other studies argue that small open
economies possess consensual decision-making procedures and state interventionist
mechanisms: see Eisenstadt, "Reflections on Center-Periphery Relations"; and Kuznetz,
"Economic Growth of Small Nations," 14–21. See also Francis G. Castles, *Australian
Public Policy and Economic Vulnerability: A Comparative and Historical Perspective* (Boston:
Allen and Unwin, 1988).

[17] Castles, *Australian Public Policy*, 61–79.

[18] In *Small States in World Markets*, Katzenstein looks at the number of banks among the
world's largest transnational financial institutions, the proportion of domestic versus
foreign investments, and the number of employees abroad.

[19] Ibid., 105–120.

tria has a domestic-oriented business community, and its government is less reluctant to modify market developments. Sweden is a mixture of the two, in that international business dominates, although its activities are checked by a powerful, united labor movement.

The partnerships taken for granted by the small-state literature have not fared well during recent periods of dramatic international changes. This statement especially holds true for countries in which business has a more international orientation, considering how national tripartism crumbled in Belgium and the Netherlands. It appears that social partnerships can only survive in an environment of relatively moderate globalization and financial integration because Austria is the only country in which social concertation has not experienced serious, life-threatening challenges. The reasons for this are the same as outlined above. Governments can only pursue a policy of flexible adjustment and adaptation if state officials possess a large degree of policy autonomy. With industrial restructuring and financial interdependence, the economic vulnerability of small states has increased while policy alternatives have decreased. Liberal corporatist countries, that is, countries in which business is largely transnational and government intervention is market-driven, are the first to notice the constraining influence of capital mobility because they possess already relatively liberalized capital markets and financial systems. Further, they are home to a large number of international firms; countries with large enclaves of international business display greater structural dependency on international capital.[20]

## Empirical Evidence from the Four Countries

My thesis takes the assumptions and findings of the two debates described above in another direction. It takes for granted that social concertation can exist only if both business and labor simultaneously seek a social compromise. Class compromises fall apart or never come into existence if either labor or business perceives them to be contrary

[20] For other studies on the impact of capital mobility and multinational business on the behavior of the business community and state capacity and domestic policies, see, for example, Robert Gilpin, *U.S. Power and the Multinational Corporation: The Political Economy of Foreign Direct Investments* (New York: Basic Books, 1975); and Peter Evans, *Dependent Development: The Alliance of Multinational, State, and Local Capital in Brazil* (Princeton, N.J.: Princeton University Press, 1979). In British politics, there has been an ongoing debate on the role of finance in domestic and foreign economic policies as well as the difficulties of the British state to go against the interests of the City. See, for example, Stephen Blank, "Britain: The Politics of Foreign Economic Policy, the Domestic Economy, and the Problem of Pluralistic Stagnation," in *Between Power and Plenty*, ed. Peter Katzenstein (Madison: University of Wisconsin Press, 1978), 89–138; or the Marxist treatment of a similar theme in Geoffrey Ingham, *Capitalism Divided: The City and Industry in British Social Development* (London: MacMillan, 1984).

to their interests. This book also affirms the main contention of the small-state argument; class compromises emerged in the four countries of this study, and variations in compensation policies or government intervention mechanisms depended on the nature of business and its international connections. However, central premises of each debate are rejected. First, with regard to the small-state argument, this book shows that small open economies have qualitatively different relations to international markets and, thus, that their attendant sensitivity to external shocks is also very different. Second, while criticizing the class compromise theories, I argue that the power resources of capital have exceeded, by all accounts, those of labor, even if the labor movement can call upon sympathetic governments.

Social concertation is only viable in relatively closed economies where the costs for firms wishing to defect are comparatively high and cumbersome. Capital in general enjoys low exit costs because money knows no national boundaries and has no special qualifications that would interfere with its conversion into shares or other currencies. But small countries differ in the way in which they are linked to the global economy and international financial markets, and this difference defines the extent to which capital can move from one market into another or from one form of investment into another.

To confirm this thesis, I selected four countries—Austria, Belgium, the Netherlands, and Sweden—which constructed tripartite arrangements after 1945 and which specialized in international trade. These small, open economies all built consensual mechanisms to buffer the national market from external disturbances. Toward the end of the 1960s, governments in these four countries firmly endorsed redistributive incomes policies, legislated numerous social programs, and used their budgetary powers to bridge labor-business animosity. Leftist and Christian democratic cabinets actively promoted consensual concertations. Less than two decades later, by the early 1980s, Belgium and the Netherlands had moved resolutely away from the institutions of tripartism and announced the adoption of neoliberal principles of policy making. Deregulation of labor markets, private enterprise, and the public sector is supposed to restore the beneficial impact of free-market forces and to recover business profitability. Similar changes are under way in Austria and Sweden, but they began later than in Belgium or the Netherlands and did not bring social concertation to an end in the 1980s.

Because these four countries engaged in redistributive incomes policies, spent large sums of money on social programs to improve the situation of less-advantaged social groups, and abided by the rhetoric of social solidarity and universal social entitlements, they are suitable for a study on the impact of capital mobility and financial integration on distributive tripartism, despite the fact that class compromise theories usually dismiss Belgium and the Netherlands as two countries that failed to institutionalize tripartite exchanges.

Empirical descriptions of the postwar settlement in Belgium and the Netherlands contradict the conclusions of the power resource model. Labor and business in Belgium and the Netherlands agreed to a system of political exchanges. In Belgium, since the end of the war, the joint declaration on productivity and collective bargaining, has been the foundation for subsequent compromises agreed to by business and labor and incorporated into the country's political system.[21] Redistributive wage bargaining and the existence of tripartite bodies characterized Dutch neocorporatism.[22]

Measurements drawn from a variety of studies provide some justification for excluding the Low Countries (Luxembourg is not included, although it is a Low Country) from the category of small nations with durable class compromises. In neither the Netherlands nor Belgium do citizens regularly cast their ballots according to class identification. These societies are divided along religious or cultural lines, a segmentation that is stronger than class divisions. Social democratic parties have never won a straight electoral majority and so govern in coalitions with stronger Christian democratic parties. Because workers identify with different cultures, unionization rates, particularly in the Netherlands, are low. Low rates of organization, competing trade union confederations, and smaller labor movement parties are usually invoked by scholars to eliminate Belgium and the Netherlands from those states with class compromises and with successful industrial adjustments and strong economic records.

At the same time, studies that use a mixed scale of economywide bargaining and consensual incomes policies give Belgium and the Netherlands a high neocorporatist score.[23] Both countries appear reg-

---

[21] More information is given in the next chapter. Cf. Armand Spineux, "Trade Unionism in Belgium: The Difficulties of a Major Renovation," in *European Industrial Relations: The Challenge of Flexibility*, ed. Guido Baglioni and Colin Crouch (Newbury Park, Calif.: Sage, 1990), 42.

[22] Jelle Visser, "Continuity and Change in Dutch Industrial Relations," in *European Industrial Relations*, ed. Baglioni and Crouch, 232.

[23] For example, Gary Marks, "Neo-corporatism and Incomes Policy in Western Europe and North America," *Comparative Politics* 18 (1986): 253–77. He looks at degree of participation in consensual incomes policies. Belgium is fourth, the Netherlands sixth. Michael Bruno and Jeffrey Sachs (*The Economics of Worldwide Stagflation* [Cambridge, Mass.: Harvard University Press, 1985]) create a rank ordering of countries according to the degree of labor market centralization. The Netherlands is third, Belgium ninth. Lars Calmfors and John Driffill ("Bargaining Structure, Corporatism, and Macroeconomic Performance," *Economic Policy*, 6 [1988]: 18) define centralization as the extent of inter-union and interemployer cooperation in wage bargaining with the other side. The Netherlands is seventh and Belgium eighth, and both belong to the intermediate group of countries.

ularly on scales measuring the extent to which workers and employers are represented in centralized trade union organizations and settle wages nationally.

Belgium and the Netherlands also fit the definitions of how class compromises are related to the developments of the public sector and the intensity of industrial conflict. Both countries administered many generous social programs and began to construct large public sectors while industrial conflicts decreased in Belgium after the institutionalization of consensual tripartitism in the 1960s. Industrial conflict stayed very low in the Netherlands throughout the postwar period.

Undeniably, class compromises in the Low Countries were embedded in an environment different from the working-class mobilization and militant employer actions that marked the rise of national concertation in Sweden and Austria. Workers were assimilated in competing sociocultural structures, headed by a political party. The party system mirrored the cultural or religious segmentation of society. Political elites, in response to strong subcultural divisions, sought to settle conflicts by calling for political compromises. The integration of culturally distinct groups into policy-making institutions also brought labor parties into national politics and coalition governments. Class relations and electoral contests turned into cross-ideological collaboration in which the social democratic parties were part of the pact and could elevate working-class concerns to national politics.[24]

The Netherlands is a typical example of a country that has cultural pluralism and centralized political agreements. (Austria is also commonly placed in this category.)[25] In fact, by many other standards as well, such as the degree of industrial conflict, social spending, and labor-business mediation mechanisms, the Netherlands possesses all the characteristics of a neocorporatist, tripartite society.[26] Even Bel-

[24] Gerhard Lehmbruch, "Consociational Democracy, Class Conflict, and the New Corporatism," in *Trends toward Corporatist Intermediation*, ed. Phillipe C. Schmitter and Gerhard Lehmbruch (Beverly Hills, Calif.: Sage, 1979), 53–61.

[25] Gerhard Lehmbruch, "Introduction: Neo-Corporatism in Comparative Perspective," in *Patterns of Corporatist Policy-making*, ed. Gerhard Lehmburch and Philippe C. Schmitter (Beverly Hills, Calif.: Sage, 1982), 16–32. The Netherlands is a strong case of corporatism; Belgium is not mentioned. Phillipe C. Schmitter, "Interest Intermediation and Regime Governability in Contemporary Western Europe and North America," in *Organizing Interests in Western Europe*, ed. Suzanne Berger (New York: Cambridge University Press), 294. He uses two measurements: organizational centralization of trade unions and the number of competing national federations. Of the fifteen countries, the Netherlands is sixth and Belgium seventh. See also Klaus Armingeon, "Determining the Level of Wages: The Role of Parties and Trade Unions," in *The Impact of Parties: Politics and Policies in Democratic Capitalist States*, ed. Francis G. Castles (Beverly Hills, Calif.: Sage, 1982), 225–82.

[26] For example, Heikki Paloheimo, "Distributive Struggle and Economic Development in the 1970s in Developed Capitalist Countries," *European Journal of Political Research* 12

gium, despite its problematic status in the literature, created a large public sector, established hundreds of advisory bodies to draw labor and business into the process of policy-making, and formulated consensual incomes policies.[27]

Why then did class compromises fail to protect employers and unions from external shocks in the Low Countries? Are Belgium and the Netherlands simply aberrant cases to be dismissed on the grounds that they failed to protect their national economies from external shocks in the past and now confront the costs of that failure?[28]

One obvious result of past decisions is that the Dutch and Belgian economies are extremely open. Too much openness interferes with social bargaining and social protection policies. Such criticism does not explain why Belgium and the Netherlands allow themselves to be too open for their own good. Francis Castles suggests that some small nations because of their acute perception of vulnerability or a greater concern for its consequences may be determined to take action against the effects of the international political economy.[29] Decisions in the 1960s and 1970s did undoubtedly increase the external vulnerability of Belgium and the Netherlands, and subsequent policy choices increased constraints on policy initiatives to mitigate external threats. Still, this does not explain why the Netherlands and Belgium acted in the way they did. I must start my investigation by asking how the domestic market is absorbed into the international political economy and what accounts for differences in the way small states relate to global markets.

A country's external relations are defined by the international and export activities of business and finance in the global economy. The greater the international orientation of business and finance, the more open the economy is. What makes business and finance more internationally oriented and therefore less anchored to domestic institutions?

---

(1984): 175–76; Francis G. Castles, "The Impact of Parties on Public Expenditures," in *The Impact of Parties*, ed. Castles, 21–96.

[27] One study finds that Belgium behaves as if it is a corporatist country though it is classified in the comparative tables on inflation and unemployment as liberal. Colin Crouch, "Conditions for Trade Union Restraint," in *The Politics of Inflation and Economic Stagnation: Theoretical Approaches and International Case Studies*, ed. Leon N. Lindberg and Charles S. Maier (Washington, D.C.: Brookings Institution, 1985), 105–40. Walter Korpi and Michael Shalev ("Strikes, Power, and Politics in the Western Nations, 1900–1976," *Political Power and Social Theory* 1 [1980]: 323) have an equal problem with the Netherlands, which has a level of industrial conflict resembling that of a class compromise country, but leftist mobilization and union militancy was throughout history low.

[28] For example, the corporatist measures developed by Cameron, which is reproduced in other studies, give the Netherlands and Belgium a low score. David R. Cameron, "Social Democracy, Corporatism, Labor Quiescence, and the Representation of Economic Interest in Advanced Capitalist Society," in *Order and Conflict in Contemporary Capitalism*, 165.

[29] Castles, *Australian Public Policy*, 49.

Two complementary factors are considered: (1) business and finance evolved distinct interests at the time of industrialization, with some national business or financial communities acquiring strong international connections, and (2) state policy encouraged business and finance to focus on international expansion. The first point is historical. In some countries, industry and banking acquired important international connections by the beginning of the century and had a global presence from their first growth spurt. The second point refers to the political choices of state officials. In some countries, state officials formulated explicit policies to encourage the internationalization of business and finance. However, the inclination of state officials reflects the already existing predilection of business and finance to compete aggressively, not from the home market, but from wider global markets.

This means that class compromises, seen from the perspective of business, differ indeed among small states. This difference is not, however, reducible to government compensation programs or market intervention mechanisms. Nor are the differences a function of the weakened power resources of labor. The difference rests with the power resources of capital, which because of its higher mobility is less wedded to social concertation, more independent from employer associations, and more inclined to shift its physical plant and financial assets abroad.

Other consequences are derived from the international roots of finance. In particular, central banks, partly in response to the interests and activities of financial institutions, advocate a monetary framework congruent with the main orientation and focus of banks and nonbank financial corporations. In countries with well-connected international banks and financial institutions, the central bank enacts fewer barriers against capital and financial movements and seeks quicker integration into international financial markets.

No country is an island, and no country can opt for autarky. Small, open economies are eventually affected by the continuous increase in movement of capital and the growth of global diversification.[30] Business globalization and financial integration have not entirely bypassed Austria and Sweden. The historical traits of business and finance and postwar state policy account for the different timing of troubles in consensual tripartism, which occurred earlier in Belgium and the Netherlands. But deepening financial integration and the movement toward global business actors have also weakened the Swedish and Austrian variants of social partnerships. Thus, the historical proclivities of

[30] For example, compare the study of Louis Pauly, *Opening Financial Markets: Banking Politics on the Pacific Rim* (Ithaca: Cornell University Press, 1988).

capital and biases in state policy must be complemented by another set of factors associated with the altered conditions in the international economy and with the encroachment of external developments on domestic institutions and policy practices.

The positions of present-day Belgium and the Netherlands in the world economy reflect the historical inclination of capitalist groups, which built transnational connections to global markets during the early phase of industrialization. In the postwar period, state agencies reinforced the transnational activities of business and finance by implementing foreign trade and monetary policies conducive to international expansion and growth of transnational networks. Class compromises were achieved, but employers were only loosely wedded to the system of social exchange and compromise since their profit maximization gave them a global reach.

A critical role is always performed by the state agency most closely identified with the financial community, the central bank.[31] The extent to which monetary authorities tolerate the opening of domestic capital markets and unregulated capital movements depends on the preferences of financial agents and the space in which a central bank acts, unencumbered by political interference.[32] As a rule, independent central banks, that is, central banks with a considerable degree of autonomy from government, act as conservative monetarists with little sympathy for full employment objectives, economic justice, and social spending programs. Rather, their priorities are price stability, disinflation, and growth of international transactions. Such policies contradict attempts by governments to keep social concertation alive and enhance capital mobility, which in turn, hinders consensual deliberations. Central banks in Belgium and the Netherlands conducted monetary and exchange rate policies inconsistent with the efforts to preserve social concertation and to restructure industrial manufacturing in the late 1970s and 1980s.

Membership in the European Community (EC), which was the most important foreign policy decision for Belgium and the Netherlands, complemented the postwar objectives of furthering the internationalization of business and finance. As original members, the Netherlands

[31] John T. Woolley, "Central Banks and Inflation," in *The Politics of Inflation and Economic Stagnation*, 338–39.
[32] This definition is the most common one. Gerald A. Epstein and Juliet B. Schor, "The Political Economy of Central Banking" (Cambridge, Mass.: Discussion Paper no. 1281, Harvard Institute of Economic Research, 1986); King Banaian, Leroy L. Laney, and Thomas D. Willett, "Central Bank Independence: An International Comparison," *Economic Review, Federal Reserve Bank of Dallas* (March 1983), 1–13.

and Belgium accepted OECD and EC rules governing financial and capital market liberalization and deregulation. They were more likely to trade policy autonomy for coordination. For smaller members of the Community, coordination of policy has often meant subordination to the objectives and ambitions of more powerful countries. With the creation of the European Monetary System (EMS) in 1979, member states adopted a semifixed exchange rate pegged to the German mark. The results were twofold. First, international traders and investors gained further from this monetary regime because it brought currency stability or predictability and promoted capital movements.[33] The losers were domestic-oriented industries and organized labor because independent policy action in an economy of full capital mobility is severely restricted. The second consequence of EMS membership was to give central bankers greater influence in macroeconomic management. Although central bankers must abide by the exchange rate agreements of the EMS and cannot act independently, their reputations and influence in national policy deliberations have risen.

Austria and Sweden did not join the EC in 1957 or 1973, in part because they feared that membership would compromise their neutrality and in part because the international connections of capital in Austria and Sweden were less extensive. Pressures to join the EC were moderate; neither business nor finance pushed very hard to obtain full membership status. Accordingly, the impact of global trends toward financial deregulation and liberalization was delayed.

In a similar vein, central bankers had very limited decision-making independence in Austria and Sweden. Politicians, who gave directions to central banks regarding monetary and exchange rate policies, feared the full impact of financial integration and flows, and hesitated to liberalize capital markets and movements. Thus, these national economies obtained a measure of protection against speculative financial flows and capital movements, which allowed for public compensation measures.

Each of these points is more fully examined in the following chapters. For now, it is important to stress two points. First, the differences in central bank policies, business behavior, foreign economic policy, and financial integration are ultimately traced to one source: the position of the financial sector relative to other economic actors and state agencies. Both Belgium and the Netherlands have independent financial sectors consisting of banks and nonbank financial corporations.

---

[33] Benjamin J. Cohen, "European Financial Integration and National Banking Interests," in *The Political Economy of European Integration*, ed. Pier Carlo Padoan and Paolo Guerrieri (London: Harvester Wheatsheaf, 1989), 145–70.

These financial intermediaries are above all interested in enlarging the circuit of capital and the volume of transactions. They strive for economic openness and the removal of capital flow restrictions in order to enlarge the scope of their profit-making transactions by increasing the circulation of money around the world and by providing more opportunities to mediate between buyers and sellers. In general, financial agents, especially those of small states where opportunities are limited, advocate minimal barriers. In the postwar period, such national preferences for economic openness resulted in support for the American international order, concurring with the call for multilateral trade and currency convertibility, as well as a fixed and strong exchange rate and the free movement of currencies. Economic integration and the concomitant surge in trade flows served the dual objectives of providing secure outlets for domestic producers and augmenting the scope of financial mediation of domestic banks and financial institutions.

Second, financial integration and international investments have not left Austria and Sweden untouched. The list of changes is long. For example, both countries submitted applications for EC membership in 1989 and 1991 and declared their desire to adopt EC norms and rules as quickly as possible. Central banks in both countries have enhanced their reputations and decision-making authority in anticipation of a greater need to control inflation and to manage exchange rate fluctuations. Further, Austrian and Swedish businesses have stepped up capital exports in order to catch up to or stay ahead of firms in neighboring countries and inside the EC. The most important symptoms of the changes are the tensions in the social partnerships and the declarations of politicians that a commitment to full employment and social solidarity is untenable in today's world of vanishing economic and financial frontiers.

CHAPTER TWO

# Introduction to the
# Four Political Economies

In this chapter I sketch the main features of social partnerships in the four countries after 1945. Most of the specific incidents and arrangements described are from the 1950s and 1960s. They demonstrate that social partnerships or tripartism existed until the early 1980s in some form in Belgium and the Netherlands as well as in Austria and Sweden, and they allow me to describe broadly the traits of business and finance in the four countries. In Chapters 4 to 7, I elaborate on this analysis.

The theoretical point I stress in this chapter is that business supports social pacts when such pacts concur with business preferences. State agencies or trade unions cannot directly influence business activities. They can only seek to create conditions that might move the investment strategies of business in a certain direction. Business can always refuse to accept the conditions available to stimulate reinvestments. By definition, business is free to allocate profits in any way it sees fit. State officials and labor movements cannot force business to participate in tripartite concertation. Although the electoral dominance of labor parties might persuade business to seek compromises with labor, it may, given its privileged position in the marketplace, decide on a course of confrontation.

Monetary policy is a critical tool for cementing a fruitful and durable exchange between labor and business. Whether the general orientation of monetary policy advances social concertation or not varies with the historic inclinations of finance, the degree to which central banks are independent from political interference, and the relation between the financial and nonfinancial sectors. A financial community with a domestic orientation and a dependent central bank produces a monetary policy framework that is generally sympathetic to the needs of business and, more important, lends support to the maintenance of durable tripartite arrangements. Class compromises are more robust and flexible if such instruments from the monetary arena as interest rate setting, for example, furnish business with specific incentives to continue to invest. Continuous reinvestments help cement cooperation between labor and management, and the provision of the appropriate blend of incentives makes it less likely that business will defect.

I analyze Sweden first because the establishment of the historic labor-business pact and the longevity of the Swedish model so clearly emphasize the importance of willing participation of business in and of the contribution of finance to any successful class compromise.

## SWEDEN

### *The Historic Compromise*

A number of scholars have suggested that the historic compromise struck in the 1930s delineated a fine balance between the feasibility of leftist politics and the exigencies of capitalist production.[1] During the Great Depression in the 1930s, farmers sided with workers in exchange for agricultural tariffs and subsidies. Their joint endeavor was meant to combat unemployment, falling agricultural prices, and more generally, the effects of global economic deflation. Although the electoral coalition with the Agrarian party gave Social Democrats a secure governing majority, they agreed to use state agencies to shape the environment in which production decisions were made while leaving the decisions themselves to capitalists. Economic power remained in the hands of capital; political power shifted to labor. The exchange between labor and capital was premised on the realization by both factions that capital could not defeat labor electorally and that labor could not win a contest at the workplace.

Capital's accommodation with the Social Democrats did not reflect

[1] Walter Korpi, *The Democratic Class Struggle* (Boston: Routledge and Kegan Paul, 1983); Peter Baldwin, *The Politics of Social Solidarity: Class Bases of the European Welfare State, 1875–1975* (New York: Cambridge University Press, 1990), 83–94; Gösta Esping-Andersen, *Politics against Markets* (Princeton, N.J.: Princeton University Press, 1985). For a similar analysis in which the independence of farmers and the weakness of the Right is considered critical, see Francis G. Castles, *The Social Democratic Image of Society: A Study of the Achievements and Origins of Scandinavian Democracy in Comparative Perspective* (Boston: Routledge and Kegan Paul, 1978); and Timothy Tilton, "The Social Origins of Liberal Democracy: The Swedish Case," *American Political Science Review* 68 (1974): 561–71. On Sweden's social and industrial development, see Steven Koblik, ed., *Sweden's Development from Poverty to Affluence, 1750–1970* (Minneapolis: University of Minnesota Press, 1975).

faintheartedness occasioned by the Social Democratic party's electoral victory of 1932 or compassion stirred by the lofty ideals of the labor movement. Instead, quick calculations based on a cost-benefit scale motivated business to go along with the Social Democratic Party, or Socialdemokratiska Arbetareparti (SAP), because it looked as though the SAP would be in government for a long time because it had found allies among the farmers. This reasoning prevailed especially among advanced technological export firms, which dominated the employers' federation, or Svenska Arbetsgivareföreningen (SAF). Their leadership of this national organization enabled them to influence state policy so that tax and investment programs, inspired by the drive for modernization and rationalization of exporting firms, were tailored to the needs of big business, not small domestic-oriented companies. The historic compromise, therefore, has another dimension, namely, a coalition between sections of the labor movement and certain factions in capital. Both derived benefits from centralizing pay negotiations and from the investment-oriented biases of state policy.

Since the 1930s, engineering firms have dominated SAF, which had been founded in 1902 to consolidate employers resistance to wage pressure. Inside the SAF, a struggle unfolded between home market industries, such as construction, and export firms.[2] Campaigning for centralized wage bargaining to ensure more predictable agreements for lower wages, employers in the engineering sector and the trade union that represented metalworkers formed a coalition against construction and building trade unions to prevent rapid wage increases. At that time, building trade workers could demand relatively high wages because the pressure on the construction industry was so high that employers were frequently forced to yield. But these high wages for skilled workers drove up wages in other sectors that contracted the services of the building industry, hired building tradesmen themselves, or were put under pressure by their own labor forces to match pay. Employers in the internationally exposed sectors advocated wage centralization and procedures to punish rebellious unions or employers in order to prevent upward pressure on wages and to arrest the competition for skilled workers.[3]

As they took over the leadership of the employers' association in the 1930s, the large engineering and metalworking firms forced smaller firms to comply with the central wage agreements that had been con-

[2] Karl-Olof Faxén, "Några kommentarer till SAFs lönepolitiska uttalanden under 1920-talet," in *Vingarnas trygghet: Arbetsmarknad, ekonomi och politik*, ed. Eskil Wadensjö, Åke Dahlberg, and Bertil Holmlund (Stockholm: Dialogos, 1989), 69–99.

[3] Peter Swenson, "Bringing Capital Back In, or Social Democracy Reconsidered: Employer Power, Cross-class Alliances, and Centralization of Industrial Relations in Denmark and Sweden," *World Politics* 43 (1991): 513–45.

cluded with member unions of the Swedish trade union confederation, or Landorganisationen (LO) i Sverige. They threatened to withhold financial and moral support from companies that were in confrontations with their workers over excessive demands.[4] Organizational reforms consolidated the influence of the main engineering firms in the SAF; the size of each firm's payroll determined the number of votes it had.

Offensive action against unions was subject to the SAF's control as well. Its executive council could order a general or partial lockout, but no member could engage in a lockout without the council's approval. Firms that were struck or engaged in approved lockouts were entitled to assistance from a central fund that was based on dues and assessments equal to 2 percent of each member firm's payroll. Firms that violated the SAF's rules could be deprived of assistance, fined, or even expelled. Although in practice, SAF's power may have been more nuanced, unlike the Dutch or Belgian employers federations, it did exert a considerable degree of control over wage bargaining and employers.[5]

After World War II, LO resisted the idea of peak-level negotiations because member unions did not wish to yield their independence in wage bargaining. SAF sought a central wage agreement in 1947, but at that time, LO was uninterested. During the Korean War, when inflation threatened to erode the progress in union members' earnings, LO entered into a round of collective bargaining in 1952 that was considered a one-time affair. For only this occasion was LO willing to impose wage restraints. But after 1952, the SAF imposed an ever-tighter grip on industry-level wage negotiations to enforce greater coordination, and the SAF directly and indirectly put pressure on trade unions to centralize wage bargaining. The second round of economywide bargaining took place in 1956, when the Social Democratic government requested wage restraint. After 1956, the SAF used its authority over its members to ensure the failure of industry-level negotiations and thus forced LO to negotiate centrally.[6] Since the SAF could coordinate the bargaining tactics of its affiliates regardless of whether trade

[4] Bo Carlson, *Trade Unions in Sweden* (Stockholm: Tidens, 1969), 20–30; Walter Korpi, *The Working Class in Welfare Capitalism: Work, Unions, and Politics in Sweden* (Boston: Routledge and Kegan Paul, 1978), 80–86.

[5] Peter Jackson and Keith Sisson, "Employers' Conferations in Sweden and the U.K. and the Significance of Industrial Infrastructure," *British Journal of Industrial Relations* 14 (1976): 306–23; G. Skogh, "Employers Associations in Sweden," in *Employer Associations and Industrial Relations*, ed. John P. Windmuller and Alan Gladstone (Oxford: Clarendon Press, 1984), 149–65.

[6] James Fulcher, "On the Explanation of Industrial Relations Diversity: Labor Movements, Employers, and the State in Britain and Sweden," *British Journal of Industrial Relations* 26 (1988): 251; Hans de Geer, *S.A.F. i förhandlingar* (Stockholm: Svenska Arbetsgivareföreningen, 1986), 139–46.

unions accepted centralized negotiations or not, LO, not without resistance from its member unions, claimed for itself greater authority in determining the structure of pay increases and entered into national collective agreements.[7]

Central wage determinations lasted until 1983, when they fell apart as employers in the engineering industries concluded a separate accord with their employees' union. Before this incident, however, centralized negotiations determined the framework agreements to estimate the size of wage increases. Framework agreements were supplemented by industrial contracts, which specified how the central arrangements were to be allocated among employers. In the third step of the process, companies negotiated with local branches of the unions about the individual terms. Usually, contracts lasted from one to three years, and workers pledged to solve outstanding issues through peaceful political means.

LO had to convince militant member unions to accept a loss of autonomy following the implementation of centralized wage bargaining. The answer to this dilemma of taking away power from the member unions was the idea of wage solidarity. This principle, which argued for equal pay for equal work, would set pay levels according to productivity gains in dynamic, expanding firms. Less efficient companies or sectors would either have to catch up or close down. Wage solidarity co-opted unions with lower wages into delegating the bargaining function to LO.

Over the years, wage accords gave more pay increases to lower-paid workers than higher-paid workers. Wage drift—wage increases above centrally negotiated levels—tended to nullify the egalitarian standards set by central accords and began to account for most of the workers' yearly growth in income in the 1960s. By the 1970s, LO insisted on compensation for workers hurt by the wage drift and demanded guarantees that those workers would not fall behind in pay simply because they could not bargain for more than the centrally set increases.[8] Solidaristic wage bargaining was strained before the withdrawal of the engineering employers in 1983.

At no point did the Social Democrats take the cooperation and acquiescence of business for granted. Prime Minister Tage Erlander's diaries, which covered his years in office throughout the 1950s and 1960s, reveal that the Social Democrats felt an ongoing need to speak directly with those who held economic power. Uncertain of the real

---

[7] Peter Swenson, *Fair Shares: Unions, Pay, and Politics in Sweden and West Germany* (Ithaca: Cornell University Press, 1989), 56, 132. See also Robert J. Flanagan, David W. Soskice, and Lloyd Ulman, *Unionism, Economic Stabilization, and Incomes Policies: The European Experience* (Washington, D.C.: Brookings Institution, 1983), 310–30.

[8] Flanagan et al., *Unionism, Economic Stabilization, and Incomes Policies*, 311–14.

intentions of the business community, SAP strategists realized two things: (1) they needed the cooperation of business for continued economic growth and continued social reforms, and (2) business would never totally accept the SAP and would prefer that it had no power. Forced to understand the habits and preferences of business, Erlander organized annual meetings at Harpsund, the summer residence of the prime minister, from 1955 until 1964, inviting bank directors, civil servants, individual businessmen, and chairmen of interest groups to review the important events of the past year and to speculate on future trends. Before the annual Harpsund conferences, representatives of export firms, industrial associations, farmers, small business, and the trade union confederations (LO and its counterpart in the service sector) had met every Thursday to discuss various aspects of economic policy. In the early 1960s, the annual conferences were criticized bitterly by the bourgeois opposition (because it was excluded) and by the SAP rank and file, who disliked the elitest format of the exchanges.[9]

Government officials were also made aware that business had limited tolerance for radical reform. In the late 1940s, the socialists were thinking of introducing a scheme for a planned economy and were considering the socialization of heavy industry. The employer federation went on the offensive and mobilized its members against the SAP government.[10] Socialization of heavy industries was dropped as a campaign slogan owing to the hardened opposition of business.

A more recent example of the 1970s is the debate on the wage-earners' fund.[11] LO adopted the program of a wage-earners' fund in 1976 as a way to skim excess profits from firms and to encourage wage restraint among workers in highly profitable enterprises. LO proposed to channel extra profits into a system of funds, collectively managed by employees, which would reinvest in private companies. Employers absolutely rejected the idea of collective profit sharing; they preferred to offer employees individual bonuses and profit-sharing deals to arrest spiraling wage demands.

The Right and employers attacked the plan as "a half-cooked egg which sane politicians will never swallow," and added that the international repercussions for Sweden of such an arrangement were too se-

[9] Olof Ruin, *Tage Erlander: Serving the Welfare State, 1946–69*, trans. Michael F. Metcalf (Pittsburgh: University of Pittsburgh Press, 1990), 250–53.

[10] Diane Sainsbury, *Swedish Social Democratic Ideology and Electoral Politics, 1944–1948: A Study of the Functions of Party Ideology* (Stockholm: Almqvist and Wiksell, 1980). Timothy A. Tilton, "Why Don't the Swedish Social Democrats Nationalize Industry?" *Scandinavian Studies* 59 (1987): 142–66.

[11] Rudolf Meidner, *Employee Investment Funds* (Stockholm: Swedish Institute, 1979).

vere to contemplate.[12] Parliament passed a bill in December 1983 which introduced a very limited version of five regional wage-earners' funds. The controversy surrounding wage earners' funds polarized Swedish politics and hardened the stance of employers against any further labor reformism. Discussions about the plan for workers' ownership were shelved during the rule of the bourgeois coalition, and the returning SAP government enacted an extremely watered-down version in 1983. Nevertheless, employers organized mass demonstrations in late 1983 and bombarded the media with anticollectivist messages.[13]

In summary, Sweden during the postwar period saw a series of satisfactory compromises between the world's most successful leftist party and a highly competitive business community as their interests converged.[14] Employers supported centralized wage bargaining because they feared a surge in wage costs if unions were free to bargain separately. Union rivalries to offer the highest and best wage packages to their members would put considerable pressure on all local wage negotiators to match the wage contracts of the most secure and aggressive workers. Business preferred centralized coordination of wage bargaining to prevent competitive bidding by trade unions and shopfloor representatives. Moreover, regulated wage setting and the moral obligation to resolve disputes amicably through face-to-face discussions removed the threat of labor militancy and strikes. Engineering firms and export firms gained the most from pay leveling. The compression of wage scales burdened unproductive firms the most and allowed profitable firms to pay lower wages than if workers had negotiated company by company. The second gain for engineering employers was that pay leveling transferred skilled workers from labor-intensive sectors to modern technologically advanced firms.[15]

While centralized wage bargaining moderated sharp wage fluctuations and benefited firms that were sensitive to international business cycles, it also was to the advantage of labor. Wage solidarity reinforced a common identity among workers, and a stronger identification with the trade union confederation strengthened the political links between

[12] Hugh Heclo and Henrik Madsen, *Policy and Politics in Sweden: Principled Pragmatism* (Philadelphia: Temple University Press, 1987), 269.

[13] Jonas Pontusson, "Behind and Beyond Social Democracy in Sweden," *New Left Review* 143 (1984): 69–96.

[14] See, e.g., Gregg Olsen, "Labor Mobilization and the Strength of Capital: The Rise and Stall of Economic Democracy in Sweden," *Studies in Political Economy* 34 (1991): 132–36.

[15] Andrew Martin, "Trade Unions in Sweden: Strategic Responses to Change and Crisis," in *Unions and Economic Crisis: Britain, West Germany, and Sweden*, ed. Peter Gourevitch et al. (Boston: Allen and Unwin, 1984), 206; Lei Delsen and Tom van Veen, "The Swedish Model: Relevance for Other European Countries," *British Journal of Industrial Relations* 30 (1992): 87.

union members and the SAP.[16] For organized labor, years of wage
solidarity and central framing of pay contracts generated low wage
differentials, which declined by half from 1959 to 1979. The com-
pressed wage structure gave the sixty highest wage sectors only 12.7
percent more pay than the lowest paid sectors.[17] Central negotiations
gave LO moral and organizational leverage, which it used to help the
SAP in its electoral contests. In return, the SAP formulated active labor
market programs—intensive training, relocation assistance, and social
benefits—to deal with the pockets of unemployment that resulted
when pay leveling set by the productivity gains of expanding firms hurt
less profitable firms. Manpower programs helped displaced or unemployed workers find other jobs at better pay in growing industries. In
practice, the government employed workers directly in the public sector as services expanded.[18]

*Banking and the Swedish Riksbank*

Toward the last quarter of the nineteenth century, Swedish private
banks began to supply long-term loans to fledgling entrepreneurs and
also furnished management with business advice. The iron ore and
timber industries required heavy investments, and during the 1870s
private banks sprang up to collect savings from wealthy individuals,
who regarded the new banks as safer risks than the unregulated non-
profit corporations, merchant houses, or cooperative savings banks.

The principal bank for industry was Stockholm's Enskilda Banken,
owned and managed by the Wallenberg family. It was founded in 1856,
and after 1863, when new banking legislation was passed, it was free to
compete for deposits. Merchant houses were neither equipped nor
prepared to supply large sums of money, although they raised money
abroad to finance local and national governments. Most industrial and
commercial investments, however, were financed through local capital
markets, where public officials and the wealthy invested their savings.
By 1900, private banks had become adept at attracting these savings
and began to lend money against the share issue of industrial firms.
The law prohibited banks from owning corporate shares, so the banks
held them as collateral against their loans. Opportunities for industrial

---

[16] Korpi, *Democratic Class Struggle*, 87–99.

[17] Lennart Svensson, "Class Structure in a Welfare State in Crisis: From Radicalism to
Neoliberalism in Sweden," in *Unions in Crisis and Beyond: Perspectives from Six Countries*, ed.
Richard Edwards, Paolo Garonna, and Franz Tödtling (Dover, Mass.: Auburn, 1986),
273.

[18] Bo Rothstein, "The Success of the Swedish Labor Market Policy," *European Journal for
Political Research* 13 (1985): 153–65; Fritz W. Scharpf, *Crisis and Choice in European Social
Democracy* (Ithaca: Cornell University Press, 1991), 104–7.

investments were so attractive that the Enskilda bank under Marcus Wallenberg, Sr., even founded a number of industrial enterprises.[19]

After 1945, interlocking networks among the three main banks— Enskilda bank, Skandinaviska bank, and Svenska Handelsbanken— and large engineering and metalworking firms underpinned a concentration of capital in Sweden.[20] Seventeen holding groups together employed more than four hundred thousand people in the early 1960s. Firms with more than five hundred employees accounted for two-thirds of the total private labor force. The Wallenberg group alone, the largest conglomerate in Sweden, employed approximately one hundred fifty thousand people and accounted for 7 percent of employment in the private sector.[21] Mergers and growth during the 1970s only accentuated the concentration of ownership; the five largest private enterprises, now belonging to more impersonal entities, such as investment funds, insurance companies, or foundations, employed a little more than one hundred ninety thousand people in Sweden in 1985.[22] A special tax exemption on dividends from minority holdings of 25 percent or more in other firms encouraged large firms to acquire smaller ones. In the 1970s, the total number of mergers per decade increased to about seven thousand.[23] Two commercial banks— Skandinaviska Enskilda Banken (SEB) and Svenska Handelsbanken— created special investment funds, which in turn, owned shares in large export firms.[24]

Despite this concentration of capital in holding companies managed by powerful families and institutional investors, it would be wrong to conclude that banking capital leads Swedish capitalism. Restrictive credit and monetary regulations have hampered the banks' freedom to expand their financial activities and to compete with innovations in other parts of Europe, while the institution of supplementary pension funds has created an additional source of credit for government borrowing needs. Furthermore, the central bank was an instrument for

[19] Lars G. Sandberg, "Banking and Economic Growth in Sweden before World War I," *Journal of Economic History* 38 (1978): 650–80; Kurt Samuelson, *From Great Power to Welfare State* (London: Allen and Unwin, 1972).

[20] In 1972, the Enskilda Bank and the Skandinaviska Bank formed the Skandinaviska Enskilda Bank (SEB).

[21] C. H. Hermansson, *Ägande och Makt: Vad Kommer efter de 15 familjerna?* (Stockholm: Arbetarkultur, 1989), 91–93.

[22] Hermansson, *Ägande och Makt*, 109.

[23] Olsen, "Labor Mobilization and the Strength of Capital," 117.

[24] Olsen ("Labor Mobilization and the Strength of Capital," 118) has a chart of the Wallenberg empire. The SEB directly controls minority interests in ASEA, Electrolux, Atlas Copco, Ericsson, and Volvo, and the investment funds of the bank has a minority stake in Alfa-Laval, Saab-Scania, and SKF.

government intervention and could not act on behalf of private commercial banks. Among the oldest central banks in the world, the Riksbank was firmly under the supervision of the party in power—which in Sweden meant the Social Democratic party. Owing to its influence over the monetary arena, the SAP accomplished two critical objectives: it was able to channel a large volume of credit to the public sector (primarily in housing and budget financing), and it was able to detach the domestic capital and financial markets from international ones. The latter accomplishment was critical for the pursuit of a policy of low interest rates from the 1950s until the late 1970s and for the pursuit of an adjustable exchange rate system in which frequent devaluations gave export firms a brief cost reprieve in the 1970s and early 1980s.

## AUSTRIA

In much of the scholarly literature on class compromises and political economic performance, Austria is considered to be similar to Sweden. However, there is no social democratic hegemony in the Austrian social partnership. Rather, the conservative bloc, which is not fragmented like the bourgeois opposition in Sweden, forms a cohesive countervailing force against socialism. The entrenchment of a conservative (previously Catholic) political class (the People's party, or Österreichische Volkspartei (ÖVP) propelled the Austrian trade union confederation to agree not to alter the distribution of income between capital and labor in the 1950s. After economic reconstruction, organized labor concentrated on economic growth in the 1960s and 1970s, because that seemed the surest path to material improvement for workers. Since economic growth depended on the investments made by firms, the Austrian trade union confederation, or Österreichischer Gewerkschaftsbund (ÖGB), relentlessly advocated wage moderation. Simultaneously, it shunned policies that touched on qualitative changes in the workplace. Democratic reforms and other forms of participation were unmentioned, and the ÖGB did not fight to ease the specific burdens of weaker regions and lower paid workers.[25]

[25] Raimund Low, "Von der Kreisky'schen Modernisierung zur Konterreform: 15 jahre SP-Regierung," in *Auf dem Weg zur Staatspartei: Zu Geschichte und Politik der SPÖ seit 1945,* ed. Peter Pelinka and Gerhard Steger (Vienna: Verlag für Gesellschaftskritik, 1988), 69; Helga Duda and Franz Tödtling, "Austrian Trade Unions in the Economic Crisis," in *Unions in Crisis and Beyond: Perspectives from Six Countries,* 242; Anton Pelinka, "Austria" in *Politics in Western Europe,* ed. Gerald A. Dorfman and Peter J. Duignan (Berkeley, Calif.: Hoover Institution Press, 1988), 306.

*The Social Partnership*

As soon as the war ended In 1945, the Second Republic created labor and business chambers—associations that were statutory, nationwide, and universal. One firm or employer could be a member in a half-dozen federal, regional, and sectoral chambers. These organizations are required to represent the common legitimate interests of their members and to use democratic procedures for their internal organizations. Each provincial chamber of commerce is responsible for social, economic, and technical questions concerning its province, while the federal Chamber of Commerce, or Bundeswirtschaftskammer (BWK), reviews national issues. Private and public enterprises in industry, services, transport, finance, and tourism are represented by the federal chamber and the provincial chamber where the business is located. A branch organization in each chamber is designated as the legitimate and sole bargaining agent of all employers. With a few exceptions (among them are printing, insurance, and banks), industrial firms and retail stores, whether large or small, must negotiate collective bargaining agreements within designated subcommittees of the federal and provincial chambers. The Chamber of Commerce (the federal umbrella organization) is the sole representative of business and enforces internal unity where none existed before.

Tensions inside the Federal Chamber of Commerce do exist. Each member has one vote, whatever the size of the firm. Ninety percent of all companies employ fewer than twenty workers, so the political power in the Chamber belongs to small firms. Although large private industrial firms founded their own association—the Association of Austrian Industrialists, representing about 70 percent of industry as a whole and 85 percent of private industry—this association cannot enter into wage negotiations. That function is reserved for the federal chamber and its provincial affiliates.

From the beginning, business was relatively smoothly absorbed into consensual tripartism because membership in the chambers was compulsory. Compulsory membership alone, however, would not have been sufficient to forge common interests between capital and labor. More likely, state-owned companies and the public economy assisted in bridging conflicting interests between labor and business and also lulled growing discords within capital. Until the late 1980s, politics ruled the nationalized sector, where managers and directors had to be affiliated with one of the two main parties (Socialist or People's party) and were appointed by the government. Conservative and Socialist politicians were responsible for a particular division of the state-owned firms, and each political bloc derived benefits from this situation. For organized labor, the public sector represented the heart and soul of Austrian unionism, and full-employment promises were largely realized by postponing layoffs in nationalized enterprises.[26] The state holding companies employed the workers who were the vanguard of Austrian unionism and endowed the Socialist party with the influence to make decisions on microeconomic corporate issues.

Largely, the entire labor movement cared intensely for the health of the main state holding corporation, Österreichische Industrieverwaltungs-Aktiengesellschaft (ÖIAG). Because of its involvement in the state sector, the Left was also sensitive to the day-to-day struggles of private companies or entrepreneurs. In the social partnership, labor emphasized converging interests with business rather than juxtaposing the conflicts between capital and labor in advanced capitalist societies.[27]

For private business, the nationalized sector also held interesting opportunities. Relatively large wage differentials were acceptable to the trade union confederation as long as workers in the public economy were protected against external shocks and domestic economic downturns. Because of the influence of the Socialist party on the public economy, both wages and social benefits for workers in the public sector were more generous than for workers in the private economy, which consisted primarily of small businesses. Not only were wages and supplemental benefits less generous in the private sector, but workers were also more likely to lose their jobs during cyclical movements than in the state-owned companies. The ÖGB tolerated this disparity in pay, benefits, and job security because the situation of employees in the state holding companies was so much better and more secure.

Besides paying workers less than large state-owned firms paid, small business also obtained raw material and semifinished products below world market prices from firms in the public sector. Private business, which had representatives on the boards of directors of the state holding company, moreover, was not excluded from the patronage system that surrounded the public economy. Since it derived direct benefits from the existence of the public sector, it shared with labor a concern for the survival of the family of firms of the ÖIAG and was willing to approve state subsidies to help out troubled parts of the nationalized companies. Measures undertaken to aid the public firms also were available for the private sector. Thus, Austria's business had good rea-

[26] Gerhard Klein, "Der Angestellte in der österreichischen Arbeitsrechtsordnung," in *Sozialpolitik und Sozialplanung*, ed. Oswin Martinek et al. (Vienna: Europaverlag, 1986), 204–5; Gösta Esping-Andersen, *The Three Worlds of Welfare Capitalism* (Princeton, N.J.: Princeton University Press, 1990), 47–54.
[27] Scharpf, *Crisis and Choice*, 178–79.

son to support the social partnership and the trade union federation's role in the public economy.

In summary, the presence of state-owned companies infused the labor movement with a strongly macroeconomic orientation in that Socialist-led governments and trade union leaders gave prominent consideration to the prospects for profit of business, whether private or public. Probably, the only time that the deliberations in the social and economic partnership deviated from the general macroeconomic objective of growth was when full employment was endangered. Market forces were generally left intact and were only subject to selected interventions of limited duration. The class compromise model in Austria favored national interests over the particularistic or universal, productivity over distribution, producer over consumer, and industrial export interests over those of the protected sectors. It also promulgated a clear hierarchy of goals: growth under conditions of highest possible employment, stable prices, and a hard currency.[28] After a considerable hiatus, concerns about social equality, economic redistribution, and solidarity were added.

### Austrian Banks and the Central Bank

Around the turn of the century the famous bank-industry networks arose, which Rudolph Hilferding, in *Finance Capital*, has identified as the first sign of a more advanced stage of capitalism.[29] The Austrian cartels arose as Vienna's great banks began to supply industry with long-term credit and organized mergers that turned private industrial companies into "joint-stock companies." The mixed banks were important in consolidating many small firms into corporations (Aktiengesellschaften), and in the process the banks became general business advisers to the new corporations.[30] From its infancy, Austrian industry grew under the patronage of the Vienna banks, and subsequent expansion was guided by the extensive involvement of financiers.[31] These financiers encouraged industrial enterprises to form cartels and to enter into interlocking corporate networks that would not

[28] Bernd Marin, "Austria—the Paradigm Case of Liberal Corporatism? in *The Political Economy of Corporatism*, ed. Wyn Grant (London: Macmillan, 1985), 116–17.

[29] Rudolf Hilferding, *Finance Capital: A Study of the Latest Phase of Capitalist Development* (Boston: Routledge & Kegan Paul, 1981).

[30] Richard L. Rudolph, *Banking and Industrialization in Austria-Hungary: The Role of the Banks in the Industrialization of the Czech Crownlands, 1873–1914* (New York: Cambridge University Press, 1976), 79, 96–121.

[31] Karl Socher, "Die öffentlichen Unternehmen im österreichischen Banken- und Versicherungssystem," in *Die Verstaatlichung in Österreich*, ed. Wilhelm Weber (Berlin: Duncker and Humblot, 1964), 353.

compete in foreign markets but would ensure market stability when tariffs were high and productivity low. Bankers instigated the formation of cartel agreements because they preferred to have their various protégés under one roof. Political instability and rising nationalism also motivated the creation of industrial-financial combinations and the erection of protective shelters. Most cartel agreements were aimed at restricting competition between firms in the same product branch, and they involved horizontal integration.[32]

The peace settlement of 1918 broke the Habsburg monarchy apart and cut Austria off from the important industrial regions of Czechoslovakia. Financial speculation replaced industrial innovation and the opening of new trade routes. When called to redeem the shares, banks were unable to do so and had to report enormous losses. In the meantime, foreign exchange restrictions and administrative barriers strangled international trade and depressed economic growth.[33]

Unable to honor its financial obligations, the Viennese Creditanstalt, the largest bank east of Germany, collapsed in May 1931. The Austrian government could not allow the country's largest bank to undergo bankruptcy because the balance sheet of the Creditanstalt was equal to the entire government budget of the First Republic. Since the government could not keep the Creditanstalt solvent through its own means, it borrowed money abroad. Foreign governments and private creditors were willing to lend only small amounts, and only if the state would take over the debt payments of the Creditanstalt so that their risk exposure would be greatly diminished. At the end of the political wrangling and financial deals, the reconstructed Creditanstalt was much smaller and largely in the hands of the state and foreign creditors.[34]

When other, smaller investment banks ran into trouble, the government simply merged them with the Creditanstalt, which became the only large bank in Austria. At the time of the Anschluss, the Deutsche Bank took control of the Creditanstalt, and after the defeat of the Third Reich, banks and industries nationalized before the Anschluss fell again into the hands of the new government of the Second Republic.

The currency and banking crises of the 1930s compelled the conser-

---

[32] Alan Milward and S. B. Saul, *The Development of the Economies of Continental Europe, 1850–1914* (London: Allen and Unwin, 1977), 322.

[33] Dieter Stiefel, "The Reconstruction of the Creditanstalt," in *International Business and Central Europe, 1918–1939*, ed. Alice Teichova and P. L. Cottrell (New York: St Martin's, 1983), 432–33. See also Alice Teichova and P. L. Cottrell's "Industrial Structures in West and East Central Europe during the Interwar Period" in their *International Business and Central Europe, 1918–1939*, 35.

[34] Aurel Schubert, "The Causes of the Austrian Currency Crisis of 1931," in *Economic Development in the Habsburg Monarchy and the Successor States*, ed. John Komlos, East European Monographs (New York: Columbia University Press, 1990), 89–113.

vative government to take steps to arrest further deterioration of the financial market. After 1945, the new generation of policymakers could not sell off state holdings because the private sector was too impoverished to raise the needed capital at home or abroad. It seemed logical for the state to reappropriate the banks, in part because they had not been in private ownership before the war. Probably resistance to the nationalizations would have been more intense if those banks had belonged to Austrian stockholders before.[35] In the end, public control over the large banks, and thus over the financial system, was not so much an aftereffect of the war and Austria's annexation as it was a result of prewar developments.

Many industrial corporations were also drawn into the state-controlled sphere to prevent the Soviet army from claiming firms in eastern Austria as war indemnity.[36] In relation to the overall economy (excluding agriculture), the public economy accounted for a quarter of the employed, a third of the gross domestic product (GDP), and nearly half of all investments. More important, the nationalized sector in the mid-1970s comprised 70 percent of banking, credit, and insurance transactions, 33 percent of industrial manufacturing, 23 percent of the food distributors, and 40 percent of housing construction.[37]

In the postwar era, while banks in most countries were prohibited from owning shares in industrial firms, the largest Austrian bank, the Creditanstalt, controlled a group of about twelve different industrial and manufacturing corporations. These firms employed 9 percent of the work force in manufacturing in the 1970s. However, the joint-stock banks were not geared to long-term investment financing, and the credit available was not generous.[38] Nor did they acquire a specialty in international financial intermediation. The commercial banks were domestically oriented.

Partly because of the domestic orientation of commercial banking, Austria possesses a dependent central bank. In the 1920s, political

[35] Socher, "Die öffentlichen Unternehmen," 365.

[36] After the establishment of the First Republic in 1918, socialization of the means of production was an important campaign promise of the Socialist party. Ironically, the nationalization of key industries after 1945 had nothing to do with the previous demands of the Socialists and took place with the full consensus of the conservative bloc. The Austrian government had to buy back its ownerless firms from a special corporation set up by the Soviet authorities to run the annexed property. Eduard März and Fritz Weber, "Verstaatlichung und Sozialisierung nach dem Ersten und Zweiten Weltkrieg—eine vergleichende Studie," *Wirtschaft und Gesellschaft* 4 (1978): 115–41.

[37] Fritz Klenner, *Hundert Jahre österreichische Gewerkschaftsbewegung: Entstehung und Entwicklung* (Vienna: Verlag des Österreichischen Gewerkschaftsbundes, 1981), 198.

[38] Helmut H. Haschek, "Aktienbank, Universalbanken, und Spezialkreditunternehmungen," in *Das Kreditwesen in Österreich,* ed. Konrad Fuchs and Max Scheithauer (Vienna: Manzsche Verlags- und Universitätsbuchhandlung, 1982), 83–84.

instability and economic chaos fueled a brief period of hyperinflation. In response, the First Republic established an independent central bank that was vested with the legal right to refuse the government's demand for additional unsecured credit.[39] After 1945, the Austrian central bank became incorporated in the tripartite social arrangements and thereafter lacked the persuasive power enjoyed by other central banks with links to financial communities active in international transactions. One major difference from the Swedish central bank—the other dependent central bank—is that the pegging of the Austrian schilling to the German mark in 1976 has virtually eradicated independent monetary actions. With independent monetary action largely out of the question, the social partners cannot, as in Sweden, use the financial system to promote their distributional goals. Nor can they devalue the currency to erase cost-gap disadvantages. Rather, the monetary authorities, at the behest of politicians, delayed for as long as possible opening and liberalizing the financial and capital markets, and then created numerous schemes based on subsidized interest rates to stimulate investments. In that sense, monetary policy blended with the political regulation of the Austrian market.

## BELGIUM

Since 1945, Belgian labor has been invited to participate in hundreds of advisory boards, and collective bargaining has existed sporadically. Social programmation (the name by which the Belgian version of class compromises came to be known) faltered because business and finance did not perceive that their interests were being met by the central framing of pay and economywide bargaining. Another reason that class compromises failed was that business itself was divided, reflecting the Walloon-Flemish split as well as the international versus domestic orientation of firms; in addition, employer associations were weak.

As in Austria, the first freely elected cabinet after 1945 forced the various business associations to amalgamate into one body. The result was the Confederation of Belgian Industry, or Verbond der Belgische Nijverheid/Fédération d'Industrie Belgique (VBN/FIB). This confederation accepted only professional associations as members, the most visible of which was the Flemish Economic Union, or Vlaams Econ-

---

[39] By 1922, prices were 14,153 times their prewar level. Schubert, "Causes of the Austrian Currency Crisis of 1931," 95; Thomas J. Sargent, "The Ends of Four Big Inflations," in *Inflation: Causes and Effects*, ed. Robert E. Hall (Chicago: University of Chicago Press, 1982), 48–56.

omisch Verbond (VEV), charged with promoting Flemish economic life and culture. Over time, because of its size and political connections to the dominant Social Christian party, Christelijke Volkspartij/Parti Social Chrétien (CVP/PSC), the Flemish Economic Union became a powerful voice inside the confederation and outflanked the business association of French-speaking Belgium.[40] In 1973, the nonindustrial federations amalgamated with the VBN/FIB to form a blanket body, the Confederation of Belgian Enterprises, or Verbond van Belgische Ondernemingen/Fédération des Enterprises Belges (VBO/FEB).

Neither employers nor workers were always ready to abide by the spirit of the national accords, and problems with wage bargaining synchronization undermined the legitimacy of social pacts. Compared with Austria, Belgium lacked a public sector that might have functioned as a bridge between conflicting private sector interests and between labor and business.

## Class Compromises in Belgium

During the Nazi occupation, the leaders of the trade union federations and some prominent members of the employers' association, who had gone into hiding, and the political elite had ample opportunity to ponder the postwar future. Both groups underwent something akin to a religious conversion and promised to resume their relationship on a new footing as soon as the war ended. In 1944, a few months before the return of the legitimate government from exile, the directors of the holding companies and the top officials of the Christian and Socialist trade union federations published the report "A Design for an Agreement of Social Solidarity." This report contained a joint statement on what would be negotiable, how economic growth would be translated into an improved standard of living for workers, and how labor and employers would build a more harmonious industrial relations system.[41]

Belgium's postwar settlement did not differ from those in other countries. The two main trade union federations and employer associations adopted collective bargaining procedures and created bipartite institutions to advance social exchanges. Reminiscent of the 1938 Saltsjöbaden agreement in Sweden, the social pact also aimed at preventing a resurgence of social confrontations that neither side could hope to

[40] Michel Quevit, *Les causes du déclin Wallon* (Brussels: Editions Vie Ouvrière, 1978), 145–47.
[41] Bob Hancke, "The Crisis of National Unions: Belgian Labor in Decline," *Politics and Society* 19 (1991): 468.

win and at keeping government officials out of the industrial arena.[42] The idea was that the state should vest the social actors with the authority to conclude legally binding collective contracts.[43]

Despite these explicit intentions, the result was a patchwork of economic and social consultative bodies that operated on three levels: the firm, the sectoral branch, and the interprofessional or national level. In addition, union representatives were invited to serve on the boards of the central bank, the Social Security Office, the Electricity Board, and the Directory of Coal and Steel, as well as municipal public enterprises, regional boards, and other parastatal bodies. In 1980, there were 150 advisory bodies deliberating on social, economic, and financial matters (not counting public health boards). In total, union members in 1980 were officially part of six hundred bilateral or tripartite councils, some of which had been dormant for a while.[44]

The most interesting phase in tripartite politics started in the early 1960s, when social programmation and centralized wage bargaining were routinized. The national wage negotiations were supposed to standardize working conditions and pay scales, thereby reinforcing the authority of the confederation leadership over its constituent unions.[45]

Toward the end of the 1950s, the productivity and competitiveness of Belgian industry had deteriorated while industrial conflict resurged. More and more, unions and employers favored national wage coordination and synchronization of labor conditions and pay among different sectors, regions, and companies. From 1960, after a violent unity strike against a package for tax reform failed, management and labor worked out new procedures to link wage increases to productivity

[42] B. S. Chlepner, *Cent ans d'histoire sociale en Belgique* (Brussels: Université Libre de Bruxelles, 1958), 243–44.

[43] Jan Bundervoet, "Vakbond en politiek in crisistijd," *Res Publica* 25 (1983): 219–35.

[44] Wilfried Dewachter, "Changes in a Particratie: The Belgian Party System from 1944 to 1986," in *Party Systems in Denmark, Austria, Switzerland, the Netherlands, and Belgium*, ed. Hans Daalder (London: Frances Pinter, 1987), 346; Roger Blanpain, "Labor Relations," in *Modern Belgium*, ed. Marina Boudart, Michel Boudart, and René Bryssinck (Palo Alto, Calif.: The Society for the Promotion of Science and Scholarship, 1990), 303–10; Val R. Lorwin, "Labor Unions and Political Parties in Belgium," *Industrial and Labor Relations Review* 28 (1975): 259.

[45] Michel Molitor, "Social Conflict in Belgium," in *The Resurgence of Class Conflict in Western Europe since 1968*, ed. Colin Crouch and Alessandro Pissorno (London: Macmillan, 1968), 30; Geert Dancet, "From a Workable Social Compromise to Conflict: The Case of Belgium," in *The Search for Labor Market Flexibility: The European Economies in Transition*, ed. Robert Boyer (Oxford: Claredon Press, 1988), 97–105; Xavier Mabille, *Histoire de la politique belge* (Brussels: Centre de Recherche et d'Information Socio-Politiques [CRISP], 1986), 342–47; A. van den Brande, "Neo-Corporatism and Functional-Integral power in Belgium," in *Political Stability and Neo-Corporatism: Corporatist Integration and Societal Cleavages in Western Europe*, ed. Ilja Scholten (Beverly Hills, Calif.: Sage, 1987), 109–15.

and to promote an equitable redistribution of the fruits of economic growth. National agreements guaranteed minimum standards for wage increases and work improvements that were further modified in industrywide sectoral negotiations. In exchange, the trade union confederation promised an end to work stoppages and strikes that frequently paralyzed small and large firms.

Social programmation during the 1960s ushered in the golden age of economic growth and welfare state expansion. In the national interprofessional meetings on wage determination, spokespersons for unions and employers estimated the future productivity gains for the next two years and determined the room for wage increases and social security expansion. Employers sought more predictability in estimating cost developments and demanded full cooperation from union leaders in the maintenance of social peace. Whereas employers desired more stable, multiyear wage contracts and an end to labor struggles, trade union confederations entered into centralized collective wage agreements to narrow regional and occupational pay differences. By and large, the top union leadership did not wholeheartedly support the frequent open conflicts with management. A central framework for subsequent branch negotiations would eliminate the primary motive for many strikes.[46]

Admittedly, Belgian capitalists were not totally entranced by consultative arrangements; to business, the arrangements fell short in quelling labor unrest and in delivering other precious gains, such as higher profits. In addition to the ambivalence of business (and labor), mounting economic problems and sharpening antagonism between the two linguistic communities of Belgium tore apart many political institutions, including social programmation.

The main problem, which I discuss in Chapters 4 and 6, was that Belgian capitalists did not link the maintenance of economic competitiveness to a system of political regulation of industrial relations. The failure resulted from a lack of unity and discipline in the employer associations and from the economic structure of business, which was dominated by financial holding companies. The holding companies from the French-speaking provinces invested hardly any resources in organizational representation because they had always had direct access to state agencies. Simultaneously, owing to their control over investment capital, the holding companies could broadly coordinate the activities of a wide range of industrial and service firms. They could also coordinate planning and execution of economic and social policies

---

[46] Jaak Brepoels, *Wat zoudt gij zonder 't werkvolk zijn? Anderhalve eeuw arbeidersstrijd in België* (Louvain: Kritak, 1981), 2:92.

because other firms depended on their decisions.[47] Social programmation was therefore not crucial to their efforts to improve economic competitiveness or gain access to state subsidies or support.

## Financial Institutions and the Central Bank

Belgian mixed banks were privately owned and devoted substantial capital and energy to industrial rationalization, making Belgium the workshop of the continent in the late nineteenth century.[48] The actions of the mixed banks and their early success in transforming small artisanal workshops into integrated factories resulted in an unparalleled concentration of economic resources. In 1898, 1 percent of all firms in extractive and manufacturing industries employed 50 percent of the work force. In this same year, one-tenth of all firms (two hundred firms in total) employed 23.5 percent of the work force (160,000 workers).[49]

After the Great Depression, new banking laws ordered each mixed bank to organize its industrial assets into a holding company and to create a separate bank to manage its financial interests. Nevertheless, the new holding companies—the industrial branches of the earlier mixed banks—retained their financial character in that they brought savers and investors together. Holding companies issued securities and bought stocks in a wide range of firms in service, transport, and manufacturing. The outstanding characteristic of the Belgian holding company was its quest to control corporate wealth and strategic planning. To this end, it purchased the exact amount of stocks required to exercise discretionary control over the resource allocation of the targeted company. The resulting concentration of economic power in the hands of a relatively small group of families far exceeded what studies on conventional economic concentration would predict. Belgium's legal structures and production do not limit the proportion of industry

[47] Beth Mintz and Michael Schwartz, "Capital Flows and the Process of Financial Hegemony," in *Structures of Capital: The Social Organization of the Economy*, ed. Sharon Zukin and Paul DiMaggio (New York: Cambridge University Press, 1990), 203–26.

[48] Jean Neuville, *L'Evolution des relations industrielles l'avènement du systémes de relations collectives* (Brussels: Editions Vie Ouvrière, 1976), 97–98; Julienne Laureyssens, "Le crédit industriel et la Société Générale des Pay-Bas pendant le régime hollandais," *Revue belge d'histoire contemporaine* 3 (1972): 126. For a more general treatment of Belgium's industrialization, see Jan Dhont and Marinette Bruwier, "The Industrial Revolution in the Low Countries, 1700–1914," in *The Fontana Economic History of Europe: The Emergence of Industrial Societies*, ed. Carlo M. Cipolla (Glasgow: Fontana, 1973), 330–47.

[49] Chlepner, *Cent ans d'histoire sociale*, 110; Quevit, *Causes du déclin Wallon*, 24. The situation did not change after World War II. One-tenth of 1 percent of 140,000 firms had more than a thousand employees and employed 25 percent of the labor force in 1965. Two-thirds of these firms had fewer than five employees and employed only 8 percent of the labor force. Centre de Recherche et d'Information Socio-Politiques (CRISP), *Morphologie des groupes financiers* (Brussels: CRISP, 1966), table 3, p. 47.

*43*

sales, assets, or employment found under the command of one group of decision makers. Through their investments, often by way of sub-holdings or subsidiaries, the holding companies determined the course of Belgium's most important and largest corporations behind closed doors.[50]

In this book, I focus chiefly on the Societé Générale de Belgique (SGB) because it is by far the largest, oldest, and most respected holding company. In the late 1980s, it employed more than 150,000 people and was the major shareholder in four other holding companies: FN (weapons), CMB (sea transport), Tractebel (electricity and energy), and Petrofina (oil and chemicals). In addition, SGB controlled half the insurance market through three insurance companies: AG, Royale Belge, and Assubel-Vie. In total, it determined the management strategy of about one hundred Belgian firms and held equity shares in about twelve hundred domestic and foreign corporations. Its assets were estimated at BF 100 billion (or $3.05 billion in 1990 U.S. dollars), and it held a majority stake in Belgium's largest commercial bank, Société Générale de Banque.[51]

Belgian capital, led by the large French-speaking trusts, had no compelling reasons to form specialized pressure groups.[52] Its contact with government was facilitated by the active involvement of holding company officials in politics and by the sheer size of its economic activities. On the other hand, employers and businesses in the Flemish-speaking provinces competed with the holding companies for access to state agencies, financial resources, and markets.

Driven by its desire to overcome its subordinate position, the Flemish entrepreneurial class developed into an astute pressure group with a sophisticated bureaucratic machinery which slowly succeeded in extracting concessions from French-speaking capitalists. In 1908, the Flemish-speaking bourgeoisie established the Flemish trade association with the dual goals of spreading the use of Dutch in commerce and

[50] Many studies try to sketch and estimate the corporate control of the holding companies. For a theoretical and empirical exposition, see Herman Daems, *The Holding Company and Corporate Control* (Boston: Nijhoff, 1978).

[51] Geert van Istendael, *Het Belgisch labyrint: De schoonheid der wanstaltigheid* (Amsterdam: Arbeiderspers, 1989), 310–13.

[52] In this book I do not deal at any great length with the convoluted conflictual history between the French- and Flemish-speaking populations. For some standard interpretations see Val R. Lorwin, "Belgium: Religion, Class, and Language in National Politics," in *Political Opposition in Western Democracies*, ed. Robert Dahl (New Haven, Conn.: Yale University, 1966), 147–84; and André P. Frognier, Michel Quevit, and Marie Stenbock, "Regional Imbalances and Centre—Periphery Relationships in Belgium," in *The Politics of Territorial Identity: Studies in European Regionalism*, ed. Stein Rokkan and Derek W. Urwin (Beverly Hills, Calif.: Sage, 1982), 251–78.

*44*

industry, and to further economic growth.[53] In 1926, the Flemish Trade Association was reconstituted as the Flemish Economic Union, or Vlaams Economisch Verbond (VEV), and reiterated its demands.[54] Obviously, the VEV was not an ordinary employers' or business association. From the start, its goals were explicitly political—to win full recognition for the Flemish language and culture. Questions concerning industrial relations or labor conflicts took second place because the Flemish Economic Union acted more like a Belgian chamber of commerce, and did not engage in wage bargaining.

On the other hand, French-speaking capitalists and owners of holding companies did not launch their own influential employers' associations. Because this faction of capital was present at the time of Belgium's founding in 1830, the mixed banks located in Wallonia played a very important role in staffing and building the new state institutions. Their history is intertwined with that of Belgium to such an extent that, as the Belgian government was fleeing to London in May 1940 as the German army approached, the prime minister told the chairmen of the three largest financial groups, "To you we entrust Belgium."[55]

After 1945, the holding companies lost some of their prestige and economic influence. Collaboration with Nazi Germany during the war, the loss of the Belgian Congo two decades later, and the economic decline of the industrial heartland of Belgium, where many of the holding companies' industrial interests were located, helped erode the power they had had before 1945. This is not to say that they were totally eclipsed by Flemish or foreign capital, but only to point out that the influence of the original builders of the Belgian economy after 1945 was limited to selected industrial or financial sectors.

One lasting legacy of the political influence of mixed bank holding companies before the war can be traced to the 1935 central bank act. At that time, neither political nor financial leaders desired a strongly independent bank. The new legislation of 1935 circumscribed the authority of the central bank in order to enable politicians and financial groups

[53] Theo Luykx, *Economische bewustwording in Vlaanderen: Veertig jaar Vlaams economisch verbond 1926–1966* (Antwerp, Belgium, Uitgeverij De Nederlandse Boekhandel, 1967), 19. For some writings on the Flemish national movement, see Kenneth D. McRae, *Conflict and Compromise in Multilingual Societies: Belgium* (Waterloo, Ontario: Wilfrid Laurier University Press, 1986), 22–33; J. Deleu et al. *Encyclopedie van de Vlaamse Beweging*, 2 vols. (Tielt, Belgium: Lannoo, 1973–75); Antoon Roosens, *De Vlaamse kwestie: Pamflet over een onbegrepen probleem* (Louvain: Kritak, 1981), 42–47; Jan Craeybecks and Els Witte, *Politieke geschiedenis van België sinds 1830: Spanningen in een burgelijke democratie* (Antwerp, Belgium: Standaard Wetenschappelijke Uitgeverij, 1981), 151.
[54] Theo Luykx, *Economische bewustwording in Vlaanderen*, 37–38.
[55] Quoted in John Gillingham, *Belgian Business in the Nazi New Order* (Ghent, Belgium: Jan Dhondt Foundation, 1977), 26.

to take advantage of the narrow range of activities of the bank. Financial groups escaped auditing and strict regulation, and governments escaped having to call on the central bank for additional budget financing.

## THE NETHERLANDS

The Netherlands, like Belgium, possesses a powerful financial community and, like Austria, constructed a formalized version of tripartite consensual policy-making. Like Sweden, it created a social welfare state that purported to close income gaps and gave handsome financial assistance to the disadvantaged. Social transfer payments and an extensive coupling of social benefits to the average pay has created a relatively egalitarian income distribution. In terms of social spending, the Netherlands was (and still is) among the leading countries.

Although public spending reached close to 60 percent of the gross domestic product in 1982, approximating the high level of public spending in Sweden, business and finance have strong international inclinations, and state policy leans toward noninterference. The combination of highly mobile capital and market-compliant state action inhibited the formulation of decisive measures to steer employers toward social concertation and accords. Instead, state officials, whether their inclinations were left-wing or right-wing, tried only to discipline trade unions.

Yet employers, lacking unity and internal cohesion, needed the heavy hand of a state agency. Because of late and scattered industrialization, a multiplicity of organizations representing different kinds of clients and handling different issues emerged.[56] In the late 1960s, the two branches of the nondenominational or general employer federation amalgamated to form the Verbond van Nederlandse Ondernemingen (VNO), or Association of Dutch Enterprises. The Calvinist and Catholic business communities, which had set up their own separate bodies to deal with social and economic issues in the 1930s, operated independently until 1970, when they merged to form the Christian Employers' Confederation, or Nederlandse Christelijke Werkgevers (NCW).[57]

[56] John Windmuller, *Labor Relations in the Netherlands* (Ithaca: Cornell University Press, 1969), 232; Abram de Swaan, *In Care of the State: Health Care, Education and Welfare in Europe and the U.S.A. in the Modern Era* (New York: Oxford University Press, 1988), 210–12.

[57] William van Voorden, "Employers Associations in the Netherlands," in *Employers Associations and Industrial Relations*, ed. Windmuller, 207.

Nonetheless, the deepest schisms among employers were not on religious or cultural lines in the 1960s but rather between those with an international orientation versus those with a domestic orientation. The transnational corporations frequently ignored central bargaining agreements and struck independent accords. Employer federations also lacked mechanisms to enforce solidarity. Not until 1973 did the employers' association create a mutual fund to aid firms caught in industrial conflicts.[58]

## Corporatist Mediation

Not long after the liberation of the Netherlands from Nazi occupation, government officials and labor representatives came to believe that the Netherlands would face mass unemployment unless more jobs were created. In addition, the loss of the Dutch East Indies in 1949 meant the loss of invisible earnings that had routinely paid for chronic trade deficits in the balance of payments. Essentially, government and labor believed that both the problem of unemployment and current account deficits could be easily brought to a manageable size if the Netherlands would rapidly industrialize. Industrialization would generate jobs for a growing population and for expatriates returning from newly independent Indonesia, and it would also solve the emerging problem of large trade deficits. Incomes policy was the tool to achieve the twin goals of creating jobs and strengthening the foreign trade sector. Unions were asked to exercise wage restraint in order to enable firms to reap comfortable profits for new capital investments.

While the legitimate Dutch government was still waiting for the end of the war in London, employers organized an extended dialogue with labor to frame the parameters of state actions in industrial relations. These discussions, secret in that they took place during the Nazi occupation, resulted in a draft declaration that called for the formation of the Foundation of Labor, or Stichting van de Arbeid, a private bilateral forum to discuss social questions. The preamble to the establishment of the Foundation of Labor specified a return to normal labor relations, the recognition of full employment as a legitimate economic policy priority, and the participation of labor in bilateral consultations in exchange for the unions' agreement to ban strikes. Union leaders also agreed to suppress demands for codetermination so as not to hinder a

[58] Jelle Visser, "Continuity and Change in Dutch Industrial Relations," in *European Industrial Relations*, ed. Guido Baglioni and Colin Crouch (Newbury Park, Calif.: Sage, 1990), 215.

*47*

return to normal labor relations.[59] The Foundation of Labor became a venue for bilateral wage negotiations and an efficient instrument for a coordinated incomes policy.

Further deliberations between the different political parties led to the establishment in 1950 of the Netherlands' second major economic policy institution, the Social Economic Council, or Sociaal Economische Raad, which was to be a central advisory body to the government. The council, whose participants included representatives of trade unions, employers' associations, and the government formulated a set of goals: price stability, balance of payments equilibrium, and full employment. In the 1960s, the council added two more: balanced economic growth and fair income redistribution.[60] These goals defined economic policy until the mid-1970s.

Dutch labor, with its religious divisions and low membership ratio, was not the main reason for the willing participation of business in either the Foundation of Labor or the Social Economic Council. More likely, Dutch business, realizing that the era of pure laissez-faire government was gone, accepted the tripartite arrangements to determine wage trends (but nothing else) as congruent with its own interests.[61] Moreover, the ultimate objective of the incomes policy deliberations was to keep labor costs artificially low to spur a quick export recovery. After 1963, when trade union confederations could no longer accept the idea of an extremely low wage structure, a complicated productivity formula was applied with the intention of keeping economy-wide collective bargaining alive and of moderating wage increases. But estimating productivity gains for individual companies or separate sectors proved to be impossibly cumbersome, and wage levels began to rise rapidly by the late 1960s regardless of productivity increases.

Consensual tripartism in the Netherlands never fostered strong loyalty among large export-oriented firms or transnational companies. One drawback of the policy of low wages was that it subsidized the least efficient firms and hampered the ability of expanding firms to hire

[59] For some standard publications on Dutch industrial relations, see Ger Harmsen, *Voor de bevrijding van de arbeid* (Nijmegen, Netherlands: SUN, 1975); Windmuller, *Labor Relations in the Netherlands*; Steven B. Wolinetz, "Socio-economic Bargaining in the Netherlands: Redefining the Post-war Policy Coalition," *West European Politics* 12 (1989): 79–98; and J. P. Windmuller, C. de Galan, and A. F. van Zweeden, *Arbeidsverhoudingen in Nederland*, 6th rev. ed. (Utrecht, Netherlands: Het Spectrum, 1987); Robert J. Flanagan, David W. Soskice, and Lloyd Ulman, *Unionism, Economic Stabilization, and Incomes Policies*.

[60] Peter de Wolff and Willem Driehuis, "A Description of Postwar Economic Developments and Economic Policy in the Netherlands," in *The Economy and Politics of the Netherlands since 1945*, ed. Richard Griffiths (The Hague: Nijhoff, 1980), 37.

[61] Ton Appels, *Political Economy and Enterprise Subsidies* (Tilburg, Netherlands: Tilburg University Press, 1986), 170–185.

skilled or specialized personnel. Low wage costs were much more important to small inefficient firms in labor-intensive manufacturing than to mobile transnational corporations. Because moderate labor costs favored the growth of labor-intensive manufacturing and increased the demand for both skilled and unskilled workers, labor markets became very tight in the 1960s. An upward readjustment of labor costs was therefore unavoidable. Rising labor costs hurt labor-intensive manufacturing and led to widening unemployment. Job losses worried trade union federations, which pushed for legislation in the mid-1970s to strengthen the monitoring capabilities of workers to predict impending factory closures. The insertion of nonmaterial demands into centralized negotiations angered employers and complicated the calculation of wage increases, which then resulted in further friction and disillusionment among unions and employers.

## Dutch Banking and the Netherlands Bank

In the nineteenth century, the global orientation of the Dutch bourgeoisie led to massive investments abroad in the Dutch East Indies (where they stimulated the growth of oil and rubber industries as well as sugar plantations), in Austrian and Russian state bonds, and in American railway bonds.[62] Revenues from colonial investments covered the chronic deficit in the Netherlands' merchandise trade and accounted for the large surplus of invisible earnings on the balance of payments.[63] From roughly 1850 to 1914, receipts on foreign investments in the form of dividends and interest equalled approximately 10 percent of national income.[64] Much of this invested surplus came from unrepatriated revenues. By the eve of the Nazi invasion, Dutch firms and households had assembled $2.7 billion in foreign securities, the equivalent of about 85 percent of the national income in 1939. The lion's share was in the East Indies, where total gold reserves of local banks, corporate cash reserves, fixed capital and portfolio investments came to 3 billion guilders ($1.66 billion). In addition, Dutch firms and individuals also held approximately 300 million guilders ($166 million) in Canadian and a variety of Latin American government securities. The total nominal value of Dutch holdings in the United States was

[62] Hans Baudet and Meindert Fennema, *Het Nederlands belang bij Indië* (Utrecht, Netherlands: Aula, 1983); K. D. Bosch, *Nederlandse beleggingen in de Verenigde Staten* (Amsterdam: Elsevier, 1948), 10, 81.

[63] F. A. G. Keesing, *De conjuncturele ontwikkeling van Nederland en de evolutie van de economische overheidspolitiek, 1918–1939* (Utrecht, Netherlands: Het Spectrum, 1948), 41, 137, 210, 268.

[64] J. C. van Zanten, "Economische groei in Nederland in de negentiende eeuw. Enkele nieuwe resultaten," *Economischen sociaal historisch jaarboek* 50 (1987): 53, 60.

assessed at $850 million. By comparison, U.S. investments in the Netherlands came to a meager $18.2 million.[65]

Industrialization at home advanced little; the moneyed bourgeoisie and the state were either indifferent or openly hostile to manufacturing. In the first half of the nineteenth century, Dutch financiers and merchants opposed the introduction of new credit facilities that were meant to promote industrialization. Subsequently, a plan to establish a French-type Crédit Mobilier in 1850 fell on deaf ears and was defeated before it had begun to operate because bankers refused to supply the starting capital. The same group of financiers also refused a loan for the construction of a canal connecting Amsterdam to the North Sea.[66] Once credit institutions became more involved in industrial financing, starting at about the turn of the century, credit was generally advanced in the form of short-term loans and overdraft accounts, which firms used to invest in expansion and modernization. Corporate networks between industry and banks did not evolve.

Nor did a strong sentiment in favor of economic nationalism and protectionism emerge in the Netherlands. Throughout the nineteenth and early twentieth centuries, spokespersons for the bourgeoisie advocated pacifism, international justice, and above all, political neutrality in the face of increasing European militarism.[67] Protectionist legislation on behalf of infant industries, specialized credit facilities and trade barriers were nonexistent. The belief in free trade and classical liberalism prevailed over and over. State action was driven by the same holy trinity that ruled Britain: free trade, the gold standard, and balanced budgets. The chief traits of state agencies of the Netherlands, like those of Britain, were their small size and their reputation for being fortresses of conservative ideas.[68]

Considering the prominence and reputation of the financial sector, the Netherlands' central bank enjoys a large degree of independence from political interference. Without doubt, the Dutch central bank is the only one of the four central banks in this study which articulated a distinct doctrine stressing two principles: price stability and a strong exchange rate. Correspondingly, monetary policy inclined toward re-

[65] Hendrik Riemens, *De financiële ontwikkeling van Nederland* (Amsterdam: Noord-Hollandsche Uitgeverij, 1948), 127–29.

[66] Bosch, *Nederlandse beleggingen in de Verenigde Staten*, 61.

[67] Joris Voorhoeve, *Peace, Profits, and Principles* (Boston: Nijhoff, 1979); C. B. Wels, *Aloofness and Neutrality: Studies on Dutch Foreign Relations and Policy-Making Institutions* (Utrecht, The Netherlands: H&S, 1982); J. C. Boogman, "Achtergronden, tendenties, en tradities van het buitenlands beleid in Nederland," in *Nederlands buitenlandse politiek* (Baarn, The Netherlands: In den Toren, 1979), 16–18.

[68] Hans Daalder, "Consociationalism, Center, Periphery in the Netherlands," in *Mobilization, Center-Periphery Structures and Nation-Building*, ed. Per Torsvik (Oslo: Universitetsforlaget, 1981), 188–95.

strictiveness throughout the postwar period. From around 1972, the guilder was pegged to the German mark (via the snake, which lasted from 1972 until 1977, and via the EMS since 1979). To preserve the exchange rate parity, the central bank made sure that inflation would not be higher than the low rates of the Federal Republic of Germany. Interest rates were set to stabilize the parity alignment and were never used to stimulate domestic investments.

As this short discussion reveals, variations in national class compromises were substantial in the 1960s. Each of the four countries—Sweden, Austria, Belgium, and the Netherlands—constructed some variant of social exchanges, although two characteristics differentiated them. From the beginning, finance communities in each country were either integrated into or detached from tripartite arrangements. Second, business in the four countries also related differently to social concertation. It either perceived social concertation to be fully congruent with its own interests, or it never warmed up to the idea of centralized consensual bargaining. In other words, business accepted social concertation as a reasonable concession to workers but did not base its own corporate strategies on the existence of such arrangements.

In Sweden, economywide collective bargaining was spearheaded by highly organized employers from expanding engineering and exporting firms, who were eager to centralize collective bargaining and keen to compress intersectoral wage differentiation. Their rationale was that home market industries such as construction drove up pay scales in the trade-dependent industries and that the existence of piece-rate earnings and wage drift enabled employers in engineering and export sectors to pay different wages. Centralized wage bargaining and pay leveling conserved internal unity in the labor movement and strengthened the electoral fortunes of the Social Democratic party.

All this was accomplished with the active consent of Swedish capital, which benefited directly from collective wage bargaining. In addition, state policy was geared to provide various forms of assistance to large employers, most of which were engineering and export firms. Taxation was tailored to minimize the corporate taxes of expanding and reinvesting firms, and the legal system encouraged concentration of capital. Further, monetary policies, particularly the management of interest and exchange rates, enabled export firms to raise capital cheaply or to avert the consequences of relatively high labor costs.

In Austria too the social partnership answered the needs of private capital. Wage restraint and procrastination in legislating welfare benefits for private-sector employees depressed workers' earnings for long periods of time. Unions accepted this inegalitarian distribution of wages and social benefits because the public economy guaranteed full employment and because organized labor wielded some measure of influence in the management of state holding companies. Subsidies protected the state holding companies from the consequences of international competition. Their state-mandated practice of supplying the private sector with goods below world market prices buffered private companies. Private firms, organized labor, and politicians relied on the public economy to cement the cooperation and consensus without which the social partnership could not exist.

Belgium and the Netherlands differ in two important respects from Sweden and Austria. Monetary policy in the Low Countries was more often than not harmful to the conservation of tripartite or corporatist exchanges. And the postwar arrangement did not succeed in welding business to social concertation.

In the Netherlands, governments used social programs based on transfer payments to enlist the cooperation of unions to hold back wage demands. But governments did little to provide incentives to capital or employers to renew social exchanges, with the exception of promising low wages. Since that was increasingly difficult to achieve, governments pleaded with unions to exercise wage moderation in return for expanded social services. Financing of these services came from payroll taxes and social security charges and thus contributed to the upward trend in labor costs. While labor-intensive firms were unable to cope with rising labor costs (and many folded), international firms turned to corporate globalization.

Belgian experiments in social programmation met with only moderate success because deep economic divisions in business and the dominant position of the financial holding companies interfered with the execution of central accords. Although they controlled a substantial portion of domestic manufacturing, holding companies were only minimally involved in social concertation. The absence of holding companies from tripartite conferences, despite their direction of investment decisions of employers who did participate, made it difficult for the government or any parastatal body to enforce or administer central accords. Unions were reluctant to abide by the rules of social concertation, and their hesitation reinforced the attitude of many employers not to take tripartism too seriously. Moreover, in Belgium, as in the Netherlands, monetary policy regularly conflicted with the spirit and execution of concessions made by government and labor. In the 1970s, the monetary authorities in both countries were above all preoccupied with price stability and maintaining confidence in the currency, while coalition cabinets tried to tailor economic policies to conform with these two goals.

# Part II

# ECONOMIC RECESSION
# AND POLITICAL CHANGE

CHAPTER THREE

# From Social Concertation to
# Neoliberal Restructuring

European labor movements in the 1980s struggled to defend real wages and social benefits against aggressive cost-cutting measures of conservative governments (or leftist governments with a conservative outlook) and against the more assertive politics of business. Industrial restructuring and slack labor markets helped sap the bargaining power of labor and reduced membership in trade union federations. Public opinion, influenced by the rhetoric of employers and their political allies, frequently blamed unions for the economic stagnation that many countries experienced after 1982. This mood also contaminated tripartism. Neither unions nor employers were anxious to renew centralized wage negotiations year after disappointing year.

National concertation ran into trouble first in Belgium and the Netherlands. Central accords ceased to matter in national economic policy-making since the late 1970s. Periodically, a governing administration cajoled and threatened labor market actors into signing economywide accords on pay and wages. These events, which took place under coercion, did not resemble the voluntary deliberations and concessions of the previous period of tripartism. Coupled with the decline of tripartism, the Left experienced a lengthy electoral impasse. Out of office for most of the 1980s, the socialist parties returned to power as junior allies of Christian democratic parties in 1989 and 1990. However, the return did not imply the end of neoliberal restructuring of state agencies, the public sector, and market forces.

In Belgium and the Netherlands, the break with the past gained momentum with the ascendance of center-right coalitions in 1982.[1] In

---

[1] Wilfried Martens formed his center-right coalition in Belgium after the parliamentary election of November 1981, and a similar coalition of Christian Democrats and liberals assumed power in May 1982 in the Netherlands.

Sweden and Austria, the Left continued to be in power. There, business and conservative parties tried to curb welfare spending and promoted labor market reforms, but restructuring took place at a slower rate, and important adjustment measures were not undertaken until the 1990s. By the year 2000, therefore, the four countries will again show marked likenesses in domestic spending patterns and social arrangements to cope with changes in the international political economy. But in the 1980s, the four countries showed striking dissimilarities.

In this chapter I examine the economic challenges and ensuing political reversals in the Low Countries and the relative political and social continuities in Austria and Sweden. Both Belgium and the Netherlands suffered an industrial crisis during which manufacturing jobs disappeared and there were fewer new job opportunities in the service sectors. But growing unemployment was only one aspect of the economic deterioration starting in the mid-1970s. Belgium and the Netherlands endured both absolute and relative economic misery (see Tables 1 and 2). In a comparison of eighteen OECD countries, economies were ranked according to their average year-to-year change in real GDP, average level of unemployment, and average year-to-year change in the consumer price index during separate periods. Belgium was grouped with the strong economies between 1960 and 1973 with a rank of 4.5, while the Netherlands fell in the middle with a score of 7. For the period of 1980–84, the Netherlands slid down the list to 13.5, and Belgium to 12. Austria kept its place among the best-performing countries, scoring 2.5 for both periods. Sweden climbed from among the weaker economies, with a score of 11, to among the stronger reaching a score of 7.[2]

In Belgium and the Netherlands, mass unemployment led to a remarkable increase of social welfare claimants and put enormous pressure on government budgets at the same time that economic growth and tax revenues slowed down. Center-right coalitions tried aggressively to rename or relabel the categories needy individuals deserving of state assistance in order to reduce the number of claimants. Concurrent with the pruning of social program expenditures, center-right governments stressed the restoration of business profitability. Social reforms and labor participation in economic councils, according to the view of conservative politicians and business leaders, interfered with healthy profits. Labor representatives found themselves plainly at odds with the new spirit. Nevertheless, the ceremony and symbolism of

[2] Francis G. Castles, *Australian Public Policy and Economic Vulnerability* (Boston: Allen & Unwin, 1988), table 2.2, p.24.

*Table 1.* Real growth of GDP (per capita average annual changes in percent)

|             | 1973–79 | 1979–86 | 1989 |
| ----------- | ------- | ------- | ---- |
| Belgium     | 2.1     | 1.4     | 4.0  |
| Netherlands | 1.9     | 0.6     | 4.1  |
| Austria     | 3.0     | 1.7     | 4.0  |
| Sweden      | 1.5     | 1.6     | 2.1  |

*Source:* OECD, *Historical Statistics, 1960–1990* (Paris: OECD, 1992), 44.

broad consensual concertation had lasted through the difficult decade of the 1970s, but the pretense of consultation was finally dropped at the beginning of the 1980s.

The rejection of social solidarity, collectivism, and universalism—the three mottoes of the welfare state and trade union movement—by state agencies and employers cannot be traced to the failing power of organized labor. This leaves two troubling questions. First, if the Left is politically subordinate and organizationally fragmented, how can pro-labor programs exist at all? Second, if the fortunes of the Left have changed over time—it was capable of winning social and industrial battles in earlier periods—what led to the present changes? Conventional labor-centered paradigms fail to address these two questions whether applied to the defeat of labor in the Low Countries or the current challenges to labor in Austria and Sweden. Considering that organized labor in Europe has confronted its greatest challenge in the postwar period, we need to look at the systemic level for a more comprehensive explanation.

State-centered frameworks also fail to shed light on why outcomes in the 1980s among similar kinds of European democracies vary substantially. State-centered explanations account for individual failures and missed opportunities for specific legislation or government action, but they do not coherently explain why the Netherlands and Belgium were

*Table 2.* Change in real private final consumption (per capita average annual changes in percent)

|             | 1973–79 | 1979–86 | 1982–86 | 1989–90 |
| ----------- | ------- | ------- | ------- | ------- |
| Belgium     | 2.7     | 1.0     | 1.2     | 2.6     |
| Netherlands | 3.3     | −0.1    | 0.6     | −0.05   |
| Austria     | 3.3     | 1.6     | 2.0     | 2.5     |
| Sweden      | 1.5     | 0.9     | 1.6     | 0.3     |

*Source:* OECD, *Historical Statistics, 1960–1990* (Paris: OECD, 1992), 56.

Table 3. Rate of unemployment as a percentage of the labor force

|            | 1968–73 | 1974–79 | 1980–86 | 1989–90 |
|------------|---------|---------|---------|---------|
| Belgium    | 2.3     | 5.6     | 11.2    | 9.0     |
| Netherlands| 1.5     | 4.9     | 10.1    | 7.9     |
| Austria    | 1.4     | 1.6     | 3.3     | 3.2     |
| Sweden     | 2.2     | 1.9     | 2.8     | 1.4     |

Source: OECD, Historical Statistics, 1960–1990 (Paris: OECD, 1992), 43.

forced to abandon their diluted versions of Keynesian economic policy-making for an entirely new approach of government intervention based on market-driven considerations.

One startling indication of how official ideology and voters' perceptions have changed is the reelection of conservative parties despite enduring mass unemployment (see Tables 3 and 4). The irrelevance of continuous unemployment in deciding whether conservative parties return to office reveals the extent to which the content of ideological discourse in Belgium and the Netherlands has changed.[3] Effects of the new reasoning have also spilled over into social reforms. While social spending is still comparatively high, the welfare safety net is much more responsive than before to private-sector incentives and competition. Socialist parties have returned to power in Belgium and the Netherlands in 1992, but they have agreed to execute the austerity programs of the conservative bloc. They are presiding over the replacement of a social citizenship with a social market state.

## BELGIUM

Belgium has always had a substantial manufacturing base which grew around steel, iron, non-ferrous metals, glass, and ceramics. The lack of innovation and of opportunities for export growth resulted in massive closures and redundancies in the most heavily industrialized areas of the country which were concentrated in the Walloon provinces in the 1970s. Economic decline underpinned a resurgence in "communal" or linguistic conflicts between the Flemish- and French-speaking communities.

Alongside the sharpening antagonism between Flanders and Wallonia, labor unions rose against the bureaucratization and centraliza-

[3] Wessel Visser and Rien Wijnhoven, "Politics Do Matter, but Does Unemployment? Party Strategies, Ideological Discourse, and Enduring Mass Unemployment," European Journal of Political Research 18 (1990): 71–98.

*Table 4.* Rate of total employment as a
percentage of population, ages 15 to 64

|  | 1980–86 | 1989–90 |
| --- | --- | --- |
| Belgium | 56.7 | 56.9 |
| Netherlands | 52.8 | 61.8 |
| Austria | 64.5 | 65.3 |
| Sweden | 78.7 | 81.8 |

*Source:* OECD, *Historical Statistics, 1960–1990*
(Paris: OECD, 1992), 42.

tion of collective wage agreements in the early 1970s. Under pressure from the rank and file, which organized strikes and factory occupations, the socialist trade union confederation demanded greater economic democracy and greater scrutiny of central accords. Employers could not respond to these new demands, and some of the most powerful employers in the steel industry called for a new industrial relations structure in which workers, via their unions, would have less influence over collective bargaining. By 1976, employers and observers spoke of a crisis in labor relations, and governments imposed a 100 percent tax on any wage increases agreed upon for 1976. No central accords were signed after 1975. In the late 1970s, governments began to set agendas for negotiations, moved toward deregulating the labor market, and generally intervened in an area that had been considered the exclusive terrain of unions and employers under the terms of the social pact.[4]

Openly aggressive employers increased the authority of management. Thus, in contrast to before the breakdown in social concertation, industrywide contracts exclude small- and medium-sized firms and can be approved despite the nonratification of one side. Agreements at the company level can modify the scope of binding provisions of the law or the national contract, and the unions' monopoly on worker representation in management councils has been broken because candidates can be recruited from among the nonunionized work force. Although discreet talks between unions closest to the governing parties and government did take place, these consultations excluded the Flemish and Walloon wings of the socialist-affiliated General Federation of Belgian Workers, or Fédération Générale des Travailleurs de Belgique (FGTB), and despite the close ties between the different branches (trade union confederation and political party) of the Catholic community, govern-

[4] Bob Hancke, "The Crisis of National Unions: Belgian Labor in Decline," *Politics and Society* 19 (1991): 463–87; P. Gevers, "Arbeidsverhoudingen in België," in *Als in een spiegel? Een sociologische kaart van België en Nederland,* ed. Luc Huyse and Jan Berting (Louvain: Kritak, 1983), 72.

ments did not halt or modify designs for budget consolidation and social security retrenchment.[5]

The continuing economic crisis, with its high unemployment, has inhibited labor militancy but has not removed government intervention from the labor market. National agreements within the framework of centralized collective bargaining were signed again in the late 1980s with the understanding that subsequent talks at industrial sector and company levels must take into account wage and price developments in Belgium's trading partners. New legislation empowers governments to intervene in setting pay if Belgium's competitiveness deteriorates.

*Industrial Crisis and Economic Decline*

Belgium's economic crisis stemmed from its weak production structure. It grew to gigantic proportions because approximately half the country's exports were in so-called shrinking sectors and world demand for Belgian goods dropped precipitously. Its foreign trade structure contained a high proportion of mass-produced manufactured goods (80 percent of merchandise trade) but virtually no specialization.[6] The loss of export markets and unadjusted specialization led to a decline in manufacturing from 30.8 percent of the GDP in 1970–72 to 24 percent a decade later. Manufacturing lost 30 percent of its employees, the equivalent of approximately 8 percent of the total private-sector employment between 1970 and 1984.[7] Construction and engineering saw a 20 percent shrinkage of their labor forces between 1974 and 1982. Job losses corresponded with a drop in fixed capital formation at an average annual rate of 5.7 percent between 1973 and 1979. For the entire period from 1973 to 1985, the growth rate of fixed capital formation hovered at an annual average of about 0.2 percent.[8]

[5] Armand Spineux, "Trade Unionism in Belgium: The Difficulties of a Major Renovation," in *European Industrial Relations: The Challenge of Flexibility*, ed. Guido Baglioni and Colin Crouch (Newbury Park, Calif.: Sage, 1990), 49–51.

[6] Robert Vandeputte, *Economische geschiedenis van België* (Tielt, Belgium: Lannoo, 1985), 164–75, 201–5; Philippe Defeyt and Evelyne Degryse, "Compétitivité et structures industrielles," in *L'Economie belge dans la crise*, ed. Guy Quaden (Brussels: Editions Labor, 1987), 279–313; François Martou, "Some Aspects of Industrial Policy in Belgium," in *A Competitive Future for Europe? Towards a New European Industrial Policy*, ed. P. R. Beije, et al. (New York: Croom Helm, 1987), 197; OECD, *Economic Surveys. BLEU 1985/86* (Paris: OECD, 1986), 18–20; Paul Kestens, "General Trends," in *Modern Belgium*, ed. Marina Boudart, Michel Boudart, and René Bryssinck (Palo Alto, Calif.: Society for the Promotion of Science and Scholarship, 1990), 225–33; Raymond Pulinckx, "Manufacturing and Construction Industry," in *Modern Belgium*, 238–46; Willy van Rijckeghem, "Benelux," in *The European Economy: Growth and Crisis*, ed. Andrea Boltho (New York: Oxford University Press, 1982), 587–92.

[7] OECD, *Economic Surveys. BLEU 1985/86*, 10.

[8] Ibid., 13.

Predictably, Belgian businesses reacted to the decline in demand for their exports by postponing new investments and closing factories. Both steps aggravated unemployment. From 1970 to 1979, more than 200,000 jobs disappeared in industry. Wage freezes and incomes policies did not seem to make a large difference, in part because wages and salaries amounted to only 29.4 percent of total production costs, while raw materials and energy represented 47 percent of the costs in certain production branches such as steel.[9] In any event, wage costs determined at the most a quarter of the value of manufacturing output, compared with 17 percent for net financial charges and 50 percent for imported goods and services.[10]

Governing cabinets did not sit back idly as more and more claimants drew ever-larger amounts of social insurance benefits. They formulated a variety of programs to reduce unemployment and to bring about structural adjustments. Needless to say, their efforts were not very effective. The programs aimed at different groups in the working population, such as younger and older workers. For example, about 36 percent of the fully unemployed labor force participated in some kind of manpower program in 1982. Most recipients of special government assistance were forced to retire early, but 2.3 percent of the labor force found employment in one of the government-financed special labor market circuits, started in 1977, in which the state covered salaries for people working in the parastatal sector. The government also hired more civil servants in the late 1970s. Manpower expenditures, apart from unemployment benefits and early retirement, accounted for BF 53.2 billion, or 1.3 percent of the GDP, in 1982.[11] Belgian efforts also went into numerous industrial policy programs that often had multiple objectives: to stem job losses, improve competitiveness, and stimulate science and technology research.

In the 1980s, policy instruments were designed to supply tax incentives but limit direct aid. In addition, constitutional reforms delegated industrial policy to the regional authorities, except for so-called national sectors—steel, coal, glass containers, textiles, and shipbuilding—which received massive amounts of state aid. Their funding was often

[9] Michel Capron, "The State, the Regions and Industrial Redevelopment: The Challenge of the Belgian Steel Crisis," in *The Politics of Steel: Western Europe and the Steel Industry in the Crisis Years, 1974–1984*, ed. Yves Mény and Vincent Wright (New York: de Gruyter, 1987), 701.

[10] OECD, *Economic Surveys. BLEU 1981/82* (Paris: OECD, 1982), 40.

[11] OECD, *Economic Surveys. BLEU 1984/85* (Paris: OECD, 1985), 35. In the 1970s, the Belgian government created state investment companies to spur capital investments and growth. Paul de Grauwe and Greet van de Velde, "Belgium: Politics and the Protection of Failing Companies," in *State Investment Companies in Western Europe*, ed. Brian Hindley (London: Macmillan, 1983), 96–124.

off-budget and difficult to gauge; their access to public funds through borrowing from public investment banks was enormous. Over a period of ten years, from 1973 to 1984, they received BF 380 billion or the equivalent of about 10 percent of the GNP in 1984.

The National Bank estimated in 1984 that total aid to business in the form of subsidies, capital transfers, loans, and equity investments averaged no less than 5.5 percent of the GNP between the early 1970s and 1990, and reached a peak of 8.9 percent in 1982. It fell to 7 percent of the GNP in the late 1980s. Aid in the early 1990s is given more frequently in the form of loans and equity investments because of the state's financial difficulties. Supplementing direct forms of financial intervention, the Belgian state has also provided various tax concessions and loan guarantees. The private sector in particular took advantage of the tax relief schemes, but its share in direct capital transfers was marginal. Capital transfers to the private sector, excluding the national sectors, was approximately 1.7 percent of the GNP in the early 1980s.

## Political Change for the Left

Despite generous state aid, the economic crisis simmered on, destroying the last remaining features of social programmation and rekindling Flemish-Walloon nationalism.[12] The crisis eventually led to major revisions of past practices and objectives. In the early 1980s, the country faced a prolonged recession, with half a million people unemployed, unsustainable public finances, and current account deficits. The fifth cabinet, led by Prime Minister Wilfried Martens from the Social Christian party (Martens V cabinet), boldly addressed these trouble spots. The cabinet decided that it could no longer work with consultative bodies of labor and business and turned to neoliberal remedies. This step required taking unpopular measures to curb public spending, bolster competitiveness, and create jobs. Martens's diagnosis of Belgium's economic woes was no longer framed in general terms of "global recession" or "international crisis" but traced the country's problems directly to the vulnerability and defects in the Belgian econ-

---

[12] For a lucid and thought-provoking analysis of the "pacification" policy, see Luc Huyse, *De gewapende vrede: Politiek in België na 1945* (Louvain: Kritak, 1984). The first reforms were enacted in 1971 and demarcated the separate cultural regions, which obtained some autonomous executive power over limited policy areas. The next round of constitutional changes took place in August 1980 and established representative institutions for Belgium's language communities and regions, which enjoy more autonomy than the earlier Regional Councils. A. Mughan, "All Periphery and No Center?" in *Centre-Periphery Relations in Western Europe*, ed. Yves Mény and Vincent Wright (Boston: Allen and Unwin, 1985), 282–97.

omy, inefficient public administration, and feuding political leadership.[13] In late 1981, the Liberal-Christian coalition requested special powers to rule by decree. War was declared on bureaucratic waste and the economic recession. The king granted Parliament extraordinary powers that enabled the government to pass legislation on public finances, social security, and unemployment. These powers were renewed until 1984.[14] What did the government plan to do with its new authority?

First, the coalition pointedly campaigned on a neoliberal platform that stressed wage freezes, welfare cutbacks, and the reduction of public employment with the goal of restoring corporate profitability. It devalued the franc to bolster export competitiveness and suspended cost-of-living indexation. Collective wage bargaining was adjourned. It placed a freeze on hiring civil servants and imposed a compulsory wage reduction of 5 percent for workers and 10 percent for managers in subsidized industries.[15] Real hourly earnings in manufacturing dropped 7 percent from 1982 to 1985.

The coalition's second line of attack aimed at controlling the burgeoning national debt and budget deficits by balancing social security accounts and transfer payments to eliminate the deficits. By 1981, gross public debt was equal to the GDP, and interest payments were about 8 percent of the GDP.[16] To achieve a meaningful reduction in public spending, social security benefits were to be brought under control. Savings measures to diminish the proportion of state contributions to social transfer payments, combined with a reduction in unemployment benefits and family allowances, made some difference. Young people were obliged to join a waiting list before they could qualify for unemployment benefits. Family allowances were reduced by BF 500 and were abolished for the first child. Pension contributions paid by employees were raised by 0.75 percent. Patients were obliged to contribute more to their health-care costs, and sickness allowances were reduced. In addition, savings on public services were instituted. Hospital care was financed through block appropriations, which administrators were

---

[13] As a note of interest, Belgium had thirteen different cabinets between 1971 and 1985. Usually, the change in government was accomplished without new parliamentary elections being held.

[14] Jozef Smits, "Belgian Politics in 1982: Less Democracy for a Better Economy," *Res Publica* 25 (1983): 181–217

[15] Bert Pijnenburg, "Belgium in Crisis: Political and Policy Responses 1981–1985," in *The Politics of Economic Crisis*, ed. Erik Damgaard, Peter Gerlich, and J. J. Richardson (Aldershot, U.K.: Avebury, 1989), 37–38; Geert Dancet, "From a Workable Social Compromise to Conflict: The Case of Belgium," in *The Search for Labor Market Flexibility: The European Economies in Transition*, ed. Robert Boyer (Oxford: Clarendon Press, 1988), 112–18

[16] OECD, *Economic Surveys. BLEU 1987/88* (Paris: OECD, 1988), 46.

free to allocate as they saw fit. Public utilities were given more autonomy and accountability, and the government offered fixed allocations for each public enterprise. The education budget was drastically cut. In 1986, the authorities created new categories of unemployment recipients in order to exclude certain groups and also reduced certain categories of payments for occupational disability and sickness.[17]

Wage restraints, partial suspension of the cost-of-living indexation, and the 8.5 percent devaluation of the Belgian franc decreased labor costs in 1983 by 27 percent compared with those in 1980, or 32 percent compared with those at the 1977 peak.[18] In 1983, the government imposed an external competitiveness norm that limited wage growth to that of its seven main trading partners. Thus, improved productivity was no longer automatically rewarded with pay raises; compensation was no longer linked to sectoral trends. When the two labor market parties were allowed to return to voluntary bargaining in 1987, the government reserved the right to intervene in wage formation if costs rose more rapidly than in the main competitor countries.[19]

One wing of the labor movement has continued to be part of national debates on economic policy-making. Although the result of its participation in macroeconomic management is all but invisible—budget cutting and government supervision over collective bargaining have continued throughout the 1980s and will continue in the 1990s—the Christian (Catholic) trade union federation or Algemeen Christelijk Verbond/Confédération des Syndicats Chrétiens (ACV/CSC), has strong bonds with Prime Minister Martens and other members of the Christian Democratic party. But the results of its involvement in austerity and recovery policies are impossible to gauge. Rather, the confederation was co-opted into endorsing the austerity package of the Belgian government and did not object to its many budget cutbacks.

## THE NETHERLANDS

The Dutch system of social concertation was based on some peculiar assumptions—one was that labor would be quiescent. Employers expected workers to trade codetermination for the right of labor leaders

---

[17] André Mommen, *Een tunnel zonder einde: Het neo-liberalisme van Martens V en VI* (Amsterdam: Kluwer, 1987), 136–38; Jozef Smits, "Belgian Politics in 1983: Communitarian Struggles despite the Economic Crisis," *Res Publica* 26 (1984): 473–91; and his "Belgian Politics in 1984: The Electoral Temptation," *Res Publica* 27 (1985): 244–56. See also Ivan Couttenier, "Belgian Politics in 1986," *Res Publica* 29 (1987): 361–72.

[18] OECD, *Economic Surveys. BLEU 1985/86*, 21.

[19] Geert Dancet, "From a Workable Social Compromise to Conflict," 113.

to participate in economic policy councils, and it was assumed that the trade union hierarchy would find no difficulty in ordering its workers to implement the tenets of the central accord.[20] Such an exceptional situation lasted until about 1963, when wages were centrally regulated, using a unified wage structure with rates established by a standardized job evaluation procedure. Wage rates in the Netherlands were among the lowest in Europe until 1963, and the wage-earners' income share in the national economy stagnated while the corporate sector recorded historically high profits.

The second assumption was that tripartite negotiations could prevent wages from rising faster than productivity. A reliance on incomes policies and central wage determination to keep inflation in check and preserve a small surplus on the current account was difficult to sustain over the long run. As a small open economy, the Netherlands could not control price rises and could only make sure that its rate of price increases would not erode its export competitiveness. Moreover, the authorities could not prevent the profitable export sector from competing for skilled labor and thereby driving up wage costs.[21]

When workers began to press for nonmaterial demands like economic democracy and greater egalitarianism in the late 1960s, the government offered to expand social benefits. However, uniformly high pay and expanding social programs clashed with price stability. The incompatible aims of economic policy—solidaristic pay structure and price stability—slowly but surely undermined the institutional foundation of the postwar order and led to a series of mandatory pay settlements after 1974.

The socialist-led cabinet of 1973–77 encouraged early wage settlements and also allowed a one-time, lump-sum payment to lower-income earners, whose pay rose proportionately more than the average income. The minimum wage was set relatively high compared with the average wage, which helped compress the wage distribution between well-paid and disadvantaged income groups.[22] Moreover, the minimum wage, which was adjusted biannually to contractual wages, served as a guideline for all social benefits. Collective wage agreements not only determined pay in the private and public sectors but also affected social

[20] Dirk Stikker, *Memoires* (Rotterdam: Nijgh and V. Ditman, 1966), 64; Tinie Akkermans and Peter Grootings, "From Corporatism to Polarization: Elements of the Development of Dutch Industrial Relations," in *The Resurgence of Class Conflict in Western Europe: Conflict in Western Europe since 1968*, ed. Colin Crouch and Alessandro Pizzorno (London: Macmillan, 1978), 174–83.

[21] This is the interpretation of Anne Romanis Braun, *Wage Determination and Incomes Policy in Open Economies* (Washington, D.C.: IMF, 1986), 272–91.

[22] For a schematic analysis of the policy framework of different postwar cabinets, see A. Knoester, *Economische politiek in Nederland* (Leiden, Netherlands: Stenfert Kroese, 1989).

expenditures and social transfer payments. By the time the worst recession hit the Netherlands after 1979, governments and employers were desperate to detach different earning scales from social benefit payments.

Because it was uncertain whether labor would voluntarily agree to hold back wage demands, the government intervened in 1980, 1981, and 1982 and left only partial freedom to union-employer negotiators in the following year. After the election of a center-right government in 1982, the tone changed and redistributive incomes policies were shelved. The coalition of Ruud Lubbers (1982–86) was the first government in ten years which openly advocated a policy of widening income differences.[23]

A central agreement was concluded in 1990, under the prodding of the recently elected center-left government of Christian Democrats and Socialists, and it committed business and labor to follow a "disciplined trend" in wage settlements. In return for wage restraint, the government agreed to raise the minimum wage after a nearly total freeze since 1984. However, the government reserved for itself the right to issue emergency controls should pay agreements be considered too high.

*Industrial Crisis and Economic Difficulties*

The Netherlands never had a strong manufacturing base, and a large part of its industry consisted of labor-intensive small firms, shipbuilding, and some transport manufacturing (cars and aircraft). None of these fared well in the 1970s, though unlike Belgium, the Netherlands had one significant advantage—the country was a major energy exporter.

In the 1940s, vast fields of natural gas were discovered, and the Netherlands became fully self-sufficient in energy in the mid-1970s. Since then, the share of natural gas in total trade ranged from 5 percent to 8 percent from 1975 to 1985 and from 4 percent to 9 percent of the GDP for that same period.[24]

Ironically, the exploitation of natural gas has been a mixed blessing and has produced the so-called Dutch disease. While analysts differ in their diagnoses, most agree that the name reflects an aberrant situation in which the economy looks buoyant from the outside but is deeply troubled within. A strong exchange rate and export performance is negated by economic stagnation, divestments, and rising unemploy-

[23] Jelle Visser, "Continuity and Change in Dutch Industrial Relations," in *European Industrial Relations*, ed. Baglioni and Crouch, 213.
[24] OECD, *Economic Surveys. The Netherlands 1986/87* (Paris: OECD, 1987), 31.

ment. According to the OECD and other analyses, receipts from the export of natural gas had the effect of raising labor incomes in all sectors. Low-productivity industries had to adjust to wage increases that were unjustified by their own performance. Tradable goods in the nonenergy sector lost their price competitiveness, not only because labor costs surged, but also because the exchange rate appreciated, with the result that the export-oriented and import-competing sectors lost market share.[25]

Whatever ailed the Dutch economy, the manufacturing industry undeniably bore the brunt of the economic downturn. Its share in the GDP declined from 26 percent to 17 percent between 1970 and 1983.[26] Naturally, the decline of manufacturing activity caused long-term unemployment among workers in textiles, clothing and footwear, basic metals, and shipbuilding. Total manufacturing employment dropped by 15 percent between 1970 and 1984.

Faced with rising unemployment, the political elite broadened the social security system to provide benefits for a large number of laid-off workers. Previously, government had habitually pledged more welfare programs to compensate unions for exercising wage restraint to overcome the adverse effects of currency appreciation.[27] Thus, while active labor market intervention was only halfheartedly pursued, the annual rate of public expenditures grew at an average of 13 percent between 1970 and 1982. By 1981, the Netherlands allocated 9.5 percent of the GDP to income support schemes for the working population (not including old-age transfers and family assistance). By comparison, Sweden spent 8.7 percent, and Belgium and Austria 5.5 percent and 2.2 percent, respectively. No less than 10 percent of the working population received disability compensation in the late 1970s because it was easier and less painful to label workers as "disabled" than "unemployed."[28] Disability payments were also more generous and continued until one's retirement, in contrast to the lower and shorter-term unemployment benefits.

[25] This is the standard view of the OECD and mentioned in every survey. See, for example, ibid., 28–31. Willy van Rijckeghem, "Benelux," 601–2.

[26] OECD, *Economic Surveys. The Netherlands 1985/86,* (Paris: OECD, 1986), 11.

[27] Robert J. Flanagan, David W. Soskice, and Lloyd Ulman, *Unionism, Economic Stabilization, and Incomes Policies: The European Experience* (Washington, D.C.: Brookings Institution, 1983), 130–31.

[28] OECD, *Economic Surveys. The Netherlands, 1983/84* (Paris: OECD, 1984), 32; Flanagan et al., *Unionism, Economic Stabilization, and Incomes Policies,* 128. In 1991, for every six workers one was "disabled," at the cost of around $12 billion. The Christian Democrats have pushed to replace the open-ended system with a five- or six-year limit that would save more than $2 billion by 1994. The Social Democrats threatened to leave the coalition if the reform was implemented. In the end, they went along. Ronald van de Krol, "Dutch Welfare Disables the Economy," *Financial Times,* 22 July 1991, 15.

## Political Change in Dutch Corporatism

As early as 1978, political parties agreed that the social security system urgently needed reform, but none of the government coalitions felt comfortable enough to override the resistance of professional groups with vested stakes in the social welfare state. Only with the first cabinet of Prime Minister Lubbers in 1982 was a turnaround in Dutch politics realized—from then on, neoliberalism guided further policy initiatives.[29] Central to the break was market liberalization and the restoration of corporate profits. Under the banner of "big operations" were three main objectives: to reduce the budget deficit and the size of the public sector, to strengthen the private sector, and to redistribute labor. Public benefits were lowered; civil servants were paid less; and restrictive regulations were removed to alter the relation between government and market.

In this new context, the Social Economic Council (founded in 1950) had no place, and the government asserted much more autonomy as it implemented more reforms of the social security system than any previous postwar cabinet. The pro-welfare state constituency lost much of its influence when the government stopped consulting with the tripartite institutions.[30] The new cabinet kicked off a veritable savings binge and promised to do what other governing parties had discussed but failed to accomplish. The public sector was forced to absorb one cutback after another in the name of reducing the budget deficit, freeing the market, and reducing unemployment. Ideological discourse was filled with references to the salutary effects of a market-led recovery that could only succeed by lowering labor costs and attaining better labor market flexibility. The underlying message was that the Netherlands should be a more hospitable home for entrepreneurs. One consequence was that the government allowed employers' and employees' organizations to frame their own sectoral and company agreements that led to a reduction of working time but without corresponding pay raises.[31] Another consequence was that wage solidarity eroded, and the

[29] Knoester, *Economische politiek in Nederland*, 153–63. Meindert Fennema and John Rhijnsburger, "Beheersing and modernisering," in *Voor en tegen de markt*, ed. Pim Fortuyn (Deventer, Netherlands: Kluwer, 1986), 44–45.

[30] J. Will Foppen, "The Netherlands and the Crisis as a Policy Challenge: Integration or Ideological Manoeuvres?" in *The Politics of Economic Crisis*, 89–106.

[31] Pim Fortuyn, "De relatie tussen economische structuur en verzorgingsstaat in Nederland in de periode 1970–1986," 51–58. Wibo Koole, "De neoliberale reorganisatie van politiek-economische regimes: Groot Brittannie, Duitsland en Nederland in de jaren tachtig," in *De theoretische grondslagen van economisch beleid*, ed. Henk W. Plasmeier (Groningen, Netherlands: Wolters-Noordhoff, 1988), 133–56. See also J. P. Windmuller, C. de Galan, and A. F. van Zweeden, *Arbeidsverhoudingen in Nederland*, 6th rev. ed. (Utrecht: Het Spectrum, 1987), 223–57.

minimum wage, which had been set at 56 percent of the average wage in the 1970s, fell to 46 percent in 1989.[32]

In 1983, the government announced its intention to shake up the social security system by reducing average benefits, lowering them further over time, and tightening both eligibility criteria and duration. The plan caused squabbles inside the governing coalition which took several years to resolve. The basic idea was to restrict unemployment benefits to those who had in fact been employed for at least half a year. Unemployment payments were still generous and were 70 percent of previously earned income (they had previously been 80 percent). The new plan, implemented in 1987, called for standard benefits to be paid out for a period that depended on number of years of full-time employment and the age of the recipient. Younger workers and new labor entrants would then run out of their unemployment entitlements and move to social assistance. Social assistance benefits were relatively paltry and fixed below minimum wage.[33]

With all these reforms, the adminstrative bureaucracy has acted on very different principles from before. It delegates authority, it is increasingly sensitive to the profit motive, and it no longer regularly consults with unions. Early studies of welfare retrenchment show that Belgium and the Netherlands, which cut back spending growth faster than other OECD-countries, are indeed the only countries that actually reduced real levels of expenditures.[34]

## SWEDEN

The fabled solidaristic wage policy had already suffered from internal strains in the late 1960s and could not cope with the continuing growth and strength of public-sector trade unions and white-collar workers. The remarkable aspect of the Swedish variant of tripartism is, however, that these tensions and frictions were contained until the end of the 1980s. Literally, it took until 1990 before a political offensive similar to that in Belgium and the Netherlands gathered steam and attacked public-sector spending and the commitment to full employment. Nevertheless, the first problems in centralized wage setting occured in the winter of 1969.

In 1969–70, wildcat strikes in northern Sweden erupted, revealing union members' deep dissatisfaction with the weak link between wages

[32] OECD, *Economic Surveys. The Netherlands 1989/90* (Paris: OECD, 1990), 106.
[33] OECD, *Economic Surveys. The Netherlands 1986/87*, 41–49, 59–61.
[34] Thomas R. Rochon, "The Political Basis of Social Policy," paper presented at the 1990 American Political Science Association conference in San Francisco.

and profits. The feeling among the rank and file was that business got away with paying wages that were too low given the profit gains. The leadership of the Swedish trade union confederation, or Lands-organisationen (LO) i Sverige, was shocked to discover the intensity of anger and tried to co-opt the loyalty of unions by demanding an extremely high wage increase for the upcoming central agreement of 1970–73. Contractual increases were set high enough to preempt wage drift and to reduce differences with white-collar workers. On top of this agreement came the wage contract of 1975–76, which increased the unit labor costs of Swedish industry by 27 percent relative to its trading partners between 1975–77. Most hurt were engineering employers or large export firms, which felt that the bargaining system had failed to restrain wages. By 1976, the large engineering companies wanted to get out of peak-level bargaining.[35]

Expecting that the newly elected bourgeois government would help them out, employers hoped to see a substantial cut in payroll or marginal taxes to bring wage developments under control. After the reelection of a second bourgeois coalition in 1979, employers organized a lockout in May 1980, refusing to negotiate with LO, which had demanded a high nominal wage increase to counteract income tax changes which favored high-income groups. Instead of supporting SAF in its conflict with LO, the coalition parties pressed employers to accept government mediators and to sign a one-year settlement. This settlement, counter to SAF's advice, entailed another wage increase, and compensation for wage drift for sectors that had fallen behind.[36]

The famous Swedish system of collective bargaining, therefore, had already run into trouble before the umbrella association of engineering companies, Verkstadsföreningen (VF), withdrew in 1983. In the following years, centralized wage bargaining took place because the government intervened to convince employers to restore peak-level bargaining. But in February 1990, the SAF board of directors publicly declared the association's rejection of centralized bargaining. A newly elected board of directors, drawn from the engineering companies, and another high-wage agreement the preceding year, broadened the support within the SAF for a new system of wage determination.

The polarization in the industrial relations system also reflected growing disillusionment among private-sector union members with the high costs of public services, as well as demands of public-sector work-

---

[35] Hans de Geer, *I vänstervind och höhervåg: SAF under 70-talet* (Stockholm: Almänna, 1989), 343.

[36] Andrew Martin, "Trade Unions in Sweden: Strategic Responses to Change and Crisis," in *Unions and Economic Crisis: Britain, West Germany, and Sweden*, ed. Peter Gourevitch et al. (Boston: Allen and Unwin, 1984), 248–50, 310–23.

ers for pay increases plus compensation for wage drift equal to that of the private sector. One conflict about wage solidarity that took place in 1986, which affected two-thirds of the country and 1.5 million workers, was started by public-sector workers who demanded higher pay and a continuation of the automatic compensation for private-sector wage drift. Finance Minister Feldt, speaking as the principal employer of public-sector workers, threatened to increase taxes or to lay off personnel unless the unions consented to automatic pay adjustments following wage drift in the private sector.[37] Alliances within and between unions were broken, permitting wages to be determined by the market and eliminating the solidaristic wage policy.[38]

All was not well, therefore, in a country that has dominated discussions on class compromises and consensual distributive tripartism. Yet Sweden, in contrast to Belgium and the Netherlands, overcame the economic crisis of the late 1970s. The move toward decentralization cannot be directly correlated to the international shocks that rocked the economies of small nations after 1979.

*Industrial Recovery and an Uncertain Future*

In pursuit of a third way, the SAP returned to power and slashed subsidies to shipbuilding and steel and abolished defensive industrial policies to switch to export-led growth. With the reelection of the SAP in 1982, the fight to preserve jobs at all costs, which had consumed the bourgeois coalition from 1976 to 1982, was abandoned. Rescuing bankrupt corporations was deemed ultimately futile; the Social Democratic government resolutely scaled back funding for troubled companies from Skr 17 billion in 1982–83 to Skr 6.5 billion in 1984–85.[39] The gradual withdrawal of subsidies to ailing firms and other restructuring trends reduced Sweden's industrial base. High-technology manufacturing took off as its share of output increased from 27 percent to 31 percent, while that of basic industries declined from 30 percent to 26 percent from 1973 to 1982.[40]

[37] Kristina Ahlén, "Swedish Collective Bargaining under Pressure: Inter-Union Rivalry and Incomes Policies," *British Journal of Industrial Relations* 27 (1989): 330–47; Nils Elvander, *Den Svenska Modellen: Löneförhandlingar och Inkomstpolitik, 1982–1986* (Stockholm: Allmänna, 1988); Lars Calmfors and Anders Forslund, "Wage Formation in Sweden," in *Wage Formation and Macroeconomic Policy in the Nordic Countries,* ed. Lars Calmfors (New York: Oxford University Press, 1990), 63–130.

[38] Peter Swenson, "Labor and the Limits of the Welfare State: The Politics of Intraclass Conflict and Cross-Class Alliances in Sweden and West Germany," *Comparative Politics* 23 (1991): 379–99.

[39] OECD, *Economic Surveys. Sweden 1984/85,* (Paris: OECD, 1985), 47.

[40] For industrial policy in the 1970s, Gunnar Eliasson and Bengt-Christer Ysander, "Sweden: Problems of Maintaining Efficiency under Political Pressure," in *State Invest-*

A shock treatment—the devaluation of the krona by 16 percent in 1982—followed an exchange rate adjustment in 1981 of 10 percent and two in 1977 of 5 percent and 10 percent, respectively. These changes provided Swedish manufacturing with a competitive edge to help it break out of years of stagnation and decline. Relative labor costs fell by 25 percent, but relative export prices fell by about 10 percent. In 1983–85, exports contributed three to four times as much to growth as during the short recovery of 1978–80.[41] The devaluation also improved the current account and generated a trade surplus for the first time since the fiscal year 1973–74. Swedish firms benefited from an extraordinary cost advantage; there was still about 20 percent left of the relative cost advantage at the end of 1986.

The decline in investments in plant and equipment was reversed and replaced by a rise approximately equivalent to 37 percent in the three years following the devaluation (1983–85). Not surprisingly, the strong recovery of investment underpinned a revolutionary turnaround in profits and production. With the export of manufactured goods expanding by 7.5 percent annually for the period of 1983–88, production in 1984 was 12 percent above the low 1982 level.[42] The return to precrisis levels of production and profitability facilitated the dismantling of various selective support schemes and subsidies. Increased business activity also lessened the pressure on the public budget as private consumption increased and employment expenditures decreased.

Leading the recovery was engineering manufacturing, which increased investment layouts by 32 percent in 1984 and continued investing at a steady annual pace of 13 percent from 1985 to 1987. The investment boom in engineering has substantially altered the profile of Swedish manufacturing from specialization in natural-resource–based industries to technology-intensive products and production. New technologies led to a high ratio of computer-aided design and computer-aided manufacturing techniques. Sweden used more robots in manufacturing per ten thousand workers than any other country, rising

*ment Companies in Western Europe*, ed. Brian Hindley (London: Macmillan, 1983), 156–91; Jon Pierre, "Central State, Local Government, and the Market: Industrial Policy and Structural Change in Japan and Sweden," *European Journal of Political Research* 20 (1991): 1–19.

[41] *Growth Policies in Nordic Perspective* (Helsinki/Copenhagen/Stockholm/Bergen: ETLA/IFF/IUI/IOI, 1987), 174.

[42] Fritz W. Scharpf, *Crisis and Choice in European Social Democracy* (Ithaca: Cornell University Press, 1991), 109–11. The figures were taken from Andrew Martin, "Sweden: Restoring the Social Democratic Distributive Regime" (unpublished manuscript, 1987), 48.

from 1.3 in 1974 to 30.0 in 1981 (corresponding figures for Japan were 1.9 and 13.9).[43]

## Political Change and New Governments

The SAP has not been immune to the international wave of budget consolidations and retrenchments and has tried to halt the growth of public expenditures. Since the mid-1980s, new programs must be paid for with existing revenues and are thus at the expense of other programs. Services are increasingly expected to be financed by their users. Another big reform changed taxation and established a new balance between earnings from wealth and income. Although the 1981 agreement between the SAP and the Liberal and Center parties reduced tax progressivity by lowering the marginal rate on income, new limits on deductions based on financial losses and debt and a higher tax on profits from the resale of real estate and other property increased the rates of taxation on wealth.[44]

It seems fair to conclude that the SAP has grudgingly departed from its earlier, emphatically progressive commitment to redistribution. Progressive income tax had justified universal flat-rate social benefits to which both the wealthy and the poor had access. The new tax reforms have given the high-income brackets greater tax relief than low-income groups. These incremental shifts in social policy by the SAP are dwarfed, however, by the breakdown in the industrial relations system. Not until the election of the bourgeois coalition government in September 1991 did neoliberal restructuring of the public sector begin to parallel the anti–social democratic mood in Belgium and the Netherlands.[45] This anti–social democratic mood is strikingly confirmed by the 1991 election, in which the SAP received 37.6 percent of the vote.

[43] OECD, *Economic Surveys. Sweden 1984/85*, 41.

[44] New tax reforms were implemented in 1990. The national income tax was abolished for 85 percent of taxpayers and retained for only the highest income groups. The shortfall in national government revenues is to be financed by extending the value-added tax to goods and services that were previously exempted and by increasing taxes on fringe benefits, capital income, and property. Swedes still pay a local income tax of about 30 percent. Diane Sainsbury, "Swedish Social Democracy in Transition: The Party's Record in the 1980s and the Challenges of the 1990s," *West European Politics* 14 (1991): 36–37; Barbara Haskell, "Paying for the Welfare State and Creating Political Durability," *Scandinavian Studies* 59 (1987): 221–53.

[45] For example, Sven E. Olsson, *Social Policy and Welfare State in Sweden* (Lund: Arkiv, 1990), especially pp. 281–87; Staffan Marklund, *Paradise Lost? The Nordic Welfare States and the Recession, 1975–1985* (Lund: Arkiv, 1988); Herman Schwartz, "Reorganizing the State in Australia, Denmark, New Zealand, and Sweden," *Administration and Society* (forthcoming).

Not since 1922 had the SAP received less than 40 percent of the national vote. The opposition parties collected a comfortable 53.3 percent, not counting the conservative Christian Democratic party which got 7 percent of the vote for the first time. In September 1992, an all-party agreement on government cuts and higher taxes ushered in a significant break with the past. Under stress, the Social Democrats swallowed fundamental changes in comprehensive welfare provisions, child benefits, housing subsidies, old-age pensions, and higher taxes on gas and tobacco. The state will save around Skr 27 billion. The agreement also deals with long-term reforms of Sweden's health and injury insurance system by shifting its costs to employers and trade unions. There is no doubt that Sweden's famous welfare system follows the path of budget reforms and cutbacks taken earlier by Belgium and the Netherlands.

AUSTRIA

In terms of inflation, growth, and employment, Austria has weathered the crises of the 1970s extremely well. Inflation and unemployment remained well below the European average, and Austria has not seen anything like the devastation of industrial manufacturing in Belgium.

The SPÖ liked to claim that Austria's solid record was due to a unique variation of Keynesian demand management. Generally this referred to the grouping together instruments such as demand management, incomes policy, and adjustment programs. The unique Austrian touch consisted of anchoring traditional Keynesian approaches to a hard currency policy in order to counter inflationary pressures and to encourage consultative decision making. The SPÖ leadership would like to claim foresight for selecting the appropriate instruments for the proper situation, but the truth is that it often muddled through, like other governing parties, yet succeeded in inspiring renewed confidence in the economy which slowed divestments, de-industrialization, and job losses.

Econometric studies have found no evidence for the superior fine-tuning of Austrian federal budgets. In general, public expenditures and fiscal policy were driven by automatic stabilizers, and discretionary measures were virtually unknown. Deficits grew in certain years and diminished in following years regardless of whether the business cycle was up or down. Although the finance minister is authorized to tap a "contingency budget" outside of regular parliamentary control to deal with pending recessions, this constitutional privilege has been utilized only twice, in 1975 and 1983. Counter cyclical fiscal spending is as little practiced in Austria as in the Low Countries; its impact on labor and production markets is therefore equally insignificant.[46] In fact, by 1983 the growing national debt prompted a reversal of priorities and ushered in a period of budget consolidation to arrest the further growth of public spending.

Some interpreters of Austro-Keynesianism stressed the centrality of institutionalized cooperation between business and labor to stabilize expectations. These analysts portrayed a system in which the fluctuations and uncertainties intrinsic to capitalist economies found an equilibrium, with the result that investments oscillated less, employment was more secure, and businesses more readily experimented with innovations because firms established fixed points in the market. Incomes policies and hard currency policies diminished uncertainties regarding export price fluctuations. Tax advantages, interest subsidies, and credit regulations stabilized investment flows. Financial speculation was also countered by an exchange rate pegged to the German mark. In effect, Austro-Keynesianism borrowed from neoclassical thinking the notion that reducing transaction costs improves economic efficiency. The Austrian partnership and government policies aimed at reducing the costs of risk taking by providing a conducive framework for rational planning and corporate decision making.[47]

It would be disingenuous not to mention that Austria did not undergo a lengthy industrial recession or export stagnation. For lack of a better explanation, this is generally attributed to exceptional historical luck.

## Economic Stability

Because Austria experienced delays in regaining its sovereignty after World War II and because it is geographically isolated, wedged between Eastern and Western Europe, business cycles in Austria followed their own timing and were dissynchronous with cycles in the rest of Europe. At the beginning of 1974, the Austrian economy was still in the midst of modernization and restructuring, whereas Western Europe had already exhausted its growth stimuli. Its late start enabled Austrian firms to import the newest technology, and a strong recovery in both output

[46] Robert Holzmann and Georg Winckler, "Austrian Economic Policy: Some Critical Remarks on 'Austro-Keynesianism'," *Empirica* 2 (1983): 183–203; Gunther Tichy, "Die Amplitude der österreichischen Konjunkturschwankungen im internationalen Vergleich," *Empirica* 1 (1986): 69–96.

[47] Robert Holzmann and Georg Winckler, "Austrian Economic Policy," 183–203; Gunther Tichy, "Austro-Keynesianismus. Gibt's den? Angewandte Psychologie als Konjunkturpolitik," *Wirtschaftspolitische Blätter* 29, no. 3 (1982): 50–64.

and employment was recorded between 1968 and 1973. Another effect of the modernization was the underdevelopment of the service sector. Only after the boom in manufacturing did retail, tourism, and public services expand, and then they faced constant personnel shortages. The service sector was the first to rehire laid-off workers from private industry.[48]

Developments in the labor market also contributed to reaching the goal of full employment. The working-age population actually declined in the 1960s by an annual average of 0.1 percent and was virtually stagnant in the 1970s. In comparison, the working-age population in the Netherlands grew by 1.4 percent annually from 1960 to 1979.[49] Moreover, in Austria full employment is not a universal entitlement—it is basically restricted to Austrian-born men. Women are generally laid off first, and in greater numbers and are discouraged from registering at their local employment agencies. Hidden unemployment among women is therefore significantly larger than that among men.[50]

The burden of labor market adjustments also fell on foreign workers. In 1973, 226,800 migrant workers were employed, accounting for 8.7 percent of the work force. Their numbers shrank to 148,345 ten years later.[51] The Austrian authorities could seamlessly manipulate the supply of foreign workers because many of them go home every year and can only return once they have obtained a working permit from the labor market board. According to some estimates, had foreign workers not been sent home permanently, unemployment would have reached 5.7 percent instead of 4.2 percent in 1985.[52]

This story of exceptional luck has a cautionary ending. Many policies no longer seem to work. The greatest change has occurred in the state-

[48] Services accounted for 40 percent of civilian employment, and agriculture employed nearly 20 percent of the working population in the 1960s. In the other three countries, the service sector passed that ratio in the 1950s, and agriculture employed a much smaller percentage. See also Scharpf, *Crisis and Choice*, 58. Hans Seidel, "Der österreichische Weg in der Wirtschaftpolitik," *Österreichische Wirtschaftspolitik, 1970–1985* (Vienna: Jugend und Volk, 1987), 20–22.

[49] OECD, *OECD Historical Statistics, 1960–1988* (Paris: OECD, 1990), table 1.2, p. 24.

[50] Margit Wiederschwinger, "Zur Bestimmung von Arbeitslosigkeit. Definition und Messung—Versteckte Arbeitslosigkeit in Österreich," in *Arbeitslosigkeit, Österreichs Vollbeschäftigungspolitik am Ende*, ed. Emmerich Talos and Margit Wiederschwinger (Vienna: Verlag für Gesellschaftskritik, 1987), 82–90.

[51] Georg Fisher, "Arbeitsmarkt und Arbeitslosigkeit. Entwickelung und Struktur," in *Arbeitslosigkeit, Österreichs Vollbeschäftigungspolitik am Ende*, 16–17. See also Felix Butschek, "Full Employment during Recession," in *The Political Economy of Austria*, ed. Sven W. Arndt (Washington, D.C.: American Enterprise Institute, 1982), 107–8.

[52] Gudrun Biffl, Aluis Guger, and Wolfgang Pollan, *The Causes of Low Unemployment in Austria*, Occasional Papers in Employment Studies, no. 7 (The Employment Research Center of the University of Buckingham, 1987), 7.

owned sector where subsidization has been drastically reduced because of falling productivity and declining competitiveness.

## Political Change

By the mid-1980s, inflation was no longer a menace, and questions regarding competitiveness, privatization, and tax reforms dominated public discussion and shaped the electoral campaigns of both the People's and the Socialist parties.[53] Corruption and waste turned voters against the public sector, and the state-owned companies were to be privatized or had already been sold. Both the Socialist and People's parties lost votes in federal election in 1990 because they were identified with political patronage in the public sector and because they seemed unable to respond to new concerns about the environment and immigration.

In the general election of October 1990, the real winner was the Freedom party, which more than doubled its parliamentary seats from 15 to 33. The Socialist party, which has since been renamed the Social Democratic party of Austria (it retained its acronym, SPÖ), kept its share of the vote because of the personal popularity of the chancellor, Franz Vranitsky, and because the Socialists presided over tax reforms and the restructuring of the state-owned sector.[54] The tone of political discussions, however, was driven by ideas on rationalization, public-sector retrenchment, and preparing Austria for EC membership, while ideological differences between the parties on the Left and Right have all but vanished.

## INTERNATIONALIZATION AND DISTRIBUTIVE TRIPARTISM

According to the small-state literature, small European democracies are more accustomed to coping with unpredictable international fluctuations in trade and markets and are therefore more adept at formulating adjustment programs. In addition, labor unions are more likely to be involved in setting adjustment policies and implementing economic recovery strategies because of existing practices of corporatist

[53] Georg Winckler, "Der Austrokeynesianismus und sein Ende," *Österreichische Zeitschrift für Politikwissenschaft* 17 (1988): 221–30. Hans Seidel coined the term *Austro-Keynesianism* and used it first in a 1979 article. In 1982, however, he stated that Austro-Keynesianism has come to an end. Hans Seidel, "Austro-Keynesianismus," *Wirtschaftspolitische Blätter* 29, no. 3 (1982): 11–15.

[54] Delia Meth-Cohn and Wolfgang Müller, "Leaders Count: The Austrian Election of October 1990," *West European Politics* 14 (1991): 183–88.

mediation. My descriptions of the Netherlands and Belgium, however, belie this simplistic image of enhanced state capacity and sensitive macro-economic fine tuning. In fact, more striking are the failures to recognize quickly the challenges confronting exporters and business, and to respond quickly to correct the situation. Once recovery cures were evaluated, not only was organized labor not party to the discussions but it was also asked to carry the brunt of the costs of adjustment.

Sweden is unique among the four countries in that it designed a recovery package within the context of tripartite consensual exchanges which seemed to work for at least a short period, until the late 1980s. How can one account for the change in tack in the Low Countries? And how can one address the growing troubles in the 1990s within the system of consensual redistributive exchange in Austria and Sweden?

Analysts of class compromises believe they have found at least a partial answer to the first question. They hold that governments will promote full employment as long as union leaders ask their members to forgo current gains in return for future job security and improved standards of living. In turn, wage moderation by workers free business to allocate new investment capital in order to remain internationally competitive. In the long run, the nation is better off because the erosion of its export competitiveness is diminished, the decline of profits is halted, and job losses are moderate. According to the leftist version of this theme, social democratic governments are more likely to extract wage concessions from unions because their governing record speaks for itself and confirms their commitment to equitable distribution of the costs of adjustment.

From the figures in tables 5 and 6, one can see that workers in each

Table 5. Rates of change in real hourly earnings and unit labor costs in manufacturing (average annual changes in percent)

| | Rate of change in real hourly earnings (%) | | Rate of change in unit labor cost (%) | |
|---|---|---|---|---|
| | 1973–79 | 1979–86 | 1973–79 | 1979–86 |
| Belgium | 3.5 | −0.1 | 7.4 | 2.1 |
| Netherlands | 0.9 | 0.7 | 3.4 | 4.2 |
| Austria | 3.7 | 0.8 | 5.3 | 2.8 |
| Sweden | 2.1 | −0.4 | 5.8 | 0.7 |
| EC | 3.7 | 1.2[a] | 10.4 | 6.2 |
| OECD | 2.0 | 0.7[a] | 8.7 | 3.9 |

[a]For the period 1980–85.
Source: OECD, OECD Historical Statistics, 1960–1988 (Paris: OECD, 1990), 90, 94.

*Table 6.* Unit labor costs and export prices in manufacturing
(in common currency, 1982 = 100)

| | Unit labor costs | | | | | Export prices | | | | |
|---|---|---|---|---|---|---|---|---|---|---|
| | 1983 | 1984 | 1985 | 1986 | 1987 | 1983 | 1984 | 1985 | 1986 | 1987 |
| Belgium[a] | 96 | 98 | 100 | 103 | 103 | 99 | 98 | 98 | 103 | 103 |
| Netherlands | 99 | 92 | 89 | 93 | 93 | 99 | 95 | 94 | 97 | 97 |
| Austria | 99 | 97 | 98 | 99 | 100 | 100 | 98 | 98 | 104 | 105 |
| Sweden | 88 | 92 | 94 | 93 | 93 | 97 | 99 | 100 | 102 | 103 |

[a]Includes Luxembourg.
*Source:* OECD, *Economic Outlook* 40 (1986):140.

country made wage concessions from 1979 to 1986. Everywhere the
prevailing norm was to hold back on wage claims until better times—to
wait until export prices, an important indicator of a country's competitiveness, stabilized over several years. Yet investment, growth, and jobs
remained sluggish and barely recovered after 1982.

Many developments stand in the way of full employment and growth
in the late 1980s after nearly a decade of sluggish investment activities.
Private investments tumbled after 1973 in most OECD countries in the
wake of the energy turmoil, inflation, and labor militance. Theorists
claim that after such a long slide in capital investments, a noticeable
recovery in the pace of capital accumulation, better employment, and
growth performance will take place only if companies believe that:
capital investment today will yield higher profits tomorrow; real investments will yield higher rates of return than financial assets; return of
foreign investments will be modest; world market pressures are manageable; and the economic future looks bright. This list of conditions is
far from complete, but it does underscore the terrible dilemmas faced
by governments. For example, take the issue of financial versus productive investments. As barriers against financial flows and innovations
have come down, more capital has been put to work to exploit the
differences in interest rates, changes in exchange rates, and new financial instruments. Governments are powerless with regard to how financial versus productive investments behave. Nor can governments
change the expectation of investors that future sales and profits on
productive investments do not justify current expenditures on capital
goods and human resources. Such expectations reflect a score of trade-
offs for investors in which financial investments are more attractive
than productive investments because of their flexibility, convertibility,
and short-term returns. This is why the regulation of wages and labor
acquiescence were not sufficient to induce continuous reinvestments in
the 1980s.

79

From the figures in tables 7 and 8, one can see that the share of machinery and equipment investment in the GDP and the investment in nonresidential construction changed little from 1974 to 1988 in all four countries. Belgium's investment rate seems to have been the worst from the late 1970s and late 1980s; both capital equipment and construction more or less stagnated over a relatively long period. Yet Belgian governments have done what they are supposed to do to stimulate investments and reduce labor rigidity (they have instituted more flexible wage setting and higher labor mobility). In this age of financial integration and liberalization, it is doubtful whether governments still possess the ability to influence business investment decisions. If governments cannot influence the conditions under which business will provide workers with improved standards of living, the rationale for unions to accede to requests for wage moderation and docility is lost.

By the end of 1988, Belgium and the Netherlands recorded real improvements in growth and investment rates as reform policies, corporate taxation and deregulation, and increased consumer demand in the European Community pulled them out of a prolonged slump. Public spending was reduced, but many antiwelfare advocates believed that the job was not yet done and that opportunities for further shrinkage still existed. The transformation from social citizenship to social market welfare state involves a gradual process of small and large structural changes, beyond fiscal retrenchment, to alter the very foundation on which the first expansion of social programs took place. The coalitions of Lubbers in the Netherlands and Martens in Belgium were as pathbreaking as the more familiar Thatcher and Reagan administrations. To accomplish their goals, Dutch and Belgian center-right governments set aside the institutions of corporatist consultations and then resurrected collective bargaining and tripartite consultation with the provision that the social partners adhere to government guidelines for wage or pay contracts and extra benefits. They went further than simply to reform budgetary allocations.

*Table 7.* Machinery and equipment as percentage of GDP

|             | 1974–79 | 1982 | 1983 | 1984 | 1985 | 1986 | 1987 | 1988 |
|-------------|---------|------|------|------|------|------|------|------|
| Belgium     | 7.1     | 6.5  | 6.3  | 6.9  | 6.8  | 7.0  | 7.1  | 7.8  |
| Netherlands | 8.7     | 7.3  | 8.0  | 8.4  | 9.4  | 10.1 | 9.9  | 10.3 |
| Austria     | 10.1    | 9.5  | 9.0  | 9.1  | 9.8  | 9.9  | 9.8  | 9.9  |
| Sweden      | 8.6     | 7.3  | 7.7  | 7.8  | 8.8  | 8.3  | 8.7  | 8.9  |

*Source:* OECD, *Historical Statistics, 1960–1988* (Paris: OECD, 1990), 70.

*Table 8.* Nonresidential construction as percentage of GDP

|  | 1974–79 | 1982 | 1983 | 1984 | 1985 | 1986 | 1987 | 1988 |
|---|---|---|---|---|---|---|---|---|
| Belgium | 7.6 | 7.1 | 6.3 | 5.7 | 5.3 | 5.1 | 5.0 | 5.5 |
| Netherlands | 6.7 | 5.6 | 5.1 | 5.1 | 4.9 | 5.0 | 5.0 | 5.5 |
| Austria | 9.2 | 7.0 | 6.9 | 6.8 | 6.7 | 6.9 | 7.2 | 7.3 |
| Sweden | 7.8 | 6.7 | 6.5 | 6.2 | 6.0 | 6.0 | 6.0 | 6.0 |

*Source:* OECD, *Historical Statistics, 1960–1988* (Paris: OECD, 1990), 71.

The puzzle is, therefore, why the assumptions on which major policy decisions were formerly based no longer operated in the Low Countries even though they lasted at least until the end of the 1980s in Austria and Sweden. What forced governments to switch to neoliberalism? And why were their achievements so disappointing? It is timely to look at how business and finance have responded to international pressures and new opportunities. Part of the recovery strategy of business and finance is to seek international connections and to become stateless entities. The neoliberal atmosphere and policy regime in Belgium and the Netherlands arose as key capitalist actors moved beyond the national jurisdiction of governments and thereby snapped the tripartite link between labor concessions, state inducements, and reinvestments.

# CHAPTER FOUR

# Holding Companies
# in Belgium and Austria

In Belgium, consensual tripartite decision making and policy proposals failed to buffer the domestic economy from international fluctuations and subsequently fell apart under external pressures. This history runs counter to the widely held assumption that social institutions in small states are specifically built to protect domestic groups and achievements from external pressures. The case of Belgium points to a more plausible inference: that class compromises in small countries *cannot* surmount and survive the combined effects of inflation, industrial restructuring, decline in world demand for exports, and currency instabilities.

One way to rescue the class compromise thesis is to argue that labor unions were too demanding on wages or insensitive to employers' competitive pressures in Belgium and that therefore the system of social exchanges and government intervention became dysfunctional. This modification of the theory of class compromises is not satisfactory. Unions and workers were equally sensitive (or insensitive) to maintaining business competitiveness in all four countries discussed here. It is not clear that unions and workers behaved radically differently in the four countries. A better approach is to investigate whether business cares at all about social concertation and therefore wishes to preserve the institutions of class compromises. If business differs about whether tripartism is worth rescuing, then we should investigate why perceptions of consensual tripartism vary over time and across nations.

In this chapter I compare business politics in Belgium and Austria; both economies are dominated by holding companies, and neither has produced world-class transnational corporations. Belgian and Austrian holding companies differ in ownership structure—they are privately owned in Belgium but state-owned in Austria. Employers were more united in Austria than in Belgium because Austrian large firms were state-owned and small business was too dependent on government to gamble on a go-it-alone strategy. In contrast, clusters of intercorporate networks exerted considerable political influence outside the employer associations in Belgium, and their presence impaired employer solidarity.

Both countries received large inflows of foreign capital and became important manufacturing locations for nonresident transnational corporations. Yet foreign capital built very different relations with tripartite institutions in the two countries. In Austria, foreign investors were absorbed into the social partnership and exerted a positive influence. In Belgium, they sharpened the antagonism between management and unions, and thus added to the distrust and friction that dismantled social programmation in the middle to late 1970s.

## THE POLITICS OF BELGIAN BUSINESS

Belgian employers accepted the principles of the social pact with the understanding that collective wage bargaining and worker representation would not encroach on management power and investment decisions. During the heyday of social programmation in the 1960s until the mid-1970s, unions had the initiative, and employers went along despite strong objections. In the mid-1970s, employers and analysts routinely referred to "almighty" unions that shackled business with high wages, unreasonable regulations, and demands for economic democracy or participation in investment decisions. Rising unemployment and industrial restructuring have enfeebled union power and hardened employers' attitudes: employers no longer accept collective bargaining and instead have moved wage negotiations to the company level. At the company level, employers insist on increased flexibility to fix wages, adjust work schedules, and determine working conditions. Unions and employers have switched places, as the unions struggle now to keep up with the changes in social legislation, workplace organization, and labor market trends.[1]

Although employers seemed to be the weaker party during the heyday of national concertation, Belgian capital has traditionally wielded considerable power. One source of structural power is the high degree

[1] Armand Spineux, "Trade Unionism in Belgium: The Difficulties of a Major Renovation," in *European Industrial Relations: The Challenge of Flexibility,* ed. Guido Baglioni and Colin Crouch (Newbury Park, Calif.: Sage, 1990), 42–71.

of capital concentration. One percent of all companies accounted for roughly 40 percent of Belgium's industrial output.[2] Control over these industrial and financial resources rested with privileged groups of managing directors and family dynasties which shaped the corporate strategies of a vast number of firms through intricate webs of cross-ownership and corporate interlocks. This concentrated ownership has endowed Belgian business with extraordinary influence and allowed it to ignore inducements furnished by sympathetic or desperate governments and accommodating labor unions. In turn, trade union delegates, noticing the futility of making concessions and the lack of reciprocity, began to lose confidence in social exchanges in the 1970s and resorted to more militant actions. Strike activities and factory occupations ruined the atmosphere for bipartite or tripartite concertation further. In retrospect, trade unions could outwit employer associations during periods of growth and full employment. Employer associations lacked unity and self-control because of cultural and economic polarization while, in addition, firm size, export intensity, and the presence of transnational corporations confounded peak-level coordination. But trade unions could not vanquish capital, that is, they could not prevent the holding companies that controlled whole sections of manufacturing industry, banking, transport, and energy from doing what they wanted to do.

From the perspective of workers and unions, the greatest uncertainty came from the fact that boards of directors of the holding companies made investment decisions for many firms in heavy manufacturing although chief executives of the holding companies were not drawn into concertation. Accords were reached with the management of a firm which belonged to the sphere of influence of, say, the Societé Générale de Belgique (SGB). But this firm had no control over critical decisions regarding long-term investments, restructuring plans, expansion or closure, and so forth. Agreements concluded during the tripartite or bilateral sessions were always based on partial information and unfulfilled promises since the actual owners of the plant were absent.

### The Holding Companies

Belgian holding companies are best defined as financial institutions that manage a portfolio of stocks in order to control the capital management of companies in which they hold equity.[3] They do this by

[2] The figure is from François Martou, "Some Aspects of Industrial Policy in Belgium," in *A Competitive Future for Europe? Towards a New European Industrial Policy*, ed. P. R. Beije et al. (New York: Croom Helm, 1987), 201.

[3] Herman Daems, *The Holding Company and Corporate Control* (Boston: Nijhoff, 1978), 2. There are about seventy holding companies, though the three most important originated

buying the minimum amount of a company's stock necessary to be the primary shareholder, thus wielding the greatest influence. Theoretically, a holding company can control the whole asset structure of an economy by purchasing the minimum portion of stocks needed to exercise control of all Belgian corporations.

The holding companies issue securities to raise capital. At the top of the affiliated firms stands the parent holding company, which creates subsidiaries through which it acquires equity shares in other companies. The structure resembles a pyramid; layers of subholdings and subsidiaries influence a wide range of companies. Savers invest in the holding companies' securities and retain indirect stakes in the assets of hundreds of firms. Unlike mutual funds, however, holding companies strive to control corporate decision making. A holding company is never a dormant partner that simply supplies a steady flow of investment capital. With their domination of the securities and capital markets, the Belgian holding companies organize the flow of capital to industry and thus shape industrial policy.

The assertive position of the holding companies in the capital market and in manufacturing defeated the first wave of industrial revitalization and economic redevelopment in the 1950s. Employers vacillated about endorsing tripartite negotiations, although the government and the trade union federations asked at various times for corporatist councils and deliberations to solve persistent industrial stagnation.[4] One area in which corporatist mediation was established in the late 1960s to facilitate industrial rationalization and restructuring was in the iron and steel industries—the backbone of the Belgian industrial miracle in the nineteenth century. Belgium still had the highest production of steel—1,299 kilos per capita in 1970, of which more than 75 percent was exported.[5] In 1975, about sixty thousand people worked in the steel sector, or 2.6 percent of total private-sector employment, and steel accounted for 7.8 percent of value added in the manufacturing industry. State aid to steel predated the European crisis of 1973/74,

---

from universal banks that existed before 1934 when commercial and deposit banking was legally separated from the financial ownership of industrial and commercial companies. See also Fernand Collin, "De Belgische financiële groepen van 1945 tot 1975," *Res Publica* 25 (1983): 621–31.

[4] Jaak Brepoels, *Wat zoudt gij zonder 't werkvolk zijn? Anderhalve eeuw arbeidersstrijd in België, 1967–1980*, part 2 (Louvain: Kritak, 1981); Geert Dancet, "From a Workable Social Compromise to Conflict: The Case of Belgium," in *The Search for Labor Market Flexibility: The European Economies in Transition*, ed. Robert Boyer (Oxford: Clarendon Press, 1988), 97–105; Roger Blanpain, "Arbeidsverhoudingen: Een momentopname van 'tripartism' in perspectief," in *30 Jaar Belgische Arbeidsverhoudingen*, ed. Roger Blanpain (Deventer, Netherlands: Kluwer, 1977).

[5] M. Installé, "L'Industrie sidérurgique en Belgique (1)," *Courier Hebdomadaire du CRISP*, nos. 660–61 (1974): 7, 24.

and 41 percent of the BF 29 billion invested in steel between 1967 and 1970 was financed through parastatal bodies.[6]

From the perspective of government officials, the chief problem in the 1970s was the pervasive discretionary control of the holding companies over capital strategies of large steel firms. Although the companies had decided to withdraw from a manufacturing industry without a future, they nonetheless refused to relinquish control over steel after 1975.[7] Before 1975, the financial holding groups imposed upon the steel industry a systematic debt policy that was financially lucrative yet crippled innovative corporate strategies and resulted in the bankruptcy of many steel firms. Once the state had taken over several steel firms, private banks and financial groups continued to delay restructuring plans until they had extracted favorable packages from the government.[8] In the meantime, the holding companies had been investigating cross-border alliances to strengthen their corporate profitability, joining the European trend in trade and financial liberalization. Steel has historically played an important role in Belgium's economic development, and the decline of steel was one of the main causes for the resurgence of linguistic conflict because most of the troubled steel mills and foundries were located in Wallonia, while Flanders was much less affected by the industrial crisis.

## The Steel Crisis

After the World War II, the holding companies fought among themselves for control of Belgium's steel industry. The largest of the giant steel companies was Cockerill in Liège, nineteenth among the world producers of steel in 1972. Seventeen percent of its shares as well as some indirect claims through another holding company were in the hands of the Société Générale de Belgique.[9] Through its equity portfo-

[6] Yves Mény and Vincent Wright, "State and Steel in Western Europe," in *The Politics of Steel: Western Europe and the Steel Industry in the Crisis Years, 1974–1984*, ed. Yves Mény and Vincent Wright (New York: de Gruyter, 1987), 20.

[7] Michel Capron, "The State, the Regions and Industrial Redevelopment: The Challenge of the Belgian Steel Crisis," in *Politics of Steel*, ed. Mény and Wright, 698. See also Jo Cottenier, Patrick de Boosere, and Thomas Gounet, *Dossier de Generale 1822–1992* (Berchem, Belgium: EPO Uitgeverij, 1989), 113–15, 176–77.

[8] Yves Mény and Vincent Wright, "State and Steel in Western Europe," in their *Politics of Steel*, 78, 85. Michel Capron, "La crise sidérurgique en Belgique et en France: Les stratégies patronales," *Contradictions* 27–28 (1981): 85–103. The steel crisis also fueled antagonism between Wallonia and Flanders. Kenneth D. McRae, *Conflict and Compromise in Multilingual Societies: Belgium* (Waterloo, Ontario: Wilfrid Laurier University Press, 1986), 149–73.

[9] Cottenier, Boosere, and Gounet, *Dossier de Generale, 1822–1992*, 114. In 1981, the heavy losses of Cockerill and of Hainaut-Sambre in Charleroi led to the merger of the

lio, the SGB shaped the business strategy and commercial development of Cockerill and exerted a correspondingly large influence in the entire industry group.[10] Competition among directors of the holding companies for control over steel spurred a series of mergers and takeovers. Cockerill, under the direction of the Société Générale, enlarged its operations by taking over or merging with other steel-producing firms in the Liège area in 1945, 1955, 1957, 1961, 1966, and 1970. This aggressive absorption of independent steel companies was premised on the view that the demand for steel would continue to rise. The Société Générale had always actively sought manufacturing assets, and it moved into basic industries quickly after World War II to preempt rivals.[11] It was not the resulting concentration of production and economies of scale, however, that brought on the subsequent difficulties.

Already in the 1960s defects in the steel industry appeared as the Belgian industry grappled with the same difficulties other European producers experienced. Rising prices for coke and surplus capacity from intensified international competition required large-scale investments in new technologies to catch up with world leaders. The heavy indebtedness of many Belgian firms during the takeover spree of the 1960s alarmed both labor and government because it meant that the steel firms were not likely to pursue renovation. Instead, debt incurred by the steel firms typically benefited the owners—a high proportion of the debt repayments went into the accounts of the financial groups that controlled the industry in the first place.[12]

In 1966, unions called for an emergency roundtable with government and steel companies to discuss plans by the steel employers' association or Groupement des Hauts Fourneaux, to close outdated plants and pour funds into the most productive ones. The outcome of the roundtable was a permanent institution for tripartite consultation on steel policy. The Consultative Committee on Steel Policy, or Comité de Concertations de la Politique Sidérurgique (CCPS) aimed at promot-

two firms to create Cockerill-Sambre. By then, the Société Générale had withdrawn from steel and reduced its share to 1.94 percent. The state was the largest shareholder with 81.4 percent.
    [10] M. Installé, "L'Industrie sidérurgique en Belgique (2)," *Courier Hebdomadaire du CRISP*, no. 662 (1974): 24. In contrast to the other holding companies, financial services accounted for a third of SGB activities, while manufacturing was nearly 60 percent. See Michel Capron, "The State, the Regions, and Industrial Redevelopment," in *Politics of Steel,*, ed. Mény and Wright, 778–80.
    [11] Anthony Rowley, "Belgium and Luxembourg: The Power of 'Les Holdings,'" in *The Barons of European Industry*, ed. Anthony Rowley (New York: Holmes and Meier, 1974), 110. See also René de Preter, *De 200 rijkste families: Geld en macht in de wereld van de holdings en de miljonairs* (Berchem, Belgium: EPO Uitgeverij, 1983).
    [12] Mény and Wright, "State and Steel in Western Europe," in their *Politics of Steel*, 9.

ing a planned program of restructuring, regional redevelopment, and reemployment for displaced workers. From 1967 to 1970, CCPS members actively evaluated investment programs, participated in the planning phase of individual firms, and proposed ways to reduce transport costs. CCPS also supervised the restructuring of several troubled firms and encouraged the Société Générale to take over another independent steel company, thereby allowing it to gain control of 41 percent of Belgian steel production. Between 1967 and 1971, CCPS also oversaw the release of nearly BF 11 billion to the steel industry in public credits (with a subsidized interest rate) through the National Public Credit Institution.[13]

After 1972, concertation fell apart. Unions justifiably complained that the actual owners of the factories—the holding companies— conveniently sidestepped the CCPS recommendations and took actions that contravened the essential purpose of tripartite consultation. The directors of the holding companies were not really part of the steel employers' federation. Top managers of the holding company, outside the formal consultative channels, determined the corporate and financial strategies of each steel firm. Despite the long history of the holding companies, Belgian corporate law does not recognize groups of companies, and judicial practice in labor law and industrial relations does not provide protection against group activities with respect to shutdowns, layoffs, and restructuring. This was a sore point for the Belgian Socialist party, which had repeatedly fought for an interpretation of company statutes and management liability that would take into account the tangled network of ownership of a large part of the Belgian manufacturing industry.[14]

The event that marked the end of tripartite concertation came when one of the holding companies informed the CCPS of a major change after it had already been implemented. Union representatives also began to notice that day-to-day affairs of the firm, such as pricing and financing, were not discussed in CCPS meetings and were off-limits to government and unions.[15] The tripartite consultations were the least effective in areas of employment and industrial redevelopment. CCPS participants were obliged to accept a series of rationalization programs

[13] Capron, "The State, the Regions, and Industrial Redevelopment," in *Politics of Steel*, ed. Mény and Wright, 703–6; Installé, "L'Industrie sidérurgique en Belgique (2)," 7–10; Jean-Pierre Pauwels, "Steel and the State in Belgium," *Annals of Public and Cooperative Economy* 51 (1980): 393–404.
[14] Willy Claes, "The European Community Is More than a Free-Trade Zone," in *Europe without Frontiers*, ed. Piet Dankert and Ad Kooyman (Assen, Netherlands: Van Gorcum, 1989), 16–17.
[15] Installé, "L'Industrie sidérurgique en Belgique (2)," 29.

involving job losses and had no means of deploying funds to create jobs in other sectors. In addition, the CCPS could not influence the long-term plans of the holding companies. These failures drained most of the energy and motivation of trade unions.

In the early 1970s, the international steel market recovered, and Belgian firms thrived, despite glaring shortcomings that would lessen their resistance against a more severe world crisis. First, Belgian production was overspecialized in bulk goods, with an underrepresentation of finished goods. Developed products represented only 11 percent of production in 1977.[16] Although Belgium had many steel producers, the holding companies had not tried to stimulate downstream diversification and integration to link raw material supplies to high value-added finished goods.

Second, the mergers were driven by the desire for quick and secure profits on safe investments. After a merger or acquisition, management did not survey the long-term compatibility of the assets of the new and the original firm. Firms were amalgamated, but outdated machinery, inefficient buildings, and incompatible assembly procedures were not pruned. Rather, outmoded equipment was allowed to mix with the most sophisticated designs, and duplication in production of hot-rolling mills, for example, was the rule. Acquisitions and mergers were not accompanied by a coherent medium- to long-term policy. With a few notable exceptions, the new management delayed the introduction of new technologies that would increase productivity and was slow to adapt the new techniques of continuous casting. In 1975, 4.1 percent of Belgium's total steel output was manufactured through continuous casting, the lowest rate in Europe.[17] Holding-company managers preferred to increase the quantity of products and to seek new markets. Cockerill, the showcase of Société Générale steel holdings, acquired the reputation of the worst-managed firm in Europe in the 1970s.

Surplus capacity and declining demand in advanced industrialized markets for steel in 1975 resulted in a rapid decline of production. Cockerill alone lost BF 4 billion. The situation deteriorated rapidly.[18] The firms needed to restructure quickly, but their debt payments made that impossible. State aid could only be obtained through the tripartite committee, and the holding companies asked for a temporary recon-

[16] Capron, "The State, the Regions, and Industrial Redevelopment," in *Politics of Steel*, ed. Mény and Wright, 699.
[17] William T. Hogan, *World Steel in the 1980s: A Case of Survival* (Lexington, Mass.: Lexington Books, 1983), 44.
[18] Cottenier, de Boosere, and Gounet, *Dossier de Generale, 1822–1992*, 170.

vening of the CCPS in the form of a separate national conference on steel in order to request subsidization. National conferences were held in 1977 and 1978.

The sums of money involved in restructuring and rationalization were so gigantic that the state took over most of the debt of the firms, bought 60 percent of the capital shares, financed investments and social security costs, and paid the interest payments. In 1979, the state paid out BF 2.68 trillion to stockholders to obtain a majority share in Cockerill and an additional BF 5 billion to acquire stock in two other companies. Servicing the steel companies' debts alone cost the Belgian Treasury BF 4.2 billion. Yet the voice of the government was not heard inside the board of directors; fragile and factious coalition governments lacked assertive economic leadership.

In addition, governments held unfounded expectations regarding the willingness of the private sector to match the sums of money for modernization channeled through public institutions. The government had signed a protocol with the holding companies in the steel industry in March 1980 whereby the private actors pledged to pay half of the proposed BF 29 billion for the rationalization plans. The fund began with BF 1 billion in capital, which was inadequate, given the originally anticipated need of BF 29 billion. Some months later, the SGB governor announced in a shareholders' meeting that his company would not spend an additional franc to support the steel industry. In 1981, Cockerill merged with Sambre, another troubled giant, to become Cockerill-Sambre. The state was left owning no less than 81.44 percent of the shares, whereas the Société Générale had reduced its holdings to 1.94 percent.

Over the years, the sums involved for rationalization and layoffs assumed staggering proportions. Between 1959 and 1979, public credit institutions invested BF 149 billion in the steel industry.[19] During that period, the state had not yet bought capital shares to become co-owner. From 1979 to 1987, the Treasury spent some BF 240 billion on steel.[20] This amount included only public funds allocated through the public credit institutions. The practice for many years had been to establish a parastatal institution that could borrow money on the capital market; the Treasury serviced the debt payments. Eventually, of course, the state had to pay off the principal to the public credit institutions.[21]

[19] Evelyne Lentzen and Etienne Arcq, "Les secteurs nationaux," *Courier Hebdomadaire du CRISP*, no. 938 (1980): 28.

[20] Jean-François Escarmelle, "Capitaux publics et restructurations industrielles," *Courier Hebdomadaire du CRISP* 1078 (1985): 1–31.

[21] André Mommen, *Een tunnel zonder einde* (Amsterdam: Kluwer, 1987), 140. For more information on public credit institutions and capital shares, see Anne Drumaux, "Priva-

Despite the futility of the endeavor to keep steel alive through public aid, the government could not afford to let Cockerill sink, because as a majority owner, the public sector would lose in depreciations and be left with further losses. The bankruptcy of Cockerill-Sambre would threaten the livelihood of nearly two hundred thousand people—workers and their families, subcontractors, ancillary personnel—and no politician wanted that on her or his record.[22]

Remarkably, the Société Générale declared losses for only one year (1981), despite Cockerill's operating deficit of BF 6.1 billion in 1980 and an equally large loss in 1981. The Société Générale outlived the steel crisis because its equity in steel was only 1 percent in the 1980s, down from 25 percent in the 1960s.[23]

SGB's survival of the steel catastrophe is remarkable but not very difficult to explain. In its dealings with the government, the chief executives of the parent company had the upper hand. Until 1980, the SGB could threaten to withdraw totally from steel by dumping its shares on the open market, which would have provoked a nasty psychological and financial calamity. After 1980, when its involvement in the steel industries had been vastly diminished, the holding company reneged on its earlier pledges to earmark a portion of its reserves to finance the restructuring program of Cockerill-Sambre. Since the bankruptcy of Cockerill-Sambre was politically unacceptable and financially irresponsible, the government covered the unpaid bills.[24] The Société Générale saddled the Belgian taxpayer with an immensely costly failure. Had government intervened sooner or had the Société Générale been more attuned to the fluctuations in the steel market, the crisis would have been shorter and less severe. But whenever governments tried to intervene, they frequently pulled at the shortest end of the stick and were often seduced into transferring tax money before they conceived of a foolproof method to oversee the final destination of public funds.

In the meantime, the holding groups' acquisitions in Europe and overseas steadily expanded. The Société had broken into the North American market by participating in Canadian mineral companies and multinational corporations in 1980, and it was the largest shareholder in the largest Belgian multinational corporation, Petrofina (which ran

---

tization in Belgium: The National and International Context," *West European Politics* 11 (1988): 74–86.

[22] Herman Todt, *Staat in ontbinding? België: De jaren '80* (Louvain: Davidsfonds, 1988), 104.

[23] Cottenier, Boosere, and Gounet, *Dossier de Générale, 1822–1992,* 171.

[24] Capron, "The State, the Regions, and Industrial Redevelopment," in *Politics of Steel,* ed. Mény and Wright, 721.

oil refineries).[25] At the same time, its withdrawal from Wallonia was spectacular. In 1958, approximately 44 percent of SGB's portfolio consisted of Walloon properties; this ratio fell to 22 percent in 1974 and 5 percent in 1982.[26]

Ironically, in late 1987, the growing international possessions of the SGB, coupled with its fragmented ownership structure, aroused the ambition of the Italian financier Carlos de Benedetti to acquire the Belgian financial group and establish the first authentic European holding company. In the end, the SGB preferred an alliance with the French SUEZ financial group to a takeover by an Italian raider. By 1988, for all practical purposes, the Société Générale ceased to be a Belgian legal entity—more than 50 percent of its share capital was owned by SUEZ.[27] With the SGB's demise, a dramatic relationship between government and the most significant faction of capital had come to an inglorious end.

### Foreign Transnational Corporations

Belgian authorities, exasperated by the dull performance of the holding companies and manufacturers, began to court American investors to bolster the domestic economy in the late 1950s. Governments offered numerous tax incentives to attract overseas investments and touted the advantage of being a member of the newly formed European Economic Community. The plan was a success. By the first oil price shock, affiliates of nonresident transnational corporations employed about 40 percent of the labor force, twice as much as domestic transnational corporations,[28] and accounted for 44 percent of total sales of Belgian manufacturing and 80 percent of all new investments from 1970 to 1976.[29]

[25] Cottenier, de Boosere, and Gounet, *Dossier de Generale, 1822–1992*, 125–29, 190–95.

[26] Bruno Dethomas and José-Alain Fralon, *Les milliards de l'orgueil: L'affaire de la Société Générale de Belgique* (Paris: Gallimard, 1989), 83.

[27] Cottenier, de Boosere, and Gounet, *Dossier de Generale, 1822–1992*, 323–24. In 1991, the swapping of shares between SGB and Groupe Bruxelles Lambert reduced SUEZ's stake to 51.1 percent and Cerus's (of Benedetti) to 9.9 percent while the two largest Belgian holding companies grew closer together.

[28] Different estimates are given by various authors. Daniel van den Bulcke ("Belgian Industrial Policy and Foreign Multinational Corporations: Objectives versus Performance," in *Governments and Multinational Corporations: The Policy of Control versus Autonomy*, ed. Walter H. Goldberg [Cambridge, Mass.: Oelgeschlager, Gunn, and Hain, 1983], 243) puts the share at 30 percent. J. Brepoels (*Wat zoudt gij zonder 't werkvolk zijn?* [Louvain: Kritak, 1978], 154, n. 3) gives a less conservative estimate of 40 percent. See also International Labour Organization (ILO), *Employment Effects of Multinational Enterprises in Industrial Countries* (Geneva: ILO, 1981), 79.

[29] Daniel van de Bulcke, "Belgium," *Multinational Enterprises, Economic Structure, and International Competitiveness*, ed. J. H. Dunning (New York: Wiley, 1985), 263.

Many affiliates of foreign subsidiaries did not merge with ailing Belgian companies but used the attractive fiscal climate, the strategic proximity to other large European markets, and the superb transport network to dominate the more advanced sectors of manufacturing—telecommunications, electronic equipment, engines, and steel tubes.[30] They shunned Wallonia; 60 percent of foreign investments and 70 percent of new jobs created by transnational companies went to Flanders.[31] Foreign investors were also more innovative than Belgian domestic companies and tended to develop products for larger markets. Foreign and domestic firms within the same high-technology production group followed different strategies; smaller domestic firms focused more on small-market niches and product differentiation. Because these smaller companies were Belgian, they were more sensitive to local politics and administrative decisions.[32]

But American subsidiaries were not absent from business politics. Coming from a different tradition and feeling strongly about the desirability of company-level bargaining, management in American subsidiaries frequently organized other employers to counter demands by workers for economic participation and investment disclosures. Many strikes in the 1970s began in the subsidiaries of U.S. companies when management denied concessions and tried to fire assertive union members.[33]

Since 1975, disinvestments by American multinational corporations in particular have quickened. Other EC governments offered similar favorable packages that matched Belgium's generosity, and neither union movements nor policymakers could persuade foreign investors to stay in Belgium, regardless of whether Belgian coalition governments were sympathetic or not.[34] But the share of foreign direct investments in industrial output has not changed because domestic firms

[30] Leo Sleuwaegen, "Multinationals, the European Community and Belgium," *Journal of Common Market Studies* 26 (1987): 265–69.

[31] André P. Frognier, Michel Quevit, and Marie Stenbock, "Regional Imbalances and Centre-Periphery Relationships in Belgium," in *The Politics of Territorial Identity: Studies in European Regionalism*, ed. Stein Rokkan and Derek W. Urwin (Beverly Hills, Calif.: Sage, 1982), 266–67.

[32] Raymond de Bondt, Leo Sleuwaegen, and Reinhilde Veugelers, "Innovative Strategic Groups in Multinational Industries," *European Economic Review* 32 (1988): 905–25.

[33] According to some observers, the most belligerent management teams came not from the old Belgian firms but from American or other multinational corporations that stepped forward to lead their production group in the fight against union delegates. Jaak Brepoels, *Wat zoudt gij zonder 't werkvolk zijn?: Anderhalve eeuw arbeidersstrijd in België* (Louvain: Kritak, 1981), 62–63, 68–70, 112–15; P. vanden Houte and R. Veugelers, "Buitenlandse ondernemingen in België," *Tijdschrift voor Economie en Management* 34 (1989): 9–34. See also Spineux, "Trade Unionism in Belgium," in *European Industrial Relations*, ed. Baglioni and Crouch, 66.

[34] Sleuwaegen, "Multinationals, the European Community and Belgium," 269.

have closed their doors at an equally fast pace. Affiliates of foreign transnational corporations still account for about 40 percent of industrial turnover, and American firms produce nearly half the industrial output of foreign firms.[35]

The atmosphere for a revival of orderly consensual programs for industrial adjustment during the mid-1970s was complicated by the unusual ownership structure of a substantial portion of domestic capital. Frequently, managers of large corporations were not the actual decision makers, yet tripartite arrangements assume by definition that the representatives of capital within a tripartite body actually speak for their firms. Once labor understood that their concessions fell into a bottomless pit—employers could not guarantee jobs and reinvestments —unions refused to accept pay sacrifices as long as general policy and the future of their jobs were indeterminate. During the steel crisis of 1973/74, foreign investments in Belgium also began to drop off, and unions once again noticed that their actions, concessions, and tactics had no bearing on the final decisions made by the local affiliate of a nonresident transnational corporation.[36]

For their part, governments were not much help in attempting to preserve concertation. Unstable coalitions tied the hands of governments, although even united and stable governments probably could not have preserved full employment against the disinvestments of foreign transnational corporations and holding companies. Governments failed to stem job losses largely because a significant segment of domestic capital and foreign investors had very tenuous ties to consensual tripartism. Investors did not view the postwar social pact as absolutely central for the improvement of their firms' competitiveness or profitability.

## The Politics of Business in Austria

Because the Austrian Chamber of Commerce compels business to act in unison in its negotiations with labor, one would not suspect, given the impressive organizational unity of Austrian capital, that it is politically subordinate.[37] Yet Austrian capital consists mostly of numerous

[35] Martou, "Some Aspects of Industrial Policy in Belgium," in A Competitive Future for Europe? ed. Beije et al., table 10.5, p. 201.

[36] Jaak Brepoels, Wat zoudt gij zonder 't werkvolk zijn?: Anderhalve eeuw arbeidersstrijd in België (Louvain: Kritak, 1981), 92. Capron, "The State, the Regions, and Industrial Redevelopment," in Politics of Steel, ed. Mény and Wright, 727.

[37] For two studies on Austrian business associations, see Franz Traxler, Interessenverbände der Unternehmer: Konstitutionsbedingungen und Steuerungskapazitäten analysiert am Beispiel Österreichs (Frankfurt: Campus, 1986); William Coleman and Wyn Grant, "The

small family-owned enterprises and large state-owned holding companies. Both these groups have tolerated a heavily regulated political economy, and neither has focused on direct foreign investments. Private business is parochial and uninterested in international diversification. The nationalized firms were discouraged from acquiring assets abroad until the late 1980s. With low capital mobility, Austria's foreign investments stood at 1.9 percent of the GDP in 1987, in contrast to 20 percent for the Netherlands and 7 percent for Sweden. About forty thousand people worked in Austrian-controlled firms abroad. Austria's share in the total OECD investment flows was a minute 0.08 percent in 1985 and 0.27 percent in 1989.[38]

In short, the historical characteristics of Austrian capitalism—its inward orientation and provincialism—were not shed in the postwar period. Austria's relations to the international political economy were "passive," in that business groups did not consciously set out to conquer global markets. The reasons for this delay in internationalization, which in the 1990s is considered a major handicap for Austria, were partly historical and partly structural. As a landlocked empire, Austria built internal trade routes to connect its different areas to its financial and trade center, Vienna. Financial calamities of the 1920s and the Nazi annexation a decade later ended the international activities of mixed banks and financial groups. The economic recovery after 1955 did not furnish Austrian private entrepreneurs with the security and means to experiment with capital exports and to become "stateless" entities. Structurally, since the state held a controlling majority of votes in most large firms, these firms were unlikely to become Europeanized corporations.[39] Austria's numerous small firms were also improbable candidates for internationalization. Instead, like Belgium, Austria received large inflows of foreign direct investment.

But because of the nationalized holding companies, foreign capital evolved a very different relation with domestic firms and corporatist

---

Organizational Cohesion and Political Access of Business: A Study of Comprehensive Associations," *European Journal of Political Research* 16 (1988): 467–87. The authors claim that Austrian business is more unified and influential than Swedish business.

[38] Margit Scherb, "Wir und die westeuropäische Hegemonialmacht. Die Beziehungen zwischen Österreich und der Bundesrepublik Deutschland in den Bereichen Währung, Aussenhandel und Direktinvestitionen," in *In deutscher Hand? Österreich und sein grosser Nachbar*, ed. Margit Scherb and Inge Morawetz (Vienna: Verlag für Gesellschaftskritik, 1990), 51–52. An exhaustive study of Austria's foreign direct investments was published in Oesterreichische Nationalbank, "Ausländische Direktinvestionen in Österreich," *Mitteilungen des Direktoriums der Oesterreichische Nationalbank* 6 (1989): 13–31.

[39] Editorial, "Die Internationalisering der österreichischen Wirtschaft," *Wirtschaft und Gesellschaft* 15 (1989): 3–9. On the inward-looking character of Austrian capital, see also Peter Katzenstein, *Corporatism and Change: Austria, Switzerland and the Politics of Industry* (Ithaca: Cornell University Press, 1984).

institutions. Foreign-owned companies accounted for 36 percent of the Austrian industrial labor force, while firms owned by the state directly and indirectly employed only 26 percent.[40] Nevertheless, this sizable group of foreign investors, as well as a corresponding dependence on the strategies of management teams from abroad, has not hurt the Austrian social partnership. Three reasons for this are: first, the state-owned sector protected both the local labor force and affiliates of foreign transnational corporations from sudden economic downturns, which engendered a sense of predictability and stability which has held down labor costs and promoted business optimism; second, foreign investors came from neighboring countries in order to transfer parts of their manufacturing industry to a country with relatively low wages and favorable investment subsidies; third, the subsidiaries and affiliates of foreign transnational corporations planted deep roots in the local business community and cultivated strong connections with the political establishment.

## Foreign Transnational Corporations

In Austria, the presence of state firms and nationalized industries diminished the chance that the social partnership would be disrupted. The regulated political economy of Austria supplied foreign producers, small business, and state holding companies with a measure of certainty that sustained centralized wage negotiations, pay moderation, investors' confidence, and continuous reinvestments. The situation was exactly the opposite to the situation in Belgium. There, foreign investments undermined the already precarious agreements among the different elements of the business community, organized labor, and government coalitions. Austria escaped this downward spiral, thanks to the central position taken by the holding companies, whose managers were political appointees entrusted with the execution of government policy.

Foreign investors came to Austria because of its political stability, nondiscriminatory investment incentives and subsidies, and comparatively favorable wage structure. Similar factors attracted foreign investors to Belgium in the 1960s.[41] One difference was that U.S. investment in Austria was moderate. The 1980 book value of U.S. manufacturing

[40] Inge Morawetz, "Schwellenland Österreich? Aktuelle Veränderungen der österreichischen Eigentumsstruktur im Sog der Internationalisierungsstrategien der Bundesrepublik Deutschland," in *In deutscher Hand,* ed. Scherb and Morawetz, 88; Hans Glatz and Hans Moser, "Ausländische Direktinvestitionen und Industripolitik," *Wirtschaft und Gesellschaft* 15 (1989):.38.

[41] Daniel van den Bulcke, *European Headquarters of American Multinational Enterprises in Brussels and Belgium* (Brussels: ICHEC, 1984).

investments per capita stood at $343 in Belgium, compared with $16 in Austria,[42] whereas the Federal Republic of Germany and Switzerland accounted for no less than two-thirds of all foreign direct investments in Austria in 1985.[43] German firms, arriving in the 1960s, were more or less compelled to seek minority partnerships with the subholdings of the Österreichischen Industrieverwaltungs Aktiengesellschaft (ÖIAG) to circumvent the special clause in the State Treaty that forbade a renewal of formal economic or political links between Austria and Germany.[44] They also set up manufacturing that continued to be part of the larger production facilities at home, and many German firms had Austrian interests dating from before World War II.[45]

Adverse effects of foreign transnational corporations were substantially deflected because foreign firms were incorporated in the federal and provincial chambers of commerce and absorbed into the social partnership, in which small business dominated. Foreign firms also joined the Association of Austrian Industry, the interest group for mostly private industrial firms, but large enterprises were often overruled in the chambers of commerce by the more numerous and politically important family-owned businesses. More important, the state-owned holding companies monopolized some parts of the economy while small business claimed other parts. Affiliates from German and Swiss companies formed a third group in the economy, wedged between small business and nationalized industries, with commercial links to both. In addition, the majority of foreign companies, which were German and Swiss, were still closely integrated into their parent companies. The pressures to move to cheaper areas or out of Austria were less severe because Austria served as a regional base for the local market or production back home.

Finally, studies on the differences between European and U.S. transnational corporations point out that European branches of European

---

[42] Leo Sleuwaegen, "Recent Trends in Foreign Direct Investments in Belgium," *Tijdschrift voor Economie en Management* 30 (1985): 14.

[43] For an analysis of the evolution of foreign direct investments in Austria, see Hans Glatz and Hans Moser, *Ausländische Direktinvestitionen in Österreich: Auswirkungen auf Beschäftigung, Wachstum und Wettbewerbsfähigkeit der Industrie* (Frankfurt: Campus, 1989).

[44] Brigitte Ederer and Wilhelm Goldman, "Mehr als verlängerte Werkbänke: Ausländisches Kapital in Österreich nach 1945," in *Auf dem Weg zur Staatspartei*, ed. Peter Pelinka and Gerhard Steger (Vienna: Verlag für Gesellschaftskritik, 1988), 214; Rosmarie Atzenhofer, "Wie das deutsche Eigentum wieder 'deutsch' wurde," in *In deutscher Hand*, ed. Scherb and Morawetz, 61–86.

[45] Siemens has had business interests in Austria since before 1930. Most of the Austrian production of German firms is reexported. One good example is Steyr Motors, owned by BMW, which manufactures engines for approximately two-thirds of all BMW cars. Inge Morawetz, "Schwellenland Österreich?" in *In deutscher Hand*, ed. Scherb and Morawetz, 107.

international corporations are on average smaller than U.S. affiliates. European companies relocate to supply the local market, while U.S. firms select a locale from which to export to adjacent countries. Accordingly, subsidiaries of European transnationals become more enmeshed with their host country and are more responsive to aggregate economic stimulation by coalition governments to increase consumer demand.[46]

### Management of the Holding Companies

The detrimental effects of foreign transnational corporations were contained because of the state-owned holding company. The ÖIAG, the Austrian state holding company, was formed in 1970 to reduce political meddling in state-owned companies. The entire group consisted of approximately three hundred firms and, including its foreign subsidiaries, employed about 115,000 people.[47] The industrial sector controlled by the banks and indirectly by the government, employed about sixty thousand workers. The total state-owned sector accounted for 10 percent of the labor force.[48]

In contrast to the private holding companies in Belgium, the Austrian public holding companies have been instrumental in stabilizing the social partnership and protecting it against international shocks. While the concentration of economic resources in privately managed conglomerates challenged the basic idea of social trade-offs and centralized bargaining in Belgium, a similar organizational structure of business has had exactly the reverse impact in Austria. The reasons for this contrast are not difficult to understand. Politicians, many of whom were sympathetic to the trade union federations, freely exercised their

---

[46] F. Haex, E. Halsberghe, and D. vanden Bulcke, *Buitenlandse en Belgische ondernemingen in de nationale industrie* (Ghent: Serug, 1978); and Daniel vanden Bulcke, *European Headquarters of American Multinational Enterprises in Brussels and Belgium* (Brussels: ICHEC, 1984).

[47] John R. Freeman, *Democracy and Markets: The Politics of Mixed Economies* (Ithaca: Cornell University Press, 1989), 178–79.

[48] The three banks are Österreichische Länderbank, Creditanstalt-Bankverein, and Österreichisches Credit-Institut. See Oskar Grünwald, "Austrian Industrial Structure and Industrial Policy," in *The Political Economy of Austria*, ed. Sven W. Arndt (Washington, D.C.: American Enterprise Institute, 1982), 135. See also OECD, *Economic Surveys. Austria 1981/82* (Paris: OECD, 1982), 23. The public sector also includes regular government services like hospitals, theaters, telephone system, railways, public utilities. Local governments run, for example, funeral homes, slaughterhouses, and garbage collection services. This book refers only to the trading and manufacturing companies owned by the federal state. The total share of employment in the public sector, including communal cooperatives and public enterprises, was 30 percent, and a little over two-thirds of the fifty largest enterprises, as measured by employment or turnover, belonged to the state-owned sector.

control over the various subsidiaries of the holding company to meet political and social objectives.

After the administrative reforms in 1970, the state, as main financier, was not saddled with the details of routine decisions but rather was involved in setting long-term goals and providing financial support. It also vetted the nominations of top managers who were recruited from the two coalition parties, the People's party, or ÖVP and the Socialist party, or SPÖ.[49] The Chancellor, representing the state, continued to be the proprietor of the ÖIAG after 1970. However, since shareholders were not empowered to instruct management, he was not entitled to formulate policy for the conglomerate. The government's mission was to appoint the supervisory board, which in turn elected the board of managers. The government was therefore one administrative layer removed from running the enterprise. Inside the board of supervisors, a member of either the Socialist party or the People's party alternated as chairperson; both parties had a more or less equal number of representatives.[50] With the appointment of representatives to the board of supervisors, the influence of each political party was checked and neutralized, and political infighting was curbed. In the past, the supervisory board had frequently been delinquent in its task of monitoring and reviewing the performance of the directors of the different companies, and the chancellor often had to step in to oversee strategic planning and investment expansion.[51]

The Austrian Parliament, which is dominated by the executive and the social partnership, receives annual reports from the ÖIAG. Parliamentary control is chiefly concerned with the restructuring plans of the state-owned enterprises. Parliament has passed a variety of acts to merge acquisitions and to reorganize existing companies into new subgroups. Legislation also completed the restructuring of the steel industry in the early 1960s and 1970s, resulting in integrated steel producers, and Parliament approved crucial financial measures such as the limit of state guarantees on ÖIAG bond issues. In 1981 and 1982, Parliament set aside money to repay both the interest and principal of ÖIAG debt.

Thus, on the one hand, manipulation of public enterprises was not a

[49] Henry Parris, Pierre Pestieau, and Peter Saynor, *Public Enterprise in Western Europe* (London: Croom Helm, 1987), 87. Alexander Van der Bellen, "Steuerung und Kontrolle staatlicher Unternehmen in Österreich," *Österreichische Zeitschrift für Politikwissenschaft* 10 (1981): 442.
[50] Helmut Dobler, "Der persistente Proporz—Parteien und verstaatlichte Industrie," in *Zwischen Koalition und Konkurrenz. Österreichs Parteien seit 1945*, ed. Peter Gerlich and Wolfgang C. Müller (Vienna: Braumüller, 1983), 319–33.
[51] Van der Bellen, "Steuerung und Kontrolle staatlicher Unternehmen in Österreich," 446.

normal policy tool or intervention instrument of the political leadership. On the other hand, public enterprises were expected to conform to the general macroeconomic goals of the government and were obliged to meet the goal of full employment. This meant extra funding during an economic downturn to postpone the dismissal of employees. Public utility companies were occasionally encouraged to initiate investment projects during a recession to reinforce a countercyclical impulse.[52] The ÖIAG especially was expected to maintain full employment. Subsidiaries could not lay off workers until they consulted local or regional politicians, the work councils, and the chancellor.[53] The ÖIAG laid off 9 percent of its work force between 1973 and 1983, while total industry shed 17 percent of its employees. Yet production in state-owned industries dropped by 8 percent, and production in total industry rose by 20 percent in that same period. The holding company's relative economic performance was worse, yet its employment record was better.[54] In the recession of 1975, the decline in production of the nationalized companies was 9 percent, yet their work force increased by 0.3 percent.[55]

In marked contrast, the Belgian holding companies could distance themselves from political demands. The organizational structure of the Société Générale long resembled a feudal kingdom, with autonomous director-generals each responsible for one portfolio.[56] This autonomy had implications for those who tried to steer or influence the corporate strategies of the parent company. Although the new governor (René Lamy) in 1980 began to shake up the old structure and to implement a modern system of management, stockholders exercised hardly any power against the ideas of the managing directors.[57] Few shares were registered in the names of the holders; the majority were anonymous bearer shares tucked away in banks. The small investors carried little weight, while significant shareholders, such as the Belgian royal family, other distinguished noble families, and the Vatican, were disinclined to question the annual reports of the governor during a general shareholders' meeting.[58] When a shareholder was adamant in

[52] Parris, Pestieau, and Saynor, *Public Enterprise in Western Europe*, 120.

[53] Van der Bellen, "Steuerung und Kontrolle staatlicher Unternehmen in Österreich," 441.

[54] OECD, *Economic Surveys. Austria 1984/85*, table 5, p. 54.

[55] Margit Scherb, "SPÖ und verstaatlichte Industrie oder: Die Angst vor dem Fliegen," in *Stahl und Eisen bricht. Industrie und staatliche Politik in Österreich*, ed. Margit Scherb and Inge Morawetz (Vienna: Verlag für Gesellschaftskritik, 1986), 163.

[56] Bruno Dethomas and José-Alain Fralon, *Les milliards de l'orgueil*, 23–24; Cottenier, de Boosere, and Gounet, *Dossier de Generale, 1822–1992*, 129, 172–74.

[57] Cottenier, de Boosere, and Gounet, *Dossier de Generale, 1822–1992*, 235; Herman Daems, *The Holding Company and Corporate Control* (Boston: Nijhoff, 1978), 80–83.

[58] Rowley, "Belgium and Luxembourg," *Barons of European Industry*, 110–11; Daems, *The Holding Company and Corporate Control*, 22. "La structure de propriété des Holdings

pressing for more information, the system of crossholdings and sub-holdings thwarted the most persistent inquiries into who owned which shares of what company. The SGB did not produce a consolidated set of profit figures because, according to one of its former finance directors, it would be misleading to add up a quarter of this, an eighth of that, and 2 percent of another company to say that this is the holding company's sales and turnover figures.[59]

Not even other Belgian financial groups could threaten or cajole the largest holding companies. With family dynasties still in command of the financial groups, the unwritten rule was not to trespass on each other's territory.[60]

During the lengthy steel crisis in the 1970s, the chief executives of the SGB could either threaten to torpedo an entire crisis package by dumping their steel stock on the open market or simply refuse to aid the government in its effort to rescue the insolvent firms. Similarly, stockholders—the actual owners of the various business affiliations of the holding companies—were unable to influence the board in order to make it conform to government intentions or to help it resist labor or political demands. In Austria, however, elected officials and other individuals not on the management board exercised some influence over the running of Austrian heavy manufacturing.

This does not mean that Austrian state companies were better run, but they met political or social criteria imposed by politicians. Partly because of this political interference, along with the decline of world demand for steel, the ÖIAG's combined steel holdings managed by Alpine-VÖEST reported losses of AS 11.8 billion ($570 million) in 1985. In the fall of that year, weekly reports announced further losses caused by dubious speculations by its trading company. In total, Alpine-VÖEST received AS 36 billion from 1978 and 1987 to cover its losses and finance restructuring programs. Part of the blame for this dismal performance rested with the board of supervisors, whose innocent reading of optimistic reports failed to uncover the shady currency deals of the trading company and the ill-timed expansion plans of the steel firm.[61]

Belges," *Courrier Hebdomadaire du CRISP* 566 (1972): 1–21. This publication traces ownership networks and shareholders' participation in twenty different holding companies.

[59] Rowley, "Belgium and Luxembourg," in his *Barons of European Industry*, 109.

[60] Dethomas and Fralon, *Les milliards de l'orgueil*, 65–69.

[61] Alexander van der Bellen, "Gewinne in der verstaatlichten Industrie," *Wirtschaft und Gesellschaft* 13 (1987): 337–52. In addition to its trading losses and faulty management, the weapons division of Alpine-VÖEST (Noricum) was subject of an intense inquiry after it was discovered in 1989 that members of the Socialist-Freedom party cabinet had permitted the export of powerful howitzers to Iran between 1984 and 1986. Melanie A. Sully, *A Contemporary History of Austria* (New York: Routledge, 1990), 152–54.

*The Private Sector and the State-owned Industries*

Political manipulation of the state holding companies did not upset
Austria's private sector. Although private employers represented the
small-business sector, the People's party articulated its preferences and,
if asked, could have pushed for denationalization or privatization; the
accommodation of private employers throughout these decades is no
indication of social democratic hegemony.[62] Rather, it is evidence of
the profound satisfaction of business with the status quo.

Many private businessleaders were recruited to the board of directors in the state-owned sector as appointees of the People's party.[63]
Private capital reconciled itself to the existence of state-owned enterprises because they posed no direct threat to the small firms. As late as
1979, 60 percent of Austria's industrial processing firms had four or
fewer employees. One-third of the firms had five to forty-nine employees, and a minuscule 0.2 percent had more than five hundred employees.[64] Most of the family companies specialized in light consumer
goods, food products, services, and electrical machinery and did not
compete with the products of state-owned firms in heavy manufacturing.

Typically, the private sector enjoyed price discounts of essential input
materials, grants for exporting finished goods, and import duties on
consumer durables, while the expansion of the state sector was subordi-
nated to other economic interests.[65] The prevailing attitude in the
1960s was to use the state-owned sector as a financial instrument for
the development of private capital. That sector, in turn, was chiefly
domestically-oriented; more than 43 percent of the firms that produced finished goods did not export at all.[66]

Since the state-owned companies mainly produced raw materials and

[62] By all accounts, Austrian socialists do not have the hegemonic influence that the
Swedish Social Democrats have. They often shared power with the ÖVP and had to make
programmatic concessions. One outcome of these compromises is a strikingly inegalitarian income redistribution. Freeman, *Democracy and Markets*, 182; Peter J. Katzenstein, *Corporatism and Change: Austria, Switzerland, and the Politics of Industry* (Ithaca: Cornell University Press, 1984), 39.

[63] Inge Morawetz, "Personelle Verflechtungen der verstaatlichen Industrie mit der
Privatindustrie," in *Stahl und Eisen bricht*, ed. Scherb and Morawetz, 112–14.

[64] Karl Vak, "The Competitiveness of the Austrian Economy," in *Political Economy of
Austria*, ed. Arndt, 166.

[65] Hans Seidel, "Die Entfaltung der Produktionskräfte der österreichischen Wirtschaft," in *Österreich im Wandel*, ed. Erich Bodzenta, Hans Seidel, and Karl Stiglbauer
(Vienna: Springer, 1985), 99. After 1970, small firms shifted from traditional consumer
goods to mechanical engineering (16 percent of total production), parts and repairs in
the automobile industry (27 percent of total domestic production), and fabricated metals
(35 percent of total production). Wilhelmine Goldmann, "Industriepolitik in Österreich," *Wirtschaft und Gesellschaft* 16 (1990): 48.

[66] Goldmann, "Industriepolitik in Österreich," 48.

some heavy machinery, they complemented the consumer goods made by small private firms by supplying cheap energy, building materials, iron and steel, and essential equipment. State policy until the mid-1960s was to compel the nationalized industries to sell processed raw materials and basic goods to Austria's small firms at about 60 percent of world market prices. Legislators went as far as to discourage state-owned industries from diversifying into finished products.[67] Losses from the delay in technological innovation and the low-price policy were tremendous. In those days, the federal government did not fund the state-owned sector generously because it did not want to upset private business, and the ÖVP deliberately subverted the growth potential of heavy manufacturing in its covert war with the SPÖ.[68] Although they formed a "grand" coalition (1945–1966), neither the Socialists nor the Conservatives wished to destroy government unity; nonetheless, each group had its own philosophy and ideological agenda. Skirmishes between the two allies centered on areas that did not threaten to rend the coalition. Thus, foreign economic policy became a site for a political contest of wills, and the general framework of the nationalized sector was a permissible subject for electoral rivalry.

The estimated revenue losses for the state-owned industries were more than AS 10 billion in the 1960s. In the 1970s, iron and steel exporters lost money because of a European Community treaty that obliged them to sell their products abroad at the same price as at home. And an artificially low price was established that favored small business; the private sector saved several billion schillings.[69] It was no surprise that the ÖVP and the association of private business mellowed their hostile views on the state-owned companies.

Such a scheme could not last forever. As attitudes slowly changed, state-owned industry spearheaded Austria's quest for modernization and competitiveness in the mid-1960s. By then, many officials had recognized that Austria would benefit from strengthening its trade relations with the EC and that the removal of import duties and tariffs might be advantageous. In 1969, the federal government presented its Structural Improvement Act, which built upon previous systems of investment funding by strengthening tax benefits and conditions for innovation. The state-owned industries were, for a change, part of this project and were integrated into the new economic plan.[70] Neverthe-

[67] Hanns Abele, "Anmerkungen zu einer Wirtschaftsgeschichte der Gegenwart: Österreich seit 1945," in *Handbuch der österreichischen Wirtschaftspolitik*, ed. Hanns Abele et al. (Vienna: Manzsche- und Universitätsbuchhandlung, 1989), 61.
[68] Wolfgang C. Müller, "Zur Genese des Verhältnisses von Politik und verstaatlichter Industrie in Österreich," *Österreichische Zeitschrift für Politikwissenschaft* 10 (1981): 398.
[69] Ibid., 400.
[70] Abele, "Anmerkungen zu einer Wirtschaftsgeschichte der Gegenwart: Österreich seit 1945," in *Handbuch der österreichischen Wirtschaftspolitik* ed. Abele et al., 67.

less, during the 1970s, the nationalized industries were still providing low-cost goods to other firms and thus contributed to the private sector's higher earnings and its willingness to reinvest. The stable pricing policy of the state-owned firms might also have had an important psychological effect in that it broke the harmful impact of the worldwide economic crisis.[71]

In addition, subsidies and capital transfers to private and public firms more than doubled in the 1970s, reaching 5 percent of the GDP in 1981 (or 6 percent of the GDP if government revenue losses from tax exemptions are included).[72] Subsidies to industrial enterprises (including tax expenditures) between 1982 and 1987 were AS 48 billion (or $4.17 billion in 1987 U.S. dollars). From 1982 to 1986, credit guarantees for export promotion amounted to an average of AS 350 billion a year ($27.7 billion in 1987 U.S. dollars) and AS 53 billion for public enterprises. Credit guarantees to the private and public sector reached AS 500 billion, or 34 percent of the GDP in 1984.[73] According to an assessment by the Austrian central bank, some 40 percent of domestic credit flows were subsidized in 1977, and the bank estimated that 30 percent of all bank credits went to industry in the early 1980s. Subsidized interest rates that were available to both private and public firms kept investments in Austria higher than in any other OECD country except Japan.[74]

### 1986 Reorganization

With the 1986 ÖIAG Act, the politicization of appointments to the board of supervisors and directors ended. The new philosophy states that the holding group must behave like any capitalist enterprise; it must strive for profit maximization and business efficiency.[75] The ÖIAG must react to the cues of the marketplace, close unprofitable or outdated plants, and resist the influence of politicians and interest groups. The new declaration actually repeated the same theme sounded in 1970 when the ÖIAG was formed to dilute political interference, but the 1986 message is taken more seriously because it is reinforced by finite financial resources. Managers must reconstruct

---

[71] Freeman, *Democracy and Markets*, 179.

[72] OECD, *Economic Surveys. Austria 1984/85* (Paris: OECD, 1985), 46.

[73] OECD, *Economic Surveys. Austria 1987/88* (Paris: OECD, 1988), 24–25.

[74] Johanna Groinig, "Aspekte der österreichischen Industrieentwicklung," in *Stahl und Eisen bricht*, ed. Scherb and Morawetz, 12–15; F. W. Scharpf, *Crisis and Choice in European Social Democracy* (Ithaca: Cornell University Press, 1991), 67. The last figure for the 1980s is from OECD, *Economic Surveys. Austria 1984/85*, 47.

[75] Morawetz, "Personelle Verflechtungen der verstaatlichten Industrie mit der Privatindustrie," in *Stahl und Eisen bricht*, ed. Scherp and Morawetz, 111.

their companies under normal market conditions and can no longer expect to obtain public aid. Some of the new managers have declared that they will resign as soon as politicians or ministers fall back into the bad habit of trying to meddle in corporate decisions.[76]

Organizational changes have created a legal footing for the new Austrian Industries consisting of six branch holdings to determine and coordinate the strategies of its subsidiaries. It has become a financial holding company that exerts corporate control over capital decisions of affiliated firms. In keeping with its new image, the federal government wants the new holding company to become a European multinational corporation because, despite its size, only 6 percent of its employees work abroad. Internationalization will be the key theme for the 1990s as the holding company becomes an ordinary corporation and Austria prepares for membership in the EC.[77]

Asset sales, so far, have been selective and limited. The companies whose main activities fell outside the reorganized production categories of the ÖIAG were partially sold in the late 1980s. The federal government also reduced its 60 percent share in the Creditanstalt and Österreichische Länderbank to 51 percent. As of the 1980s, the proceeds from the sales are about AS 24 billion (or $1.9 billion in 1988 U.S. dollars).[78] ÖIAG proceeds are returned to the holding company for financial reconstruction of its subsidiaries. Profits from the privatization of the banks and the Austrian national carrier go to the national budget, and proceeds from privatization of electric utility companies provide the starting capital for a fund to promote new technologies.[79] The banks are free to sell their industrial assets, which they did in the late 1980s at a great loss.

No matter how the reorganization takes hold, politicians, labor, and small business will have to learn to live without pliable state-owned firms. The trade union federation leadership accepted the inevitable as public opinion turned against the state firms, whose productivity continued to suffer under the various social and political requirements. For the trade union federation, privatization would also solve the widening disparities in wages and benefits between workers in the state-owned companies and in the private sector. The growing pay differen-

[76] Wolfgang C. Müller, "Privatising in a Corporatist Economy: The Politics of Privatization in Austria," *West European Politics* 11 (1988): 114.

[77] For a long and detailed description of the undertaken and planned changes in the ÖIAG, see Andrea Itzlinger, Rudolf Kerschbamer, and Alexander Van der Bellen, "Verstaatlichte Industrie (ÖIAG-Konzern)," in *Handbuch der österreichischen Wirtschaftspolitik*, ed. Abele et al. (Vienna: Manzsche- und Universitätsbuchhandlung, 1989), 436. Sully, *Contemporary History of Austria*, 56–59.

[78] OECD, *Economic Surveys. Austria, 1988/89* (Paris: OECD, 1989), 25–26.

[79] Müller, "Privatising in a Corporatist Economy," 112.

tiation had the potential to become a serious source of friction and disunity. In the 1950s, the state-owned industries were supposed to be exemplary models for progressive relations between management and unions as well as for social experiments. As recently as 1983, a significant majority of surveyed workers preferred to take a job in a state-owned company over one with identical pay in the private sector because of job security and fringe benefits.[80] It was thought that the private sector would eventually offer matching working conditions, but that did not happen, and the gap between the sheltered work force in the nationalized industries and the lower-paid, less secure work force in the private sector widened. In the public sector, where overstaffing and overpaying is endemic, laying off workers and changing working conditions are no longer taboo. While friction between the two classes of workers is thereby avoided, the trade union federation must be cognizant of the risks of exposing the sheltered heavy industries to genuine market competition. Economic steering by governments sympathetic to labor will have to do without the neutralizing influence of state-owned industries. In addition, these state-owned industries represent the heart and soul of Austrian unionism; dismissals and closures will gradually reduce the number of ideologically committed union activists and decrease membership density.

Not only must organized labor surrender economic control, but the private sector as well must adapt to a more unforgiving entrepreneurial climate in the near future. For the association of private industry (VÖI), the most urgent step was to privatize the service firms owned by municipal authorities (for example, funeral homes, health services, and garbage collection). Only later, in the mid-1980s, as public opinion turned against the perceived inefficiencies of the nationalized industries, did the Business League wholeheartedly promote general and comprehensive privatization.[81] Because selling to foreigners is the only viable option for privatizing further parts of the new Austrian Industries holding company, private capital looks to a future in which its sheltered and cozy relationship with the political establishment and economic marketplace will change beyond recognition.

Many commentators have pointed out the vast reciprocal network between the private and public sectors in Austria, and it seems logical

[80] In 1983, 53 percent of the respondents preferred to be employed in a state-owned company, and 20 percent preferred a private firm. "Die Krise der verstaatlichten Industrie 1985," *Journal für Sozialforschung* 26 (1986): 224. Freeman (*Democracy and Markets*, 184) claims that pay earnings were 10 to 15 percent higher than for similar jobs in the private sector.

[81] Müller, "Privatising in a Corporatist Economy," 104.

to conclude that political regulation of selected aspects of manufacturing and production stabilized economic fluctuation and inspired investors' and workers' confidence.

The Austrian private sector was seduced into accepting political intervention in the market because it drew direct benefits from capitalist regulation. Although Austrian workers did not live in a workers' paradise and had come to expect relatively modest social welfare gains from the long incumbency of the SPÖ, they knew for sure that full employment would be preserved. Above all, it was the taming of the labor market, with the idea of turning the state-owned industries into a progressive showcase, that induced wage restraint and disciplined union behavior. The model of progressive labor relations used in state-owned enterprises was not embraced by the private sector, but full employment was nonetheless achieved—partly because population growth stagnated and "full employment" included Austrian-born men only.

In Belgium, by comparison, the absence of a core group of businesses fully committed to central bargaining and social trade-offs undermined the fragile foundation of political bipartite institutions. The subsequent friction between the two sides of the labor market eroded the legitimacy of central bargaining and broad consensual agreements. Wages stagnated in Belgium in the 1980s; statutory incomes policies succeeded where concertation had failed. These Belgian government directives took no account of the preferences or requirements of labor and purposefully tried to bolster corporate profits by keeping wage costs down.

Wage restraints and concessions had the predictable impact on investments and employment in Austria, but only because government could convince business to step up its capital expenditures by supplying such things as subsidized interest rates and various forms of protection. Austrian business took advantage of these incentives because although it operated from a relatively small base, it was more firmly anchored to the domestic market than Belgian business. Austrian capitalists have been slow in launching cross-national ventures and international alliances and in collecting foreign assets. The detrimental impact of highly mobile foreign multinational affiliates in Austria was in all likelihood also moderated by constant government sensitivity toward business cycles. In Belgium, the inflow of foreign investment capital only intensified the suspicions of labor that current sacrifices would not provide job security or new jobs in the future.

# CHAPTER FIVE

# Transnational Corporations in the Netherlands and Sweden

In this chapter I compare the ways in which Dutch and Swedish transnational firms related to tripartite institutions. One might think that all transnational firms are alike and that their links to domestic political arrangements are therefore similar. In fact, transnational corporations in the Netherlands are more global, more dominant, and less embedded in national institutions than similar firms in Sweden. The global character of Dutch transnational corporations can be traced to their origins as colonial ventures, which produced a corporate structure and outlook different from that in firms that began locally and outgrew their home markets. The tenuous ties between transnational firms and the home market has had repercussions for the organization of Dutch business as well. Employers' associations in the Netherlands, in contrast to those in Sweden, were passive and undisciplined bodies that frequently bowed to trade union pressures and settled for redistributive wage settlements, cost-of-living indexation, and pay leveling in the 1960s. But as in Belgium, employers' associations are not an accurate indicator of the power resources of capital. Dutch organized labor was no match for highly mobile transnational firms.

In Sweden, by comparison, transnational corporations retained vested interests and deep roots in the domestic market, a situation the Social Democratic party encouraged with an appropriate blend of investment incentives. Swedish firms were also strongly beholden to the employers' association for pay coordination and for defending them against a militant and united labor force. Greater unity among employers and stronger national identification conserved the practice of social concertation into the 1980s.

## THE POLITICS OF DUTCH BUSINESS

The Association of Dutch Enterprises, or Verbond van Nederlandse Ondernemingen (VNO), is not a forceful and astute agent. The Netherlands' late and scattered industrialization enabled the elites from the two main churches, Calvinist and Catholic, to incorporate their followers in distinct life-style movements by creating a plethora of distinct social institutions. Business also fell into competing denominational camps, and its unity from the beginning was marred by religious cleavages. A factor contributing to the underdevelopment of employers' associations was that the predominance of small-scale manufacturing at the time of industrialization hindered the emergence of a united militant working class. In the absence of cohesive working-class organizations, employers did not experience strong pressure to found their own disciplined organizations.

The segmentation of society into cultural or denominational movements hurt labor more than business. Large firms did not suffer from religious rivalry, and important Catholic firms quietly held dual membership in a Catholic employers' association and in the larger non-denominational association. However, like labor, small firms, which constitute the bulk of enterprises in the Netherlands, suffered from the persistent division of society into competing blocs. Ninety percent of the Netherlands' half million firms employed fewer than ten workers in the 1980s.[1] In Austria, where class and cultural divisions overlapped, small business built its own class organizations and found a political home in the ÖVP. But small business in the Netherlands found itself divided into several nearly identical organizations. Only around 30 percent of the small firms were organized, and their owners voted for any party that was to the right of Labor party.[2] In the period of centrally guided wage policy from 1945 until the mid-1960s, small business consistently sided with large employers on wage restraints, price stability, and export orientation even though their primary orientation was the domestic market.[3] Because small businesses neglected to build their

---

[1] M. P. C. M. van Schendelen, "The Netherlands: From Low to High Politicisation," in *Politicisation of Business in Western Europe*, ed. M. P. C. M. van Schendelen and R. J. Jackson (New York: Croom Helm, 1987), 59. In 1987, 82 percent of establishments had one to nine full-time workers; 0.6 percent of establishments had two hundred to 499 full-time workers; and 0.3 percent had more than five hundred employees. OECD, *Economic Surveys. The Netherlands 1989/90* (Paris: OECD, 1990), 105.

[2] J. H. Pompe, *De kleine middenstand in Nederland* (Deventer, Netherlands: Van Loghum Slaterus, 1980), 188–95. They voted for the Liberal, Calvinist, or Catholic parties.

[3] Detailed publications on economic policy making in the first postwar reconstruction phase do not mention the position and attitudes of small business, though they were part

own political representation and dynamic associations, politicians and state officials ignored them despite their number. Indicative of this neglect was, for example, the scarcity of special credit facilities or grants for small firms despite the serious obstacles they faced in trying to raise investment money from capital markets, the lack of specific economic subsidies, and the burdens of an appreciating guilder and a high exchange rate.[4]

The large firms dominate within government circles and the business community. In the executive council of the Association of Dutch Enterprises, Shell, Unilever, and Philips each has its own representatives. The most powerful trade association is the Federation of Metalworking and Electronic Enterprises, an employers' association whose entire 1979 budget was higher than that of the VNO itself. This employers' association represented about 1,170 firms that had a total work force of about 350,000 in 1979, but 281,000 in 1986. It represented the largest firms in the Netherlands such as Philips, Hoogovens, DAF, and Fokker, but the majority of its members are small to medium-sized establishments with fewer than one hundred employees.[5]

VNO officials never acquired the power needed to enforce central agreements or motivate members to conform to central agreements. Fines imposed by the employers' association were abolished after World War II; the only tool remaining was persuasion, coupled with the threat of ostracism. After 1945, the VNO expected governments to enforce central accords. In the 1950s, at the height of centrally guided wage negotiations, government authorities could make life especially unpleasant for a firm by utilizing its judiciary powers to issue fines. But large international corporations were virtually immune to the moral suasion of employers' associations or persecution by government authorities, who were loath to punish the nation's largest firms.

Yet ruptures in the postwar collective wage bargaining system were caused by the defection of transnational corporations. In 1965, Hoog-

---

of all the debates, deliberations, and decisions. W. J. Dercksen, *Industrialisatiepolitiek rondom de jaren Vijftig* (Assen, Netherlands: Van Gorcum, 1986); F. J. Ter Heide, *Ordening en verdeling: Besluitvorming over sociaal-economisch beleid in Nederland, 1949–58* (Kampen, Netherlands: Uitgeverij Kok Agora, 1986).

[4] H. H. Eijgenhuijsen, J. Koelewijn, and H. Visser, *Investeringen en de financiële infrastructuur* (The Hague: Wetenschappelijke Raad voor Regeringsbeleid, 1987), 24–28; Ton Appels, *Political Economy and Enterprise Subsidies* (Tilburg, Netherlands: Tilburg University Press, 1986), 219–21; and Ann Romanis Braun, *Wage Determination and Incomes Policy in Open Economies* (Washington, D.C.: IMF, 1986), 276–77.

[5] P. W. M. Nobelen, *Ondernemers georganiseerd* (Ph.D. diss., University of Rotterdam, 1986), 77–79; J. P. Windmuller, C. de Galan, and A. F. van Zweeden, *Arbeidsverhoudingen in Nederland*, 6th rev. ed. (Utrecht: Het Spectrum, 1987), 341–44, 348–55.

ovens, the steel conglomerate, opened talks with the metalworkers union with the explicit purpose of going beyond the terms of central accords set by the collective wage guidelines of the tripartite Social Economic Council and offered workers more money or longer-running contracts.[6] Philips ignored conventional practices when it introduced automatic price compensation in 1967. Shell followed immediately because it competed with the other transnational corporations for technical personnel and skilled labor.[7] In the late 1970s, transnational firms called for greater wage decentralization and the fixing of pay and working conditions by the company itself. In the mid-1980s, employers of the transnational firms bypassed trade union delegates completely and signed pay agreements with their staff behind the backs of the trade unions.[8]

Large firms did not depend on the VNO or its affiliated associations for legal assistance, technical information, or financial or political support. From their establishment in the Netherlands, the multinational corporations depended on their own personnel departments and technical divisions to deal with labor and financial issues.[9] They also established their own contacts with government agencies and members of Parliament. While the rest of the business community looked on trade and employers' associations as its patrons, the transnational corporations had the political savvy to ensure sympathetic treatment in political circles.

Although individual chief executives of prominent firms had their own informants in The Hague, the business world generally was not very well connected politically. In 1978, barely 13 percent of the members of Parliament had a business background. An insignificant proportion of businesspeople surveyed, 2 percent, claimed that they had been engaged in politics, according to the findings of a 1981 survey. In a study of directors in the packaging industry, twenty-four of the eighty-three respondents "had done something for a political party,"

---

[6] John Windmuller, *Labor Relations in the Netherlands* (Ithaca: Cornell University Press, 1969), 261, 263.

[7] Frank van Empel and John Jansen van Galen, *Captains of Industry: De economie van het ondernemen* (Amsterdam: Uitgeverij de Viergang, 1985), 24. Shell and Unilever are genuine multinational firms because British and Dutch divisions own 50 percent of the parent company and headquarters are located in both countries. An example of an authentic Swedish multinational corporation is ASEA-Brown-Boveri of which half is owned by the Swiss and the other half by the Swedes.

[8] Jelle Visser, "Continuity and Change in Dutch Industrial Relations," in *European Industrial Relations: The Challenge of Flexibility*, ed. Guido Baglioni and Colin Crouch (Newbury Park, Calif.: Sage, 1990), 215–16.

[9] Windmuller, *Labor Relations in the Netherlands*, 235.

but more than 70 percent of the chief executives were basically apoliti-
cal.[10] In an interview, Lex Helfrich, the president-director of Shell
Netherlands, concluded that top Dutch managers found it difficult to
formulate a common viewpoint and disliked political activism. His explanation for their apoliticism was that in the 1950s and 1960s they had
passed through a wonderful period of rapid growth, and so did not
need to collaborate, and then during the economic downtown of the
1970s they competed among themselves.[11] All these factors—
disorganized small business, individualistic employers, and dominating
transnational corporations—weakened the internal cohesion of business and undermined the political weight of its organized bodies. As in
Belgium, however, employers' or trade associations are not the true
yardstick of the political influence of capitalist groups in society.

The power belonged to the transnational (or multinational) firms,
and they set the policy agenda of the Netherlands. With the portion of
Dutch foreign investments abroad approximately equivalent to 40 percent of the GDP, the multinational corporations have played a critical
role in the Netherlands' prosperity. Since the first oil price rise of 1973,
their outward foreign investments have been twice as large as the inflow of foreign capital. For example, the leading sources of foreign
direct investments in the United States, in the mid-1980s were Britain,
the Netherlands, and Japan.[12] Commerce, banking, and insurance invested 20 to 36 percent of their average gross investments in fixed
capital outside of the nation's borders. Industrial concerns exported
capital equivalent to 48 percent of gross fixed private investments in
the mid-1980s.[13] Government policies were constrained by the international mobility of capital, services, technology, and other factors of
production. Firms can take advantage of government inducements to
foster tripartism and subsidies to promote regional restructuring or
rationalization and nonetheless move abroad. Government policies are
hostage to the unknown calculations of international capital, raising
hard questions about the utility of social exchanges and inducement
packages.

After 1945, the Dutch establishment held two different opinions.
Dutch people had endured a terrible war and severe economic depriva-
tion. Some intellectuals and left-wing politicians pressed for a free,
unpolarized society that would show greater concern for the powerless

[10] Van Schendelen, "The Netherlands: From Low to High Politicisation," in *Politicisation of Business in Western Europe*, ed. van Schendelen and Jackson, 73.
[11] The interview appears in Van Empel and Jansen van Galen, *Captains of Industry*, 25.
[12] U.S. Department of Commerce, *Survey of Current Business* 66, no. 6 (1986): 33.
[13] René Belderbos, "Buitenlandse investeringen en internationalisering van de
Nederlandse ekonomie," *Tijdschrift voor Politieke Ekonomie* 12 (1989): 20, 21.

majority. They lost their public relations campaign, but every political party agreed to provide social security and to create venues for labor to participate in wage deliberations. The second opinion of that time, which was never fully articulated, concerned economic reconstruction. Here the liberal roots of Dutch economic doctrine resurfaced; the emphasis fell on reestablishing a strong trading niche in the postwar economic order. Export growth would reposition the Netherlands as a primary trading nation. The instrument that would achieve this was low wage costs, which would give Dutch products a small, though unmistaken, competitive advantage. Incomes policies received the support of unions, small business and transnational firms for different reasons; the unions supported the policies because they participated in formulating them; small business supported them because they would keep wage costs down; and the transnational firms supported them because they reasserted the liberal hands-off approach to markets. Both small business and labor paid a heavy price for having endorsed this prescription of market-compliant economic steering. When workers demanded pay scales that conformed with those in neighboring countries, the labor-intensive family operations—for example, textiles, clothing, shoes, and leather—were practically annihilated. These businesses could not cope with adjusted labor costs and rising social security fees. Large firms absorbed higher production costs by stepping up rationalization and modernization and by relocating operations to their export markets where they could save on transportation, servicing, and marketing costs. Organized labor, too, lost out; deindustrialization and capital exports eliminated many decently paid but low-skilled jobs, which resulted in high structural unemployment and a decline in union membership.

## International Business and the National Economy

In the 1960s 3 percent of all Dutch industrial enterprises had more than five hundred employees. Yet this minuscule cluster of companies employed half of the Netherlands' industrial work force of 1.2 million workers.[14] Five transnational corporations—Royal Shell (oil refining), AKZO and DSM (chemicals), Philips (electronics), and Unilever (food)—accounted for 70 to 80 percent of all research and development in the postwar period.[15] In 1983, Royal Shell had a turnover

---

[14] Windmuller, *Labor Relations in the Netherlands*, 237.

[15] OECD, *Economic Surveys. The Netherlands 1985/86* (Paris: OECD, 1986), 10. The remaining 30 percent of research and development is located with other large firms in aircraft, steel, and subsidiaries of U.S.-owned firms. Rob van Tulder, "Management of Industrial Change in a Small Country," *Journal of Public Policy* 4 (1985): 338.

equal to two-thirds of the Netherlands' national income. Shell, Unilever, and Philips were the second, sixteenth, and twenty-fourth largest non U.S. corporations, respectively, in the late 1970s. In 1978, Shell's share of foreign employment in its total work force was 67 percent; Unilever's, 48 percent; and Philips', 79 percent.[16] Transnational corporations also controlled industrial manufacturing. The hundred largest industrial concerns, 4.2 percent of all enterprises, claimed more than 30 percent of sales, 44 percent of exports, and 30 percent of industrial employment. Of these firms, the largest eighteen corporations had more than 50 percent of their production abroad.[17]

These corporations are absolutely critical for the prosperity of the Netherlands and the viability of tripartite arrangements and central wage agreements. Royal Shell, for example, is the largest private investor and exporter in the Netherlands.[18] It also co-manages the Netherlands' natural gas fields and thus participates in the formulation of energy policies. Its connections with the political world and policy making are through many different channels. The president of Shell is highly regarded and frequently invited to join one or another of the Netherlands' dozens of expert committees to advise (and legitimize) government decisions. Philips is the largest private employer in the Netherlands. Its Dutch work force represented 21 percent (28,500 jobs) of its entire payroll in the 1970s.[19] Foreign sales accounted for more than 90 percent of its turnover, and in the electrotechnical sector, only IBM, General Electric, and ITT had larger balance sheets. In 1980, Unilever Netherlands owned about thirty different firms in the Netherlands, which accounted for a modest 8 percent of total production of the multinational corporation. It employed fourteen thousand people in the Netherlands and had sales of 5 billion guilders in 1980. About half of its production was exported.[20] It follows that Unilever Netherlands, notwithstanding its relatively small base in the parent country, makes significant contributions to the Dutch economy and balance of payments.

The asymmetrical dependence of the home market on the competi-

---

[16] U.N. Center on Transnational Corporations, *Transnational Corporations in World Development* (New York: United Nations, 1983), 357–59, Table 2.31.

[17] H. W. de Jong, "De internationalisatie van het Nederlandse bedrijfsleven," in *Ondernemen in Nederland: Mislukkingen en mogelijkheden*, ed. Maria T. Brouwer and H. W. ter Hart (Deventer, Netherlands: Kluwer, 1984), 139.

[18] Van Empel and Jansen van Galen, *Captains of Industry*, 17.

[19] Maarten van Klaveren, "Een profiel van het Philips-concern," in *Nederlands kapitaal over de grenzen*, ed. Fred Crone and Henk Overbeek (Amsterdam: SUA, 1980), 157.

[20] Werner de Haan, Coby van der Linde, and Ferrie van der Molen, "Een zwaargewicht slankt af, Unilever 1965–1980," in *Nederlands kapitaal over de grenzen*, ed. Crone and Overbeek, 140–41; Van Empel and Jansen van Galen, *Captains of Industry*, 57, 63.

tive advantages of the multinational corporations that have the bulk of their sales, employment, and production abroad spells trouble for efforts to construct a viable and enduring foundation for social concertation. Domestic wage costs rose steeply in the 1960s and hurt many smaller firms while the transnational corporations adapted easily to the new cost developments because of higher capital-to-labor ratios, productivity curves, and mobility.[21] The interests of small and large firms increasingly diverged (as they did in the 1980s) when wage freezes, austerity measures, and a high exchange rate hurt small business, which depended on private consumption. In the 1980s, large retailers and small business criticized the economic programs of the Lubbers cabinet but their complaints fell on deaf ears and were not taken up by the more influential transnational firms.[22]

### Liberalism, Internationalization, and Labor Accommodation

After 1945, postwar coalition cabinets saw no need for direct market intervention and defined their role as providing a supportive economic environment. Fiscal and monetary policies regulated aggregate demand, and supervision of wage formation preserved the country's competitiveness. Except for using these traditional instruments, governments have taken a laissez-faire approach to industrial restructuring or adjustment. One exception to this policy was the treatment given to the shipbuilding industry, which threatened to vanish in the 1960s.[23]

Except in the case of the shipbuilding industry, the Dutch administrative elite expressed an unmistakable preference for market solutions.[24] In the 1970s, as more and more industries ran into trouble, public aid was made available to business.[25] But defensive and forward-looking expenditures on reindustrialization, industrial policy, and extra financing of capital-intensive projects in large firms never exceeded 0.5 percent of the GDP in the 1980s.[26] By comparison, in Belgium, after the government had committed itself to public spending cuts and

[21] Geoffrey Renshaw, *Adjustment and Economic Performance in Industrialized Countries: A Synthesis* (Geneva: ILO, 1986), 26.

[22] Van Tulder, "Management of Industrial Change in a Small Country," 346.

[23] A. F. P. Wassenberg, "Overheidssteun aan ondernemingen: Het voorbeeld RSV," in *Ondernemen in Nederland*, ed. Brouwer and ter Hart (Deventer, Netherlands: Kluwer, 1984).

[24] Rudy Andeweg, "Less than Nothing? Hidden Privatization of Pseudo-Private Sector: The Dutch Case," *West European Politics* 11 (1989): 121–22.

[25] Dietmar Braun, "Political Immobilism and Labor Market Performance: The Dutch Road to Mass Unemployment," *Journal of Public Policy* 7 (1987): 307–35; Göran Therborn, *Why Some Peoples Are More Unemployed than Others. The Strange Paradox of Growth and Unemployment* (London: Verso, 1986).

[26] OECD, *Economic Surveys. The Netherlands, 1985/86*, 28.

austerity, it still allocated BF 300 billion, or 7.3 percent of the GDP, to support enterprises. The national sector (mainly steel, glass, and textiles) and state enterprises obtained 17 and 60 percent, respectively, of this sum, but 23 percent, or 1.8 percent of the GDP, went to private companies.[27] In the Netherlands, by contrast, funds set aside for redevelopment and industrial restructuring went to firms that were in the midst of globalizing their production facilities. The investment subsidies, therefore, did not go to job creation or to strengthening export competitiveness but to foreign direct investment and, incredibly, to plant closures.

Along with the individual bailout efforts was legislation for more systemic investment schemes. The WIR, an investment account, disbursed basic premiums and more selective grants for different sorts of capital investments with different objectives. The WIR was launched with considerable verve in 1977 to assist in the modernization of the Netherlands' aging capital stock. Firms could apply for special tax allowances for large investment layouts, and further deductions were granted for job creation, regional development, and energy savings. In this way the government hoped to steer investments into desirable areas. Not much came from this grand plan. Application guidelines and distribution criteria were so confusing and opaque that many firms were discouraged; the basic premium came to 83 percent of total WIR expenditures, and the remaining portion was insufficient to promote social or political objectives such as regional investments, job creation, or environmentally sound projects. The WIR was used by most firms to depreciate windfall profits and to introduce labor-saving machinery. The WIR was abolished in 1988.

In the absence of strict parliamentary oversight, more than 125 different programs existed by 1981, but their impact on jobs and investments was negligible. Most of these programs were tailored to the needs and bureaucratic skills of transnational corporations—four large companies acquired more than half the funds, which they used to rationalize their production and scale back their operations in the Netherlands.[28]

Nonintervention was a basic premise for the design of any industrial stimulation package. The public credit facilities, which were supposed to compensate for the shortage of venture capital and were underwrit-

---

[27] R. Boelaert, "Overheid en bedrijfsleven" *Tijdschrift voor economie en management* 33 (1988): 221.

[28] Robert Jan Spierenburg, "Staatsinterventie en noodlijdende bedrijven," in *Interventie en vrije markt: Overheidsbeleid ten aanzien van de struktuur van de Nederlandse ekonomie*, ed. Hein Vrolijk and Richard Hengeveld (Amsterdam: SUA, 1982), 114–18. Van Tulder, "Management of Industrial Change in a Small Country," 343.

ten by private and public funds, also favored the large international corporations. Commercial considerations were used to evaluate funding applications so that loan guarantees were awarded to sound projects submitted by reputable firms.[29] The goal of job creation was regularly defeated; Rob van Tulder attributed the loss of industrial jobs mostly to the restructuring process of the transnational corporations because their access to state agencies enabled them to consume most of the public funds.[30] The thinking and execution of industrial policy favored market-compliant considerations because state officials allowed themselves to be influenced by transnational firms. Such schemes benefited the transnational corporations; they were regarded as safe risks according to the criteria developed by administrators to assess the viability of each application. That technocrats and politicians in the Netherlands adhered to such a starkly liberal interpretation of government's role in the market reflected the prominence of international firms in the Dutch business community in the first place. For them, government's hands-off approach, with its vaguely defined objectives, meant a steady supply of aid and funds, and discouraged less well-connected firms that did not command the same bureaucratic expertise and political astuteness.

The squandering of public money on the rationalization of international firms explains, in part, why in the 1980s wage moderation did not engender the anticipated shift to increased investments and new jobs. The largest corporate investors used government inducements to relocate and to export from foreign markets. Yet unions, whether out of prudence or political pressure, held back their wage claims to decelerate inflation and maintain the price competitiveness of exports until the Netherlands' relative export prices improved slightly after 1976. Real wage rates virtually stagnated between 1976 and 1982, after an annual growth rate of 3.5 percent from 1969 to 1973.[31] The trade unions virtually relinquished their right to wage growth above inflation rates, although labor income was still protected by government-guaranteed price indexation. But public-sector salaries and welfare benefits declined in real terms after 1982.

Internationalization of Dutch business accelerated in the 1970s and continued unabated into the 1980s. From 1972 to 1982, the outflow of capital tripled from 2.3 to 7.5 billion guilders. On average, 12 to 20 percent of domestic gross capital formation was invested outside the

[29] A. G. de Boer, "Investeren en participeren: De financieringsproblematiek van ondernemingen en de rol van de overheid," in *Ondernemen in Nederland: Mislukkingen en mogelijkheden*, ed. Brouwer and ter Hart, 83–93.

[30] Van Tulder, "Management of Industrial Change in a Small Country," 339.

[31] Renshaw, *Adjustment and Economic Performance in Industrialized Countries*, 28.

country.[32] Dutch foreign investments had always been considerable; in 1967 the value of Dutch investments abroad was $2.2 billion In the 1970s, two changes took place. First, Dutch foreign investors redirected their attention from the less developed countries, where three-quarters of foreign direct investments went in the 1960s, to the OECD, which received three-quarters of Dutch foreign direct investments in the 1970s.[33] The second change was the absolute growth in foreign direct investments at the expense of domestic capital formation. The outflow of capital climbed from 3 billion guilders in the early 1970s to 10 billion guilders a decade later. At about 2 percent of the national income, the outflow was twice as large as the inflow of capital by foreign transnational corporations in the 1980s.[34] Larger capital outflows and consistent reinvestments of foreign-earned income abroad multiplied the total sum of foreign direct investment abroad from 60 billion guilders in 1979 to 144 billion in 1984.[35] The trend has continued unabated; the net outflow of capital was more than 8 billion guilders in 1989, half of which was accounted for by the service sector.[36]

Domestic factors do affect to some extent a firm's decision to internationalize, but it is very questionable whether labor costs and social security contributions are the primary culprits. Domestic factors, insofar as they mattered, were related to the monetary and budgetary policies of governments, not wage costs. Austerity programs convinced potential capital exporters to leave the Netherlands; the combination of a strong guilder and depressed consumer demand justified the gamble of seeking alternative markets and cross-border ventures. Monetary policies aimed at stabilizing the value of the guilder and the pegging of exchange rate parity to the German mark might well have discouraged domestic expansion and encouraged capital outflows.

High capital mobility and a preference for diversified acquisitions abroad collided with national-based collective agreements on wage costs, working conditions, and social programs. The contradiction was sharpened, furthermore, by the twin circumstances of ineffective business representation and governments's unfaltering belief in market-driven public allocations. The result was that the firms with the best public relations departments and the closest connections to the state

[32] De Jong, "De internationalisatie van het Nederlandse bedrijfsleven," in *Ondernemen in Nederland*, ed. Brouwer and ter Hart, 134, 137.

[33] Henk Overbeek, "Nederlandse direkte investingen in het buitenland," in *Nederlands kapitaal over de grenzen*, ed. Crone and Overbeek, 61.

[34] Belderbos, "Buitenlandse investeringen en internationalisering van de Nederlandse ekonomie," 17–18.

[35] Ibid, 14.

[36] De Nederlandsche Bank, *Annual Report, 1989* (Amsterdam: Kluwer, 1990), p. 30, table 6.5.

administration appropriated the largest portion of the available funding. They used these financial windfalls to expand abroad and thereby contributed very little to employment or investment recovery.

## THE POLITICS OF SWEDISH BUSINESS

Industry and industrialists have always enjoyed enormous prestige in Sweden, whereas trade and finance have played a more humble role.[37] Unlike students in the Netherlands, students in Sweden rated civil engineering and a technical education second only to medicine for prestige, social usefulness, and intellectual challenge. Apparently, the trade union confederation (LO) and the Social Democratic party have identified with the basic values of industrialism; they regard economic rationalization as necessary and unavoidable. Wage policy aimed at structural change to improve the standard of living of blue-collar workers as well as to boost the profitability of privately owned firms. In the 1960s, union leaders expressed greater concern for the pockets of poverty which resulted from rapid change and the 1967–68 recession. Nevertheless, the way in which inequality was to be fought consisted of increased spending on employment programs, not slowing down structural change.[38]

Many studies comment on LO's ingenious combining of egalitarian ideals with private capitalist production. Yet were it not for the readiness of the Swedish employers' association (SAF) to submit to this resourcefulness, the Social Democratic experiment would have quickly drawn to a sorry end. The policies of the strongest labor movement in the world are dependent on, and constrained by, the most strongly organized employers in the world.[39] In the 1980s, the movement and its programmatic goals ran into many difficulties. The exhaustion of the Swedish model manifested itself in the widening schism between private and public sector workers, the ceiling on further welfare state growth, and the government offensive to control pay expenditures.[40]

Concurrent with the strains in the industrial marketplace, the nature of Swedish capitalism has changed as well in that capital exports for

[37] Peter Lawrence and Tony Spybey, *Management and Society in Sweden* (London: Routledge and Kegan Paul, 1986), 57. See also Richard F. Tomasson, *Sweden: The Prototype of a Modern Society* (New York: Random House, 1970), 136–40.

[38] Rudolf Meidner, "Swedish Union Strategies towards Structural Change," *Economic and Industrial Democracy* 7 (1986): 85–97.

[39] James Fulcher, "Trade Unionism in Sweden," *Economic and Industrial Democracy* 9 (1988): 131.

[40] Nils Elvander, *Den Svenska modellen: Löneförhandlingar och inkomstpolitik, 1982–1986* (Stockholm: Almänna, 1988).

global diversification are increasingly characterizing the activities of Swedish firms in the late 1980s. A set of questions emerges that must be understood in the light of the politics of business in other countries. Why did Swedish business ever consent to the spirit of the agreements forged in the late 1930s and renewed after the late 1950s? How did organized labor ensure capitalist accommodation to egalitarianism and welfare state expansion? By 1990, employers decidedly rejected further participation in the Swedish model, but what spurred this shift in their preferences and perceptions?

That employers feel differently about the Swedish model is beyond doubt. In November 1990, during its SAF triennial conference, the SAF announced its aim to destroy the sacred cow of collectivist values of equality and solidarity. Besides lowering social expenditures and taxation, the plan involved privatization of state-owned firms, railways, and utilities and the introduction of market mechanisms in the distribution of health care, child care, and education. National wage agreements would be replaced by differential pay contracts based on productivity.[41] The group of firms most antagonistic to central wage determination was the Association of Engineering Employers, or Verkstadsföreningen (VF), to which the most multinationalized firms in Sweden belong.[42]

But until this shift in attitude, organized labor had succeeded in forging a fruitful modus vivendi with business, because capital exhibited certain features that made it receptive to these bargains with labor. Unlike Dutch firms, Swedish business actors depended more on the state (and Social Democrats) for various benefits and subtle market protection. And above all, Swedish transnational corporations had greater stakes in the domestic economy than Dutch firms had. In the end, this delayed the onset of rapid globalization and the crumbling of industrial pacts and social accords.

### The Character of Swedish Business

Sweden's largest firms moved production abroad early in their existence; and six of the ten transnational companies that would be the largest by 1975 already owned foreign subsidiaries by 1910. From archival research on individual corporations we know that the most com-

[41] The Financial Times, 8 November 1990, p. 2.

[42] Jonas Pontusson, "Radicalization and Retreat in Swedish Social Democracy," New Left Review 165 (1987): 24. Göran Brulin, Från den "svenska modellen" till företagskorporatism (Lund, Sweden: Arkiv Tryck Studentlitteratur, 1989). Andrew Martin, "Wage Bargaining and Swedish Politics: The Political Implications of the End of Central Negotiations," Center for European Studies Working Papers, no. 36, Harvard University, 1991.

mon reason for producing abroad was to exploit unique technical capabilities based on domestic inventions and the redesign of imported technology. The positive reaction of international markets to product improvements or innovation in safety matches, ball bearings, steam turbines, centrifugal separators, telephone equipment, and air compressors led to a growing dependence on exports. Direct investments abroad were therefore market-oriented in the sense that they were meant to reduce export dependency by establishing sales subsidiaries abroad first and then manufacturing companies. In general, Swedish foreign direct investments did not go abroad to ensure access to raw materials or semimanufactured products for the home market.[43] Other factors for international expansion were changes in the structure of demand and new technologies of mass production and standardization, with the exception of the match industry.[44]

In contrast, the main reason Dutch companies went abroad was to secure raw materials or to exploit regional wage differentials. Most of the Dutch international firms and practically every commercial bank began in the Dutch East Indies. As a major producer of rubber, oil, sugar, tin, exotic spices, tea, and coffee, the overseas territory offered tremendous opportunities for Dutch corporate enterprises. The cultivation of plantations and the beginning of raw material exploitation coupled with the use of new financial forms, such as the limited liability firm, stimulated large capital investment after 1870. In addition, the expansion of industry and commercial activities in the Dutch East Indies stimulated demand for business services because the colony sustained a wide trading network around which Dutch shipping, insurance, storage, and wholesaling thrived. The majority of colonial products were destined for the North American market, and Dutch firms arranged the sales, storage, insurance, and transport. Calculations estimated that the loss of the overseas territory would have reduced national income by 14 percent in 1938.[45]

By comparison, considerable natural resources at home first gave Swedish firms their taste for adapting technology and manufacturing inventions to exploit comparative advantages. These advantages were based on Sweden's endowment of timber and iron ore, the foundation for the paper/pulp and metal industries. The second natural or comparative endowment of Sweden was human capital and skilled labor.

[43] Lars Håkanson, "Organization and Evolution of Foreign R&D in Swedish Multinationals," *Geografiska Annaler* 63B (1981): 47–56.

[44] Håkan Lindgren, *Corporate Growth: The Swedish Match Industry and Its Global Setting* (Stockholm: LiberFörlag, 1979), 17–30.

[45] Hans Baudet and Meindert Fennema, *Het Nederlands belang bij Indië* (Utrecht: Het Spectrum, 1983).

Before the end of the century, Swedish authorities funded technical universities to supply upcoming firms with engineers and scientists.[46] Alongside these natural and human capital resources, highly developed bonds between banks and manufacturing fostered corporate interlocks and dulled the impulse to export capital. Such firms as Swedish Match would not have been successful as international ventures had it not been for ready access to banking capital.[47]

Compared with Sweden, fledging firms in the Netherlands had no specialized client relations with commercial banks and financial houses. Most of the Netherlands' industrial expansion was financed through retained profits and occasional short-term loans. Overlapping networks between banks and international firms continued to exist in the postwar period but only because executives of banks and transnational corporations served on one another's boards of directors. But Swedish banks, in contrast, lent their own equity capital to finance the undertakings of industrial companies, and thus became closely involved in their future. During World War I industrial companies borrowed banking capital from Swedish banks, and then in 1922 the depression caused bankruptcy failures among the industrial firms. The large banks could either stand by and watch their clients go under or continue to supply funds until the situation improved. The big banks, such as Svenska Handelsbanken, wrote off accounts with no future whereas others were pulled closer into the bank's orbit of responsibilities. Handelsbanken organized a special department with accountants and engineers to oversee the affairs of various industrial projects in which the bank had a large stake. The bank often asked its own staff to sit on the board of directors or to advise the firm. By 1936, the department was abolished because the links between industry and the bank were routinized to such an extent that special personnel were no longer needed. Different commercial banks had connections with different industries: Handelsbanken, for example, had ties to forestry and paper industries, and to L. M. Ericsson.[48]

The Great Depression saw the collapse of aggressively expansionist international firms, and legislation of the 1930s restricted the volume

[46] Birgitta Swedenborg, "Sweden," in *Multinational Enterprises, Economic Structure and International Competitiveness*, ed. John H. Dunning (New York: Wiley, 1985), 223.

[47] Björn Gäfvert, *Kreuger, Riksbanken och Regeringen* (Stockholm: LiberFörlag, 1979), 272, 287. Lars Hassbring, *The International Development of the Swedish Match Company 1917–1924* (Stockholm: LiberFörlag, 1979); Lindgren, *Corporate Growth*.

[48] Karl-Gustaf Hildebrand, *Banking in a Growing Economy: Svenska Handelsbanken since 1871*, trans. D. Simon Harper, (Stockholm: Esselte Tryck, 1971); Lars Jorberg, "Structural Change and Economic Growth in Nineteenth-century Sweden," in *Sweden's Development from Poverty to Affluence, 1750–1970*, ed. Stephen Koblik (Minneapolis: University of Minnesota Press, 1975).

of equity capital and industrial lending by banks. Despite these restrictions, banks and corporations continued to form clusters of networks as private banks focused on long-term lending to big industrial corporations. In turn, the firms could issue bonds only through an established commercial bank, and they often recruited bankers as board members to manage retirement funds.[49] Volvo was associated with Handelsbanken, and Saab-Scania, L. M. Ericsson, Electrolux, and Swedish Match belonged to the sphere of the Skandinaviska Enskilda Banken.[50] Incidentally, the SAP perceived the banks as agents of economic rationalization and encouraged bank-industry links.

It would be dangerous to attribute the much greater internationalization of Dutch transnational corporations to only a few variables since countless other factors contributed to the growth of the Netherlands' foreign assets. Nonetheless, two facts are incontestable. First, Dutch international firms had looser connections to the home market, financial institutions, and interest group organizations than similar kinds of Swedish companies. Second, tripartite exchanges between business, labor, and goverment faltered sooner and faster in the Netherlands because Swedish firms were generally smaller, less globalized, and more numerous.[51]

Owing to its strong bonds to the parent country or home market, the economic elite of Sweden played a direct role in politics from the late nineteenth century. This role has been replaced by less visible and more controversial indirect political activity in the modern era. Many distinguished businesspeople led the employers' federation or the industry association from its foundation to the present. Similarly, the Liberal and Conservative parties recruited leading businesspeople as parliamentary deputies. Such ties between political and corporate worlds are more common in Sweden than in the Netherlands.[52] After 1945, the corporate world utilized many political bodies to influence public opinion and politicians. About nine hundred organizations represented industrial interests in parliamentary politics, as well as social and economic legislation. Large companies had their own public relations de-

[49] Jonas Pontusson, *Public Pension Funds and the Politics of Capital Formation in Sweden* (Stockholm: Arbetslivscentrum, 1984), 61.

[50] Skandinaviska Banken and Stockholms Enskilda Banken merged in 1971 to form Skandinaviska Enskilda Banken (SEB). For an exhaustive analysis of who owns what, see Larry Hufford, *Sweden's Power Elite* (Washington, D.C.: University Press of America, 1977), 30–100. See also C. H. Hermansson, *Ägande och Makt: Vad kommer efter de 15 familjerna?* (Stockholm: Arbetarkultur, 1989), 101–2, 159, 167.

[51] One source with earlier figures is Peter J. Buckley, "Testing Theories of the Multinational Enterprise: A Review of the Evidence," in *The Economic Theory of the Multinational Enterprise*, ed. Peter J. Buckley and Mark Casson (London: Macmillan, 1985), 196–210.

[52] Hufford, *Sweden's Power Elite*, 92–97.

partments, yet the administrative committees and state commissions were staffed by the transnational corporations, which in turn relied on the acumen and connections of business associations and federations for assistance and representation.[53] Not until the wage-earners' fund controversy of the 1970s, which promised to increase employees' influence over capital formation, did a part of the business community go outside the SAF framework to attack organized labor and the SAP.

### Transnational Corporations and the National Economy

The second important difference between Dutch and Swedish transnational firms is that the Swedish firms are smaller and more numerous. As a result, the asymmetry between the national collectivity and internationally mobile capital is less stark and more manageable.

The number of people employed by Swedish foreign subsidiaries is equivalent to a third of total manufacturing employment in Sweden. In the 1970s, foreign direct investments stood at around Skr 5 billion per year, but it has more than doubled between the early 1980s and 1988. In 1983, the flow of foreign direct investment corresponded to approximately 60 percent of total industrial investment in Sweden. The twenty most internationalized firms accounted for about 80 percent of employment in Swedish foreign subsidiaries, and in recent years, they have invested abroad about 70 to 80 percent of their total investments.[54] Most of their funds went to the acquisition of foreign firms and to marketing rather than to manufacturing production.

Yet Swedish transnational corporations are, by international standards, not very large, and the asymmetry between the market power of business and the political resources of labor were better matched. In a 1983 study of the 806 largest industrial firms in the world, the Netherlands was home to nine companies (not counting Shell and Unilever because they are Anglo-Dutch firms) with sales figures of $36.1 billion. In contrast, nineteen Swedish companies had $44.1 billion in sales.[55] Employment figures demonstrate the same high degree of concentration among Dutch transnational companies: nine Dutch corporations employed nearly as many people as fourteen Swedish corporations

---

[53] Roger Henning, "Sweden: Political Interference with Business," in *Politicisation of Business in Western Europe*, 18–38. Thomas Bresky, Jan Sherman, and Ingemar Schmid, *Med SAF vid Rodret. Grankning av en kampororganisation* (Stockholm: Liber-Orlag, 1981).

[54] OECD, *Economic Surveys. Sweden 1984/85*, 43.

[55] The two Anglo-Dutch corporations, which are in a separate column, had sales of $100 billion in 1983. John H. Dunning and Robert D. Pearce, *World's Largest Industrial Enterprises, 1962–1983* (New York: St. Martin's, 1985), table 2.2, p. 25.

(528,000 people in Dutch firms and 570,000 people in Swedish firms).[56]

Five Dutch companies, but more than twenty Swedish companies, account for roughly three-fourths of industrial research and development in their countries. These figures show that each individual Swedish company is not only smaller but also plays a less dominant role in the national economy than similar firms in the Netherlands. Further, each firm is less internationalized than similar firms in the Netherlands. To give two examples, in turnover, Volvo was the largest Swedish firm and exported more than 80 percent of its production in 1983. Most of its manufacturing and 75 percent of its work force were in Sweden. The largest paper/pulp firm, SCA, had 70 percent of its sales but only 35 percent of its work force abroad in 1983.[57]

In all likelihood, because of their less extensive global reach, Swedish transnational corporations have taken advantage of the growth-oriented export strategy of the Social Democratic government, which returned to power in 1982. Since the 1982–83 fiscal year, business and fixed investments expanded steadily—even in the late 1980s. Manufacturing investment increased by 13 percent in 1987 and 10 percent in 1988. These figures excluded intangible investments in marketing, quality improvement, and research and development, which also rose strongly in the 1980s. In fact, the Social Democrats' recipe for restructuring and improved competitiveness was so successful that capacity utilization in industry in 1988 was the highest recorded since 1980.[58] Firms reported a shortage of skilled labor, and an extremely low unemployment rate drove up wage rates and strained the industrial relations system in the late 1980s.

## Organizational Features of Business and Public Policy

The development of Swedish industry very likely facilitated organizational unity and sophisticated bureaucratic skills that were of help to government officials when they conceptualized and drafted investment programs. In the late 1930s, the SAF proposed tax breaks that favored large and efficient firms and also legislated the first tax deduction for investment and inventory reserves as well as 100 percent first-year

[56] Dunning and Pearce, *World's Largest Industrial Enterprises, 1962–1983*, table 2.7, pp. 35–36.
[57] The figures are taken from Reinhold von Essen, *The Seven Swedes* (Stockholm: Almqvist and Wiksell, 1984), 48, 79, 93.
[58] OECD, *Economic Surveys. Sweden 1988/89*, 25.

depreciation write-offs.[59] In contrast to the way in which Dutch business retained its laissez-faire mentality through the 1930s and 1980s, Swedish export industries have been active in politics. In 1933, the five leading export firms—AB Separator/Alfa Laval, SKF, Electrolux, ASEA, and L. M. Ericsson—formed a directors' club to promote common economic interests. The club played an interesting role in Sweden's foreign trade policy during World War II—it advocated political neutrality in order to sustain commercial relations with both the Axis (Germany) and the Allies (Britain and the United States). The directors' club also agreed, after some controversy, to declare the SAF nonpartisan in 1931 to ward off political interference by the Social Democratic government.[60] Organizational reforms in the SAF increased the centralization of executive authority and redistributed voting strength according to a firm's payroll size. Employers from the growing export firms, such as the five mentioned, gained more influence and were instrumental in the rise of a professional and articulate employers' association. The directors of the large companies endorsed the lockout as a weapon of last resort against striking or uncooperative unions.[61]

These early and successful attempts at organization and lobbying have prompted a significant number of scholars to propose a positive association between export specialization, economies of scale, and centralization or concentration of capital in small advanced industrialized states. In other countries—the Netherlands is the best counterexample —industry was predominantly composed of tiny firms. In Sweden, however, the size distribution of manufacturing enterprises was quite different from that of the Netherlands. Firms with less than ten employees constituted only 14 percent of the total industrial establishment.[62] This breakdown in size of firms has important implications for cementing alliances with private capitalism. From the perspective of social democracy, a partnership with large and internationally aggressive companies was prudent because such firms indeed represented the

[59] Sven Steinmo, "Political Institutions and Tax Policy in the U.S., Sweden, and Britain," *World Politics* 41 (1989): 524.

[60] Klaus Wohlert, "Multinational Enterprise—Financing, Trade, and Diplomacy: The Swedish Case," in *Historical Studies in International Corporate Business*, ed. Alice Teichova, Maurise Levy-Leboyer, and Helga Nussbaum (New York: Cambridge University Press, 1988), 77–85.

[61] Sven Anders Söderpalm, *Direktorsklubben: Storindustri i Svensk Politik under 1930 och 40-talen* (Stockholm: Raben and Sjögren, 1976), 12–15; Peter Swenson, *Fair Shares: Unions, Pay, and Politics in Sweden and West Germany* (Ithaca: Cornell University Press, 1989), 47.

[62] OECD, *Economic Surveys. Sweden 1990/91*, table K, p. 134.

majority of establishments of Swedish capitalism. Although neither country believed that "small is beautiful," the presence of so many artisanal workshops and family-owned businesses should have raised some questions in the Netherlands with regard to the ultimate payoff of big business favoritism. Subtle discrimination against small firms endowed the export firms with further advantages and political weight. Yet large Dutch firms, most of which are transnational, did not metamorphose into champions of collective wage bargaining and the broadening of workers' participation in economic life. Large Swedish firms did; and they also worked for legislation to strengthen their market power and competitiveness at home and abroad. The Social Democrats were willing partners of big business and designed mutually satisfactory deals that would benefit both workers and capitalists.

A principal requirement of every government is to maintain the investment capacity of the corporate world; the SAP clearly mastered the art of compromise and business promotion. The tax system penalized consumption but not the possession of working capital. The wealthy were taxed heavily if they held nonproductive assets (e.g., housing) or spent their money on luxury goods. An egalitarian income redistribution was achieved by taxing everybody without offering any deductions or exemptions. In contrast, corporations, which determine Sweden's prosperity, pay an exceptionally low rate. The principle of the tax system is to compress incomes in the middle- and lower-income brackets and to shield the high-income groups as long as they shift their capital into productive investments. In 1979, the average tax burden of Swedish industrial firms was between 3 and 13 percent, and corporate taxes contributed 3 percent to the total collected revenues. This is a minuscule amount because the total taxes collected by the state amounted to more than 50 percent of the GDP in that year.[63] In the mid-1970s, companies transferred the equivalent of 1.4 percent of GDP in corporate taxes to the state budget. Similar figures for Belgium and the Netherlands were 3.0 and 3.3 percent, respectively, of the GDP for the period 1974–76.[64] In the 1980s, the overall marginal tax rate, depending on the rate of inflation, was anywhere between 0.2 percent and −2.6 percent. Taxes on corporate income as a percent of total taxes was 2.5 percent in Sweden but 6.6 percent in the Netherlands in 1980 (see Table 9).

Not surprisingly, Pehr Gyllenhammer, the chairman of Volvo, con-

---

[63] Villy Bergström, *Studies in Swedish Postwar Industrial Investments* (Stockholm: Almqvist and Wiksell, 1982), 12.
[64] OECD, *Public Expenditures Trends* (Paris: OECD, 1978), 48.

*Table 9.* Source of tax revenues for 1971, 1980, and 1987 (as percentage of GDP)

| | Personal income taxes | | | Corporate taxes | | | Consumption taxes | | |
|---|---|---|---|---|---|---|---|---|---|
| | 1971 | 1980 | 1987 | 1971 | 1980 | 1987 | 1971 | 1980 | 1987 |
| Belgium | 9 | 15 | 15 | 2.6 | 2.6 | 3.0 | 12.7 | 10.9 | 10.5 |
| Netherlands | 9 | 12 | 9 | 2.9 | 3.0 | 3.7 | 10.5 | 10.4 | 11.4 |
| Austria | 7 | 9 | 9 | 1.6 | 1.4 | 1.4 | 13.0 | 12.5 | 13.2 |
| Sweden | 17 | 20 | 21 | 1.5 | 1.2 | 2.3 | 12.3 | 11.1 | 13.1 |

*Source*: OECD, *Revenue Statistics of OECD Member Countries*, 1983, 1989.

siders his home country to be a genial place for an international businessman like himself.[65] The system works in favor of large profitable firms with large inventories or depreciable assets because the fiscal incentives are, for the most part, tailored to their strengths. Studies have shown that the Swedish Social Democrats have contrived to stimulate economic concentration and centralization of wealth in the hands of the international firms that are most efficient and therefore the most likely to succeed. Investment rules and tax benefits encouraged concentration of production, and nearly four thousand mergers affecting 360,000 employees took place in the period 1970–79.[66] In the 1980s, industrial concentration progressed further. Firms with five hundred employees or more accounted for 60 percent of industrial employment in 1984, up from 53 percent ten years earlier. The tax treatment of real capital gains, income, and wealth has often made it more profitable to sell a small company than to continue operations and receive taxable income.[67]

Another puzzling outgrowth of the incentive system for big business is the survival of the Wallenberg empire. Social Democratic Sweden has never objected to a large accumulation of assets by one family. In the early 1960s, the Wallenberg empire employed approximately 13 percent of workers in the private sector and was responsible for a little over one-fourth of industrial processing value. Of the ten largest private companies, only Volvo and Skånska Cement were not even partially owned by the Wallenberg family. Moreover, this family holding group also owned a large portion of the voting shares of Skandinaviska Enskilda Banken.[68] At the end of 1990, the Wallenberg dynasty accounted

[65] Quoted in Steinmo, "Political Institutions and Tax Policy in the U.S., Sweden, and Britain," 519. See also Henry Milner, *Sweden: Social Democracy in Practice* (New York: Oxford University Press, 1989), 137.
[66] Joachim Israel, "Swedish Socialism and Big Business," *Acta Sociologica* 21 (1978): 350.
[67] OECD, *Economic Surveys. Sweden 1984/85*, 44.
[68] Hufford, *Sweden's Power Elite*, 57.

for more than 35 percent of the total capitalization of the Swedish stock market and included four of the world leaders: Electrolux, the manufacturer of household appliances; ASEA of ASEA-Brown-Boveri, the electrical engineering firm; SKF, the maker of ballbearings; and L. M. Ericsson, a telecommunications firm. What is most peculiar is that the law explicitly sanctions the concentration of the nation's economic resources under the control of one family. Sweden has a system of different classes of stock shares with unequal voting rights (as in Belgium), which allows one family to control an entire corporation with just a handful of shares. Thus, Electrolux, L. M. Ericsson, and SKF issue some shares with one thousand times as many votes as others. Although the Wallenbergs own only a 16-percent share in Electrolux, they control 95 percent of the votes.[69]

These conglomerates, however, do not function and are not constituted like the Belgian group of holding companies. Belgian financial groups collected seemingly random possessions in a large variety of industrial firms, raw material processors, financial institutions, utilities, and transportation. The Swedish group is clustered around a core group of engineering firms, cultivating a synergy which is usually lacking in the Belgian version of cross-ownerships. Moreover, the Belgian holding groups trace their origins to the mixed banks before World War II. Belgian executive boards of the largest holding companies still think of their possessions as portfolio investments and engage in financial asset management.

In Sweden, banking capital is subordinate to industrial capital, and authorities have guaranteed that industrial manufacturing will continue to be treated as the primary engine of growth and economic well-being. All sorts of compensations have been available to industrial firms to help them cope with competitive challenges. Foreign ownership of Swedish firms was prohibited in order to prevent hostile takeovers by nonresidents. While Swedish investors had the freedom to invest anywhere in the world, foreigners were carefully screened so that control of domestic assets and manufacturing could be kept in the friendly hands of Swedish capitalists. It should be noted that this protectionist rule offered a reprieve to both Swedish firms and Social Democrats—tax rules would have been considerably less effective if many firms had been owned by nonresident transnational corporations with their capital mobility and diverse interests.

Rewarding firms for large size and growth potential does not stop with tax privileges and favorable corporate legislation. Other incentives include the policy of armed neutrality during peacetime so that

[69] "The Wallenbergs: The Empire Strikes Back," *The Economist*, 2 March 1991, p. 2.

Sweden can remain free of alliances during war. This policy has had various implications for foreign economic policy and government procurement decisions. Since Sweden is nonaligned, it spends a relatively large proportion of its budget on military defense. On average, in the 1960s defense received about 12 percent of budget allocations, and total defense spending was about 7 percent of the GDP. Budget deficits lowered defense spending to about 8 percent of total budget expenditures and 3 percent of the GDP in the 1970s.[70]

Most of this money is spent in Swedish companies; reliance on foreign defense suppliers would compromise neutrality. With a large number of firms excelling in electrotechnical manufacturing, it stands to reason that not many are left without a defense contract. Saab produces fighter planes; L. M. Ericsson is a large supplier of electronics and computers, while ASEA, Bofors, and Volvo manufacture anti-aircraft guns, antisubmarine weapons, missiles, armor plate, artillery ammunition, mines, bombs, military vehicles, military electronics, and other related equipment.

Until now, the government aimed for self-sufficiency combined with high performance at affordable prices.[71] Both goals have increasingly strained Sweden's financial and technological capacities. The best example of how such incompatible goals were reconciled was the torturous discussion of whether Sweden should build its own replacement for the Viggen, its chief fighter jet, or buy one of the new generation of foreign-manufactured models. After a decade of indecision and inconclusive research reports, the cabinet in 1982 settled for a domestic multipurpose aircraft that would be cheaper than a totally new air defense system. Central to this outcome were pressures from the two trade union federations, LO and the TCO, the white-collar trade union federation, and the public pledges by the international export firms to create more jobs in the civilian sector to offset losses in military production as long as they received at least the funds to develop a less sophisticated and cheaper new aircraft.[72] With prominent firms and unions united, the cabinet felt compelled to authorize a new but less expensive replacement. The development of the JAS-39 Gripen, led by a Swedish consortium, was not an unqualified success. Cost overruns have exceeded Skr 7 billion, partly because of unforeseen technical problems,

[70] Hufford, *Sweden's Power Elite*, 215–23.
[71] John Logue, "The Legacy of Swedish Neutrality," in *The Committed Neutral: Sweden's Foreign Policy*, ed. Bengt Sundelius (Boulder, Colo.: Westview Press, 1989), 35–66.
[72] W. J. Taylor, "Sweden," in *Nordic Defense: Comparative Decision Making*, ed. W. J. Taylor and P. M. Cole (Lexington, Mass.: Lexington Books, 1985). An earlier study of business and defense expenditure decisions is by Ingemar Dörfer, *System 37 Viggen: Arms, Technology, and the Domestication of Glory* (Oslo: Universitetsförlaget, 1973).

and in late 1990, after having placed an order for thirty aircrafts, the government refused to release more money for the project. A second order of more than one hundred planes, to be delivered at the end of the 1990s, was postponed.[73] Predictably, because money spent on defense is recycled to the private sector, more than twice as many people as not supported an increase in defense spending in 1986.[74] The policy of neutrality, combined with defense spending, is another example of the fruitful understanding between big business and Social Democratic governments, but it also underscores changing conditions in Sweden that might complicate such deals in the future. Budget constraints and the end of the Cold War have reduced Sweden's need for and capacity to produce fancy military goods.

### Changes: Employer Offensives and Internationalization

Whenever the SAP deviated from the path acceptable to business, the business community rallied its forces and organized a frontal attack against social democracy. In the 1940s, the ideological stalwarts of the party toyed with the idea of creating a planned economy, and in the 1970s, the SAP election campaign contained a promise to install a diluted version of the original wage-earners' fund. In each instance, the business community adopted a far more partisan agenda than it normally acted upon and openly challenged the SAP.[75]

In the 1980s, the political struggle was led by the transnational firms, particularly engineering firms, which argued that wage bargaining should take place at the company level. Engineering firms rejected centralized wage negotiations, claiming that they set wages too high and that they establish too rigid wage differential guidelines. Wage leveling, according to the engineering firms, results in general wage drift for all, and a lack of pay differentiation hinders the recruitment of skilled labor. Inside the employers' association, the VF since the mid-1970s has waged a slow campaign to persuade other employer groups to abandon central wage bargaining. But through the 1970s support for drastic changes among many other industry sectors was lukewarm, and the frightening economic turmoil of that decade discouraged many employers from dismantling the existing postwar industrial rela-

[73] John Burton, "Sweden Postpones Saab-Scania Order," *The Financial Times*, 23 November 1990, p. 2.
[74] Joseph Kruzel, "Sweden's Security Dilemma: Balancing Domestic Realities with the Obligations of Neutrality," in *The Committed Neutral*, ed. Sundelius, 86.
[75] Nils Elvander, *Den Svenska Modellen: Löneförhandlingar och Inkomstpolitik, 1982–1986* (Stockholm: Almänna, 1988).

tions system.[76] The mood changed in the 1980s, and the VF decided to be more independent of the SAF regardless of what the rest of business plans to do—it enlarged its own strike insurance fund. The employers' association feared a further decline in organizational unity and allowed affiliates greater formal authority for independent action. The SAF adopted the VF platform and declared in 1990 that central bargaining was a thing of the past.[77]

The push for decentralization was subtly reinforced by the proliferation of company bonuses, profit-sharing schemes, and employee share ownership. These nontransparent benefits foster workers' loyalty to the firm and undermine wage solidarity. Neither LO nor the SAP government, even assuming it returns to office soon, is likely to infuse new life into the collective bargaining system and solidaristic wage policies. Consistent with engineering's new emphasis on high-technology manufacturing, the workplace accommodates workers with multiple skills and thereby blurs traditional distinctions between blue- and white-collar workers and undermines centralized pay setting. In any event, the SAF has disbanded its negotiating secretariat with the clear intention of continuing to work toward decentralized, company-level wage bargaining.[78]

The rebellion against central wage determination is motivated not only by the drive to reshape the workplace to introduce flexible automation and employees with multiple skills. Not far behind economic and technological innovations are the political motives of employers to overpower organized labor by exacerbating ever-greater fragmentation and disunity inside LO and between LO and white-collar workers. With the dissolution of labor cohesion, the SAP will see its electoral support decline to an ever-smaller core group of loyalists, until the defection of even a small minority of union members could put it out of power for a long period.[79]

The talent of engineering firms at dodging the countermoves of workers and other groups in the SAF reflects the new international market opportunities for transnational corporations. Since the early 1980s this industry has accelerated its net direct investment abroad; it

[76] Hans de Geer, *I vänstervind och högervåg: SAF under 1970-Talet* (Stockholm: Almänna, 1989), 225–72.
[77] For an account of the internal struggles in the SAF, its motivation, and the combativeness of the VF, see Martin, "Wage Bargaining and Swedish Politics," 137–64; Kristina Ahlén, "Swedish Collective Bargaining under Pressure: Inter-Union Rivalry and Incomes Policies," *British Journal of Industrial Relations* 27 (1989): 330–47.
[78] Rianne Mahon, "From Solidaristic Wages to Solidaristic Work: A Post-Fordist Historic Compromise for Sweden?" *Economic and Industrial Democracy* 12 (1991): 305.
[79] Martin, "Wage Bargaining and Swedish Politics," 18.

grew from Skr 4 billion in 1981 to Skr 19.8 billion in 1987.[80] The exodus of corporate investments has meant that in 1989 for the first time ever, Sweden invested more abroad than at home. In 1990, outflow of foreign direct investment was calculated at an annual rate of Skr 46 billion ($7.5 billion), more than ten times the 1985 outflow.

From the perspective of engineering firms and their representatives, gains from welfare spending and demand management no longer justify toleration of public-sector expansion and labor market accords. While the transnational firms have done exceedingly well in the 1980s, the Swedish market nonetheless absorbs increasingly fewer products and accounts for fewer sales. Figures on the distribution and proportion of sales inside and outside Sweden by twenty-seven firms since 1965 show that foreign production, as a percentage of total production, increased from 28 percent to 47 percent from 1965 to 1986, while home sales, as a percentage of total sales, declined from 47 percent to 23 percent.[81] A direct correlation between global diversification and attitudes toward central bargaining is difficult to prove, but many highly internationalized firms, such as Volvo, L. M. Ericsson, Electrolux, and SKF, act increasingly independently of social concertation.[82]

Transnational firms have no choice if they want to remain competitive. They must transfer a progressively larger portion of their production from the parent country to important import markets. To some extent, this has already been accomplished. There is a surprising lack of correlation between business's substantial research and development spending and the proportion of high-technology goods in Sweden's foreign trade balance. Swedish firms carry out most of their research and development in Sweden but produce their high-tech products outside Sweden so that they can stay close to their import markets. Technology is transferable across national borders and through intrafirm trade; hence, Swedish transnational corporations have grown in international competitiveness, yet Sweden's competitiveness has fallen.[83]

[80] OECD, *Economic Surveys. Sweden, 1988/89* (OECD: Paris, 1989), table 3, p. 17. See also Lennart Petersson, "Den Svenska Ekonomins Internationalisering," in *Makt och Internationalisering*, ed. Göte Hansson and Lars-Göran Stenelo (Stockholm: Carlssons, 1990), 54.

[81] Petersson, "Den Svenska Ekonomins Internationalisering," in *Makt och Internationalisering*, ed. Hanson and Stenelo, 58; Gregg Olsen, "Labor Mobilization and the Strength of Capital: The Rise and Stall of Economic Democracy in Sweden," *Studies in Political Economy* 34 (1991): 120–24.

[82] Gösta Rehn and Birger Viklund, "Changes in the Swedish Model," in *European Industrial Relations*, ed. Baglioni and Crouch, 321.

[83] Magnus Blomström, "Competitiveness of Firms and Countries," *Skandinaviska Enskilda Banken Quarterly Review*, nos. 1–2 (1991): 8–14; OECD, *Economic Surveys. Sweden 1984/85*, 49–51.

If Swedish transnationals are indeed increasingly thriving beyond the nation's borders, the pact between social democracy and private capitalism is bound to face incongruities. Social democracy needs the cooperation of capitalists, but the reverse is not true at all. This is confirmed in a recent study of the 1981–82 currency devaluations and economic policy measures introduced by the returning Social Democratic cabinet after 1982. Deep devaluations totaling 25 percent lowered relative unit labor cost to 20 percent below the 1973 level. The purpose was to halt the shrinking of the tradable sector and to spur a shift in resources from the sheltered and public sectors to the manufacturing industry. Initially, the fall in relative unit labor costs occasioned by devaluation expanded profit margins and increased demand for skilled labor. But the longer view shows that the tradable sector has not expanded.[84] Although LO and its workers fulfilled their part of the agreement during the first few years after the devaluations, the economic structure of Sweden has not changed, and the manufacturing or tradable sector has continued to shrink.

In the age of international production, business's commitment to social concertation and dependence on national state policy has diminished. Government packages geared to influence corporate decision making have become largely ineffective. As we saw in this chapter, this process started earlier in the Netherlands, where social exchanges eroded faster. Transnational business has had no compelling economic or political rationale to enter into long-term pacts with labor or national governments.

It is ironic that the social democratic movement in Sweden has been very slow to realize that the assumptions of the 1930s—the dependence of business on the domestic labor force and markets—has changed irrevocably. The SAP, at least until 1987, hesitated to break out of its familiar framework, with perhaps fatal implications. Sweden has not escaped the neoliberal fight against "excessive" public sector spending and "inhospitable" investment climates. Until these tensions surfaced, concertation in Sweden was expedited by a number of structural and incidental developments. First, the business community formed a cohesive unit until the late 1980s. It did not shrink from forming a united bloc to fight for favorable policy outcomes, and its organizational cohesion was better. Second, the less intense globalization of large export firms enabled government officials to offer big business certain incen-

---

[84] Magnus Henrekson, "Did the Devaluations of 1981 and 1982 Induce a Structural Shift in the Swedish Economy?" *Skandinaviska Enskilda Banken Quarterly Review*, No. 4 (1990): 90–99. Hans Bergström, "Sweden's Politics and Party System at the Crossroads," *West European Politics* 14 (1991): 15.

tives and advantages that kept them anchored to the domestic economy. Third, in the absence of small business, government cabinets could focus on only one sort of public intervention, one that was particularly favorable to big business, knowing that it would encompass a large array of firms and companies. Fourth, military spending in the context of neutrality had a mild Keynesian effect because state expenditures went to transnational corporations and meshed very well with their civilian specializations in electronics, engineering, and metallurgy. Fifth, tax policy had a similar discriminatory impact and also benefited export firms. None of these five factors was present in the Netherlands. Economic uncertainty and more attractive global investment opportunities led Dutch firms to abandon social concertation and to fault collective wage bargaining and social spending for the resulting economic mess.

To summarize the findings of the last two chapters, business politics in Belgium and the Netherlands share several outstanding features. First, employer federations were weak bodies, but business did not rely on these organizations to protect its privileged position and communicate with government agencies. Second, in both countries, the asymmetric dependence of a small market on a cluster of transnational corporations (the Netherlands) or networks of holding companies (Belgium) complicated the conservation of social concertation in periods of economic uncertainty and expansion of financial investments and activities. Third, the high capital mobility of large business aroused the suspicion of labor that current sacrifices are insufficient guarantees for future improvements in the standard of living.

However, the changed structure of the international political economy has also sharpened the contradiction between national-based social pacts and internationally mobile capital in Sweden, while Austria may yet see the repercussions of privatized firms that are drawn ever more tightly into international markets.

# CHAPTER SIX

# Central Bank Independence in Belgium and the Netherlands

Central banks influence economic policy because they control the monetary sphere. The extent to which a central bank is able to act independently from government supervision defines the degree to which central bankers can influence monetary policy and affect economic outcomes. Central banks that are independent of political pressures are able to resist demands for monetary expansion and can prevent politicians from timing an expansionary cycle to coincide with an upcoming election.

Central banks look after the country's foreign monetary relations. They decide how far liberalization or deregulation of capital and currency flows can proceed, when to intervene in foreign exchange markets, and what privileges to grant to nonresident financial institutions. Independent central banks, which claim financial independence from government and possess final decision-making authority over monetary issues, have the institutional means and moral suasion to bring about a reduction in budget deficits and regulate or deregulate domestic financial and money markets.[1]

Dependent central banks, by contrast, are less likely to withstand political demands for the monetization of fiscal deficits and are more

[1] Michael Parkin, "Domestic Monetary Institutions and Deficits," in *Deficits*, ed. James M. Buchanan, Charles K. Rowley, and Robert D. Tollison (Oxford: Blackwell, 1987), 310–31. According to his ranking, only the Bundesbank and the Swiss National Bank are independent. See also Thomas D. Willett, King Banaian, Leroy O. Laney, Mohand Merzkani, and Arthur D. Warga, "Inflation Hypotheses and Monetary Accommodation: Postwar Evidence from the Industrial Countries," in *Political Business Cycles: The Political Economy of Money, Inflation, and Unemployment*, ed. Thomas D. Willett (Durham, N.C.: Duke University Press, 1988), 200–38; Alberto Alesina, "Politics and Business Cycles in Industrial Democracies," *Economic Policy* 8 (1989): 55–98.

ready to tax voters through inflation. Their response to fiscal deficits and wage increases in excess of national productivity trends is to be accommodating—to supply more money to the economy. Countries with dependent central banks tend to have higher-than-average inflation and better employment records. Dependent central banks are more easily absorbed in social partnerships while less likely to allow international finance access to the domestic market.[2] Ordinarily, dependent central banks prefer to delay the removal of capital and exchange rate controls to protect government budgets, interest rates, and domestic financial markets from exposure to international shocks.

From the figures in Table 10, one may observe the slow changes in the consumer price indices of Austria, Belgium, and the Netherlands, as opposed to Sweden, which is the only country in this study where the central bank is fully under the control of elected officials. The Austrian central bank is classified as dependent, not because of its statutory rules, but rather because the two sides of the social and economic partnership direct the decisions of the bank's board and because the commercial banks focus on domestic retailing instead of on international transactions and cannot draw upon special expertise or needs to protect the central bank against political intrusion.

Where central banks do not have to act in response to the aspiration of domestic commercial banks with strong transnational inclinations, capital and exchange controls are more likely to be enforced by state officials. That is to say, the different degrees of internationalization—and therefore, the exit options for business—are to a large extent determined by the central bank in conjunction with the Finance Ministry or Treasury. These institutions decide how to create the most advantageous conditions to abet the international expansion of commercial banks. In turn, the decision whether or not to promote capital and financial flows determines the extent to which the domestic market is shielded from international fluctuations.

Dynamic financial communities, especially in small European countries, are passionate advocates of joining the global circuit of capital because foreign transactions and international banking are profitable supplementary activities. Such a financial community enhances the political influence of the central bank.[3] Central banks whose independence is augmented by the presence of internationally connected banks and nonbank financial institutions tend to be persistent champions of

[2] Jukka Pekkarinen, "Keynesianism and the Scandinavian Models of Economic Policy," in *The Political Power of Economic Ideas: Keynesianism across Nations*, ed. Peter Hall (Princeton, N.J.: Princeton University Press, 1989).

[3] John B. Goodman, *Monetary Sovereignty: The Politics of Central Banking in Western Europe* (Ithaca: Cornell University Press, 1992), 8.

*Table 10.* Consumer price indices (average annual changes in percent)

|  | 1960–68 | 1968–73 | 1973–79 | 1979–84 |
|---|---|---|---|---|
| Belgium | 2.8 | 4.9 | 8.4 | 7.3 |
| Netherlands | 3.6 | 6.9 | 7.2 | 5.0 |
| Austria | 3.6 | 5.2 | 6.3 | 5.5 |
| Sweden | 3.8 | 6.0 | 9.8 | 10.3 |

*Source:* OECD, *Economic Outlook* 45 (1989).

financial integration and liberalization. They also like to issue restrictive credit and monetary policies.

Of the four countries studied in this book, the Netherlands has the most independent central bank (De Nederlandsche Bank), both in how it has been expected to operate and how it actually has operated. Belgium's central bank (Banque Nationale/Nationale Bank) is handicapped because its credit supervisory functions were handed over to other institutions, but it can tap the support of the financial community in any dispute with the government. In both the Netherlands and Belgium, the financial community makes an important contribution to growth, trade, and employment and has multiple connections with international finance.

The Austrian central bank (Oesterreichische Nationalbank) is incorporated in the social partnership, and commercial banks generally focus on the domestic market. Yet Austrian officials value price stability highly and are extremely averse to fluctuating price levels (see Table 10). This fear of inflation, however, was perceived as consistent with harmonious social agreements; low inflation was not regarded as a precondition for strengthening the international activities of domestic financial institutions. In the Netherlands, in contrast, low inflation was supposed to promote the international business of banks and the international circulation of the guilder.

The Swedish central bank (Riksbank) is considered the most dependent because Parliament appoints a seven-member board of commissioners and the governing party sets the broad direction of monetary and credit policies.

All four central banks have seen a noticeable rise in political power just as their economic power has declined. Although international financial integration and speculative financial markets overwhelm the activities of most central banks in the advanced industrialized world, the need for exchange rate stability and low inflation nevertheless elevates the bureaucratic standing of central bankers in their dealings with elected officials and other parts of the state administration.[4] Monetary policy in all four countries is increasingly driven by developments in international markets because the formation of the European Monetary System (EMS) has encroached on national monetary policy and economic outcomes for both European Community members and nonmembers. The impact of these contradictory trends varies among the four countries. The tension between independent central bank actions and dependent monetary policy decisions is least apparent in the Netherlands and most visible in Sweden. The reason for this, as I explain in this chapter, is that the Dutch central bank largely derived its authority after 1973 from its encouragement of strong bonds between the guilder and world financial markets and because it is formally vested with the duty to preserve the external and internal value of the currency. To achieve this, the guilder was pegged to the German mark, and price stability (i.e., low inflation) was regarded as the top priority.

At the other end of the spectrum, deepening financial integration has had the most radical impact on the Swedish Riksbank, where intrusive methods of monetary and credit intervention were abolished in the light of speculative financial flows after capital and exchange controls were removed. A revolutionary break with the past was signaled by the decision to informally link the Swedish krona to the exchange rate mechanism of the EMS in 1991.

For Belgium and Austria too, the growth and spread of international financial forces have undermined independent monetary action, although they have bolstered the prestige of central bankers. In all four countries, policy agendas are increasingly dominated by monetary targets linked to developments in the EMS. Since the Federal Republic of Germany is without doubt the key actor in the EMS, monetary policy simply means following German decisions and ensuring that monetary aggregates such as inflation and interest rates do not diverge too far from German levels.

In this chapter I examine the impact of the Dutch and Belgian central banks on economic recovery strategies and the social democratic promises of full employment and redistributive justice in the early 1980s. It should be noted that the heritage of the Belgian central bank is quite different from that of the Dutch. Neither the Belgian government nor private financial groups wanted a strongly independent central bank to emerge. In the midst of the Great Depression, new banking statutes created a porous bureaucratic structure that invited financial

---

[4] Gerald A. Epstein, "A Political Economy Model of Comparative Central Banking," Working Paper, no. 3, Department of Economics, University of Massachusetts, 1990.

groups and government coalitions to take advantage of the central bank's narrowly defined scope of activities. Politicians exploited the circumscribed authority of the central bank; they borrowed extensively on capital markets to finance social programs and pacify rising linguistic antagonisms. Financial groups exploited the loopholes in banking supervision to escape auditing and regulation.

## THE STATUTORY POSITION OF DE NEDERLANDSCHE BANK

According to the Bank Act of 1948, the Dutch central bank, De Nederlandsche Bank (DNB), is to regulate and stabilize the value of the guilder in the manner most conducive to the country's welfare. Other duties are to put money into circulation and to supervise the credit system. Exchange rate policy is determined by the minister of finance together with the central bank. In other respects, the bank is independent, although its actions are not supposed to conflict with government objectives.[5]

The organizational structure of the bank consists of a Directorate, a Board of Commissioners, and a Bank Council. The Directorate is the policy-making body. It is chaired by the president of the bank and composed of a director-secretary and four directors. All are appointed by the government for a tenure of seven years, which exceeds the incumbency of any government. Members of the directorate can be reappointed and usually serve more than one term. The Board of Commissioners supervises and approves the annual account of the bank. The Bank Council is composed of seventeen representatives of business, labor, and the government. The Council advises both government and the bank. The minister of finance can overrule the central bank in the event of a dispute over monetary policy, but the minister must make his or her decision and reasons public, which could produce a parliamentary vote of no confidence. So far, the Ministry of Finance and the central bank have never clashed, and the government has never invoked its powers to overrule the bank's policies.[6]

The main actors in the Dutch financial system are universal banks and instititutional investors as well as smaller agricultural cooperatives, savings banks, credit unions, and security credit institutions. Three universal banks act as stockbrokers, issue shares, grant loans, and take

[5] Bank for International Settlements (BIS), *Eight European Central Banks* (London: Allen & Unwin, 1963), 233–40.
[6] Don Fair, "The Independence of Central Banks," *The Banker* (October 1979), 37; Jane Welch, *The Regulation of Banks in the Member States of the EEC* (London: Nijhoff, 1981), 201.

deposits. In the early 1980s, the two largest commercial banks—AMRO and ABN—accounted for 60 percent of the combined balance sheet totals, and the three largest accounted for 75 percent of the balance sheet total of commercial banking.[7]

Both Dutch and foreign-registered universal banks are eligible for membership in the Netherlands Bankers' Association. Cooperative credit institutions and savings banks have their own representation. De Nederlandsche Bank is obliged to consult the bankers' association before it takes any action in credit regulation. Only if the consultations do not lead to an informal agreement is the bank empowered to issue a general directive to the industry, and then it must obtain the approval of the ministry of finance. So far, it has always been possible to reach a common understanding.[8]

## The Autonomy of De Nederlandsche Bank

Although the central bank was nationalized in 1948, the way in which directors are appointed, their term of office, the payment and pension schemes for banking officials, the settlement of disputes between bank and government, and the definition of the bank's functions classify it as independent.[9] Its main task is to safeguard the value of the currency and to maintain price stability. The latter goal depends heavily on fiscal, social, and budget policies, and the central bank is automatically drawn into discussions on domestic spending programs and government financing needs. Moreover, financial institutions have historically had a striking reputation for being among the more dynamic and outward-oriented sectors.

Most comparative studies rate the independence of DNB as "medium," somewhere below the central banks of Germany and Switzerland but above that of the very unsovereign central bank of France.[10] Yet any reading of economic policy-making in the Netherlands leads to a

[7] In 1990, ABN and AMRO signed a merger agreement to prepare for the coming of the Internal Market. The amalgamated bank is one of the twenty largest in the world.
[8] Peter Coffey, *The European Monetary System: Past, Present, and Future* (Boston: Nijhoff, 1989), 74. Welch, *Regulation of Banks*, 206–8.
[9] Jan Q. T. Rood, "The Position of the Netherlands: A Lesson in Monetary Union," in *Monetary Implications of the 1992 Process*, ed. Heidemarie Sherman, Richard Brown, Pierre Jacquet, and DeAnne Julius (London: Pinter, 1990), 136–37.
[10] Alesina ("Politics and Business Cycles," 81–83) ranks the Dutch central bank in the same group as the Belgian and Swedish central banks and defines them as dependent. Parkin, "Domestic Monetary Institutions and Deficits," 310–31, claims that the Swedish Riksbank has less autonomy in financial matters because the government determines profit allocation but that Belgium, Sweden, and the Netherlands have equally dependent central banks with respect to policy authority. See also Gerald Epstein and Juliet Schor, "The Political Economy of Central Banking," mimeo, Harvard University, Department of

very different conclusion; DNB often has had the final word in policy deliberations. Where does its influence originate? Certainly, a not insignificant factor is the highly visible role of finance and trade in the Netherlands' economic history. Partially for this reason, DNB was invited to take part in numerous tripartite committees of the Social Economic Council (1950), with the result that delegates of social interest groups in the 1950s and 1960s modified their views on distributive justice or full employment to meet the bank's criteria and objections. Top DNB administrators induced unions and employers to evaluate the effects of wage negotiations on the exchange rate or price stability. Many discussions revolved around how the balance of payments and price development would react to pay increases during the period of guided income policy, until 1963, and subsequently during the era of productivity-linked wage increases.

In the 1950s and early 1960s, the bank's influential voice was reinforced by the disunity among business groups and the erstwhile conservative thinking among spokespersons for organized labor, who preferred to emphasize the greater macroeconomic framework of economic justice or wage solidarity. Moreover, Catholic-led coalitions were willing to delegate authority over monetary issues to the central bank because they basically agreed with the bank's stress on price stability and a strong currency.

DNB carried so much weight in incomes policy deliberations because price stability was by far the most urgent objective for government leaders and because the tripartite exchanges were established to ensure a measured and orderly rise of incomes. Neither unions nor employers could be expected to display self-restraint, given their internal divisions. Dutch incomes policy, with its recurrent statutory wage controls, aimed at controlling price developments in an open economy with low union membership and acute organizational fragmentation. The central bank, together with the first coalition government elected after 1945, strongly believed that price stability could be achieved as long as the rate of increase in nominal spending was not permitted to exceed the potential for real income growth. Carefully attuned monetary and fiscal policies could guarantee stability of the domestic price level, with incomes policy serving to prevent money wages from rising faster than productivity.[11]

Economics, 1986. Dutch commentators hold very different views; see A. Knoester, *Economische Politiek in Nederland* (Leiden: Stenfert Kroese, 1989), 179. The Economist Intelligence Unit (EIU) reports that the Dutch central bank is among the most independent in Europe, second only to Germany's Bundesbank. *Country Profile. Netherlands* (London: EIU, 1991).

[11] Ann Romanis Braun, *Wage Determination and Incomes Policy in Open Economies* (Washington, D.C.: IMF, 1986), 272–73.

In the 1950s and 1960s, this very conservative institution was a strong supporter of consensual wage negotiations. Since the original objective of centralized negotiations was to keep pay artificially low, DNB perceived the tripartite Social Economic Council and bilateral Foundation of Labor as fully compatible with price stability and export competitiveness. In the consultative frameworks, reports that gave elaborate projections of future productivity trends and current account developments defined the parameters for wage increases. The central bank, as a technocratic agency skilled in deciphering economic forecasts, led the discussions. Because only banking officials and the nominally independent Central Planning Bureau had the sophisticated knowledge to draft these reports in the first place, they tended to monopolize a discussion that they themselves had initiated. Unions and employers waited for the reports prepared by the technocrats of the central bank and the Planbureau and then relied on the same people for a detailed exposition of what these forecast models were saying. The trade union federations were supposed to calculate permissible pay increases based on this information.

The bank's role in wage formation discussions went beyond the presentation of obscure models. In the late 1950s, low pay led to tensions in the labor market as employers competed to hire more and more workers. Marinus Holtrop, the first postwar president of the bank, salvaged the system of guided wage policies by formulating a compromise solution that satisfied both labor market parties.[12] In the 1960s, Holtrop lobbied for a mixed wage system that permitted general supervision over labor cost developments but gave room for productivity and profit differentials in different production branches.[13]

To a large extent, monetary policies also intersect with social spending programs; budget deficits are a direct concern to the monetary authorities. In the Netherlands, any budget deficit had to be financed through the domestic capital market. Supposedly, this would control the size of the deficit, and its inflationary impact would be diminished.[14]

With its involvement in economic policy making and tripartite delib-

---

[12] John Windmuller, *Labor Relations in the Netherlands* (Ithaca: Cornell University Press, 1969), 300.

[13] M. W. Holtrop, "On the Effectiveness of Monetary Policy: The Experiences of the Netherlands in the Years 1954–69," *Journal of Money, Credit, and Banking* 9 (1972): 283–311. The author was president of DNB from 1945 until 1967.

[14] OECD, *Why Economic Policies Change Course* (Paris: OECD, 1988), 92. Nout Wellink and Victor Halberstadt, "Monetary Policy and Control of Public Expenditure with Special Reference to the Netherlands," in *Public Expenditure and Government Growth*, ed. Francisco Forte and Alan Peacock (Oxford: Blackwell, 1985), 185–86. In the 1970s, a budgetary deficit of 4 percent of net national income was calculated to be consistent with the domestic savings rate and with a small surplus on the current account.

erations, the central bank could request that inflation and balance-of-payments equilibrium, not full employment or demand stabilization, be the first concern of government in the 1970s. Governments attempted to moderate wage trends through the implementation of nationally coordinated incomes agreements precisely because it might arrest inflationary pressures and protect the guilder. Jelle Zijlstra, the second postwar president, proclaimed repeatedly that inflation was "the greatest evil afflicting the economy." [15]

From 1976 onward, DNB has pursued a restrictive monetary regime in order to retain parity with the German mark and to block further fiscal expansion. In 1977, it imposed credit restrictions to decrease the liquidity ratio by 1 percent per year. When the current account registered small deficits in 1978 and 1980, the short-term interest rate peaked at 24 percent to preserve the exchange rate parity.[16] From 1979, the bank has simply refused to finance budget deficits through monetization. The state was not allowed to borrow abroad and had to finance its budget deficits by borrowing in the domestic capital market.[17]

Studies on Dutch public policy and the demise of social accords claim that the Nederlandsche Bank has acted as a brake on macroeconomic policy making.[18] After 1978, the Dutch government increasingly directed attention toward the control of inflation because DNB assigned primacy to price stability and the maintenance of confidence in the guilder. Since open economies cannot control liquidity, pegging the guilder to the German mark and refusing to finance budget deficits were the best instruments available to DNB.

This policy course does not seem to differ from the concern of other small European countries with currency and price stability, but DNB has also sought to promote the internationalization of the guilder as a complementary goal. Price stability and a fixed exchange rate went

---

[15] De Nederlandsche Bank, *Annual Report 1976* (The Hague: Staatsuitgeverij, 1977), 19.

[16] OECD, *Why Economic Policies Change Course*, 93.

[17] Wellink and Halberstadt, "Monetary Policy and Control of Public Expenditure with Special Reference to the Netherlands," in *Public Expenditure and Government Growth*, 190–92. Gisli Blöndal, *Fiscal Policy in the Smaller, Industrial Countries, 1972–1982* (Washington, D.C.: IMF, 1986), 181.

[18] Dietmar Braun, "Political Immobilism and Labor Market Performance: The Dutch Road to Mass Unemployment," *Journal of Public Policy* 7 (1987): 313–14; Wibo Koole and Göran Therborn, "De Casablanca-solution' voorbij: De merkwaardige dood van het Keynesianisme en de relatieve verpaupering van Nederland," in *Socialisten in no nonsense tijd*, ed. Pim Fortuyn and Siep Stuurman (Nijmegen, Netherlands: SUN, 1987), 22–25; Wibo Koole, "De neoliberale reorganisatie van politiek-economische regimes," in *De theoretische grondslagen van economisch beleid*, ed. Henk W. Plasmeijer (Groningen, Netherlands: Wolters-Noordhoff, 1988), 138.

hand in hand with far-reaching liberalization of capital flows and the adoption of EC and OECD codes for financial deregulation. The international community was invited to treat the guilder as an international reserve currency and to compare its reliability with that of the deutsche mark. After 1973, when floating exchange rates typified the international monetary system, the guilder was pegged to the German mark to reinforce this message. To pursue a credible hard currency option, central bank personnel insisted on a small surplus on the current account. Since a surplus on the current account threatened to give the domestic market extra liquidity, the bank also promoted capital outflows and issued credit measures to block an expansionary fiscal policy at home. Eventually, restrictive credit policies generated a difficult investment climate and spurred a continuous outflow of capital at the expense of capital stock modernization, employment, and manufacturing recovery.

### The Financial Sector

In the Netherlands the Minister of Finance and the central bank traditionally see eye-to-eye on most if not all issues, and they cooperate closely. The minister of finance has never needed to invoke Section 26 of the 1948 Bank Act to remind DNB that it must "properly coordinate with the government's monetary and financial policy." To a large extent, the Dutch are as obsessed with disinflation as the Germans. The German intolerance of radical price movements has always been understood as a reaction against the painful hyperinflation waves that hit the Weimar Republic in the 1920s. Recent history in the Netherlands, however, does not yield any clues about why the Dutch are similarly obsessed with low inflation since there is no comparable episode of agonizing financial and currency instability. Hence, the most plausible explanation for this preoccupation with price equilibrium and a credible hard currency is the country's expertise and specialization in financial transactions, overseas investments, and business services. Central bank personnel interact regularly with financial experts in the private sector who fervently believe in financial deregulation, openness, and sound finance.

Moreover, the Dutch financial sector is unique both because of the size of its banks and their detachment from manufacturing production. In *Euromoney*'s 1988 rating of the world's five hundred largest banks, three Dutch banks, RABO, ABN, and AMRO, were ranked 24th, 53d, and 57th by shareholders' equity. The largest Belgian banking group, Generale Bank, was ranked 95th, Creditanstalt, 160th; but the largest Swedish bank, Svenska Handelsbanken, ranked as 328th.[19] In a 1988 list of transnational corporations compiled by the United Nations, Swiss and Dutch banks are the only financial institutions from any of the small countries to be named among the fifty largest banks according to assets less contra-accounts.[20]

Capital flow liberalization and the internationalization of Dutch assets have paid off in that the guilder claimed 0.9 percent of the offshore Euromarket in the mid-1980s, compared with 1.3 percent for the pound sterling, and was equal to the share of the French franc, even though France's GNP is triple that of the Netherlands.[21]

International transactions substitute for equity participation and industrial lending at home. In the early 1980s, share assets accounted for about 2 percent of the combined balance sheets of all the commercial banks.[22] The law forbids commercial banks from owning more than 5 percent of the capital of a nonfinancial company, but this is not the main roadblock. The prohibition was legislated to protect the banks from risky deals and to prevent cartel formations. Although DNB has a strong aversion to equity risktaking by banks, the main barrier is the tradition of the banks themselves. Commercial banks were never *banques d'affaires*, or investment banks. In the early 1980s, they lent to other banks, which accounted for about one-third of their activities, and only 22 percent of their financial transactions was with manufacturing companies.[23]

Most of the loans to manufacturers were short-term industrial cash loans, ranging from one month to two years, or were issued in the form of debt certificates, which were not transferable and had no secondary market. The universal banks, acting as brokers, bring parties together and issue fixed interest debt certificates in lieu of bonds as a way to channel long-term funds from institutional investors to borrowers.

[19] "The World's Five Hundred Largest Banks," *Euromoney*, June 1989, pp.85, 87, 95, 102. The three Dutch banks each held more than $80 billion in assets. The Generale Bank, which is partially owned by the Société Générale, had $71 billion dollars in assets in 1988. The largest Austrian and Swedish banks trailed with $39 billion and $38 billion in assets, respectively. For Dutch banking, see also Frans N. Stokman, Frans W. Wasseur, and Donald Elsas, "The Dutch Network: Types of Interlocks and Network Structure," in *Networks of Corporate Power: A Comparative Analysis of Ten Countries*, ed. Frans N. Stokman, Rolf Ziegler, and John Scott (Cambridge, U.K.: Polity Press, 1985), 112–30.

[20] U.N. Centre on Transnational Corporations, *Transnational Corporations in World Development* (New York: United Nations, 1988), 548–50.

[21] Francesco Giavazzi and Alberto Giovannini, "The EMS and the Dollar," *Economic Policy* 2 (1986): 469.

[22] Robert Jan Spierenburg, "Staatsinterventie en noodlijdende bedrijven," in *Interventie en Vrije Markt: Overheidsbeleid ten aanzien van de Struktuur van de Nederlandse Ekonomie*, ed. Hein Vrolijk and Richard Hengeveld (Amsterdam: SUA, 1982), 97.

[23] Geoffrey Renshaw, *Adjustment and Economic Performance in Industrialized Countries: A Synthesis* (Geneva: ILO, 1986), 81.

These debt certificates are not quoted on the stock exchange and are resold directly through the banks.[24] Bankruptcy laws favor bank creditors, who are more or less guaranteed to recoup their borrowed capital. Other less-secured creditors must wait until the banks have settled their financial affairs with the troubled company.[25] For this reason, despite their size, the commercial banks do not become locked into a company after they accept a part of an issue of debt certificates to the extent that they would if they made direct loans and were directly affected by the fate of their customers. Commercial banks neither acquire nor aspire to a high degree of influence. Most of their lending goes to multinational corporations, which present less of a risk. Transaction costs are lower because lending is concentrated in a few large customers.[26] The multinational corporations appoint bankers to their supervisory boards because it improves their international standing, but the bank representatives are not necessarily privy to corporate strategies. Interlocking networks among banks and industrial corporations are common but do not indicate an authentic community of interests on behalf of manufacturing.[27]

Institutional investors, not deposit-taking banks, are the main conduit for private savings in the Netherlands, but they are even less active in industrial lending than the universal banks. Life insurance funds and private and public pension funds collect about 90 percent of household and company savings. Private pension funds, claiming 39 percent of the contractual savings, invest in low-yield government bonds or loans because of their reliability. The public pension fund for government employees was obliged to place some of its capital in government bonds to finance budget deficits, but the restrictions were lifted in 1986, and the fund can now invest abroad. Life insurance funds, accounting for 28 percent of contractual savings, are free to deal in foreign currency notes. They primarily issue mortgage loans.[28]

Whether out of necessity or choice, Dutch business mostly relied on internally generated funds or retained profits to finance investments;

---

[24] E. V. Morgan and R. Harrington, *Capital Markets in the EEC* (Boulder, Colo.: Westview Press, 1976), 227–29, 230, 243.

[25] Spierenburg, "Staatsinterventie en noodlijdende bedrijven," in *Interventie en Vrije Markt*, 98, 116.

[26] *Euromoney*, May 1985 (Supplement), 19; H. H. Eijgenhuijsen, J. Koelewijn, and H. Visser, *Investeringen en de financiële infrastructuur* (The Hague: Wetenschappelije Raad voor Regeringsbeleid, 1987), 52, 61; Renshaw, *Adjustment and Economic Performance in Industrialized Countries*, 81.

[27] Stokman, Wasseur, and Elsas, "The Dutch Network: Types of Interlocks and Network Structure," in *Networks of Corporate Power*, ed. Stokman, Ziegler, and Scott, 112–30.

[28] Eijgenhuijsen, Koelewijn, and Visser, *Investeringen and de financiële infrastructuur*, 57–60.

about 75 percent of commercial and industrial companies counted on self-financing for fixed investments until now.[29] The separation of industry and finance has long-standing antecedents and existed before the political restructuring after World War II. In the late 1940s, the Catholic–Social Democratic coalition government had a chance to build a financial system that would be more tailored to industrial lending and providing long-term credit. But the government decided to furnish "appropriate" investment conditions with a variety of supply-side measures such as early depreciations, lower corporate taxation, and other comparable fiscal schemes. State action was confined to removing barriers to allow the private sector to expand, but none of the measures encompassed capital market reforms and financial innovations to bridge the historical separation between financial intermediaries and manufacturing industry.[30] Employers and business associations did not protest against the absence of financial reforms because centralized wage policies instituted after 1945 provided a steady flow of profits and thus investment capital. In the 1960s, generous profits created ample cash reserves, and Dutch transnational corporations were also able to borrow on international capital markets.

With the financial community's stake in international transactions, off-shore markets, and security investments, the central bank had sound reasons to fight to maintain confidence in the guilder and against inflation. Yet the appreciating guilder and its parity to the German mark hurt every export sector of the economy, with the exception of energy. The costs were especially harsh for small labor-intensive import-competing enterprises and shifted demand away from labor-intensive outputs to energy-related production. Large corporations substituted domestic production for capital exports to escape the crippling effect of an appreciated exchange rate, a depressed consumer market, and monetary restrictiveness. After 1976, the consequences began to appear in declining profitability, weak private investment, rising unemployment, and increasing current account deficits (excluding natural gas receipts). Fundamentally, the sequence of policies and effects arose from the unwavering commitment to price stability when no corresponding degree of stability in costs could be foreseen.[31]

[29] Renshaw, *Adjustment and Economic Performance in Industrialized Countries*, 80.

[30] Dercksen, *Industrialisatiepolitiek rondom de jaren vijftig*, 135–37; Erwin Zimmermann, *Neokorporative Politikformen in den Niederlanden* (Frankfurt: Campus, 1986), 71–74.

[31] Romanis Braun, *Wage Determination and Incomes Policy in Open Economies*, 291. René Belderbos, "Buitenlandse investeringen en internationalisering van de Nederlandse ekonomie," *Tijdschrift voor Politieke Ekonomie* 12 (1989): 32; H. W. de Jong, "De internationalisatie van het Nederlandse bedrijfsleven," in *Ondernemen in Nederland: Mislukkingen en mogelijkheden*, ed. Maria T. Brouwer and H. W. ter Hart (Deventer, Netherlands: Kluwer, 1984), 133–52.

*The "Dutch Disease" and DNB*

With borrowing abroad disallowed and the central bank refusing to extend further credits after 1979, the government was forced to raise money in the domestic capital market. The private and public sectors competed for affordable credit in the domestic market and drove up interest rates. The government concluded that spending natural gas rents would restore a more natural equilibrium in the domestic capital market and lower the costs of borrowing for everybody. In the late 1970s, the Netherlands was diagnosed as suffering from "Dutch disease" (called the petrocurrency effect in Britain). Symptoms of this disease are mass unemployment and de-industrialization, despite a surplus in the current account. The culprits in the transmission of this disease were private investors who moved resources from the tradable sector (exports) to the nontradable sector (services) as the high exchange rate lowered profit margins in the nonfuel sector. The inflow of wealth stimulated consumer demand for goods and services and put upward pressure on salaries and wages. Price adjustments could be made only by producers in the domestic, sheltered sector. Exporting firms must follow price levels set by world market trends. Labor-intensive manufacturing, which did export, closed down because it could not compete against the flow of cheaper imported goods and also lost market shares abroad.

Yet various government coalitions did not limit natural gas exports in order to reduce the demand for guilders in foreign exchange markets and to halt the appreciation of the guilder. By general consensus, monetary and fiscal authorities understood that a small surplus on the current account enhanced the reputation of the guilder as a strong and stable investment currency and that income from natural gas was a noninflationary way to finance budget deficits. One of the by-products of the current account surplus was that it repeatedly threatened to undermine restrictive liquidity and anti-inflation measures at home. The central bank was forced to clamp down on credit and fiscal spending and to encourage capital exports in order to neutralize inflationary pressures stemming from a surplus on the current account.

Wealth from a finite resource—natural gas—was used to pay for rapidly rising social transfer payments and was squandered on public consumption instead of being used to restructure industry or to reduce taxes.[32] Gas exports also led to the appreciation of the guilder and caused a worsening of terms of trade for import-competing and ex-

---

[32] OECD, *Economic Surveys. The Netherlands 1983* (Paris: OECD, 1983), 16; Renshaw, *Adjustment and Economic Performance in Industrialized Countries*, 27.

porting firms. In addition, the current account surplus undermined the noninflationary credit policies and the price stability objective of the Nederlandsche Bank so that central bankers were forced to encourage capital outflows to siphon off the extra liquidity available to consumers and investors. To promote such capital exports, the Nederlandsche Bank asked for fiscal retrenchment and restricted credit flows. The net result was depressed consumer demand that disheartened small domestic producers and ruined investors' confidence. Thus, various studies of Dutch transnational corporations have concluded that specific domestic conditions such as depressed domestic purchasing power, a strong currency, and restrictive credit policies triggered a noticeable increase in the outflow of capital.[33] Foreign direct investment abroad displayed a countercyclical pattern; domestic economic stagnation in the recession years of 1974–75 and 1980–83 quickened the outflow of capital and hastened the downward spiral of economic activities at home. This impasse could have been broken if the authorities had sent strong positive signals to the business community. Wage ceilings and pay freezes, however, only tended to strengthen recessionary trends in the domestic economy and literally chased business away to more promising pastures across the Atlantic. Between 1981 and 1985, the Netherlands accounted for nearly 9 percent of the annual average outflow of foreign direct investments from developed market economies. Much of this increase was accounted for by medium-sized firms, not the large international companies.[34]

It is difficult to say what foreign direct investment abroad has done to the Dutch labor market. One calculation estimates that an outflow of capital at an average of 2 percent of the GNP translates into a loss of production capacity of 2 billion guilders and twenty thousand jobs. The lowest estimate is a loss of 1 billion guilders and ten thousand jobs. Using the more conservative figures, net capital exports in the period from 1973 to 1982 equaled an annual loss of economic growth of 0.33 percent, or a cumulative economic loss of 3.3 percent and 100,000 jobs.[35]

[33] H. W. de Jong, "De Internationalisatie van het Nederlandse bedrijfsleven," in *Ondernemen in Nederland*, 149.

[34] The shares of France and Germany were 5.5 and 8.6 percent, respectively. U.N. Centre on Transnational Corporations, *Transnational Corporations in World Development* (New York: United Nations, 1988), 77.

[35] These figures must be treated with caution. The estimate does not take into account the nonclassical view that foreign direct investments augment the total investable income in the world and therefore exert a positive influence on the Netherlands as well. Gerard Haack and Boe Thio, "Werkgelegenheids-en produktie-effecten van direkte investeringen in Nederland," *Tijdschrift voor Politieke Ekonomie* 8 (1984): 76–77.

Repeatedly, Dutch monetary officials have warned the fiscal authorities not to deviate from the goal of price stability and to back up the international reputation of the guilder. The goals of disinflation and a strong currency received wide legitimacy because the banking industry was among the most advanced economic sectors in the Netherlands. During post–World War II reconstruction, the central bank was included as an observer or participant in tripartite institutions and during wage deliberations. Its presence in these venues propelled other social actors, particularly labor, to give careful attention to monetary developments and to weigh wage or pay settlements against their combined effect on price stability and balance of payments.

Financial interests were always hegemonic in Dutch capitalism, despite their specialization in overseas investments and international financial mediation.[36] Their preeminence was further secured because price stability was a major objective of centralized wage formation in the postwar period. Central bankers thus became the gatekeepers of economic and labor market trends. They were called upon to interpret econometric data and to evaluate the impact of incomes policy on price developments. For the central bank, price stability served to broaden the use of the guilder in international financial transactions; this dictated a constant policy of low inflation and a comfortable surplus on the current account, two not fully compatible goals. The surplus helped meet the financing needs of government yet also fueled inflationary expectations and growing budgetary spending. To ensure that the current account surplus was not consumed at home, restrictive monetary policies insofar as possible deterred business from borrowing for capital investments.

In addition to monetary restrictiveness, the appreciating exchange rate also hurt nonenergy exports both in foreign and home markets because of competition from cheaper imports. The accumulation of industrial and economic imbalances, visible in the 1970s, was not offset by state aid for industrial adjustment and modernization. As was discussed earlier, public programs were only sketchily formulated without much foresight and did not mitigate the painful consequences of international economic downturns. Hence, struggling companies obtained little relief from the economic recession, while large transnational corporations, with their natural propensity to go abroad, weathered domestic and international recessions better since they were less dependent on the Netherlands than the Netherlands on them.

---

[36] For an account of Dutch financial hegemony which complements my own interpretation, see Zimmermann, *Neokorporative Politikformen.*

## THE STATUTORY POSITION OF THE BELGIAN NATIONAL BANK

The Nationale Bank van België/Banque Nationale de Belgique (NBB/BNB) does not possess the same degree of political independence as the Dutch central bank.[37] In 1935, the authorities deliberately created a dual system in which the government retained some control over monetary policy. Fifty percent of the bank's stocks were placed in the hands of the state, and the other half was sold publicly on the stock exchange. The bank would formally share responsibility for open market operations with the Ministry of Finance, which continued to retain the veto right in certain limited cases. The central bank was prohibited by law from pursuing goals that conflict with the government's general objectives. Aside from that constraint, the central bank had no constitutional task.

The bank's labyrinthine system of appointments ensured a broad distribution of responsibility for its decision making. At the top is the governor, who is appointed by the Crown (i.e., the government) for five years and may be reappointed. The governor can be removed from office or suspended for up to three months should a conflict arise between the Nationale Bank België/Banque Nationale de Belgique (NBB/BNB) and the government. The bank's affairs are managed by a board of directors, which is assisted by a Council of Regency. The Council of Regency is chosen by government from among candidates who are proposed by the organizations that represent labor, industry, trade, and agriculture, as well as two executives from the public financial institutions and three proposed by the minister of finance. If the Council and the government clash over appointments, the Council has final authority. To safeguard the bank from political interference, neither the minister nor the Council can impose a decision on the other.[38]

The Royal Decree of 1935 vested the NBB/BNB with the right to set interest rates and direct monetary policy in general. Surveillance of the financial system was entrusted to an autonomous Banking Commission. The Banking Commission, in turn, appointed a Board of Auditors, which set ratios between assets and liabilities for each commercial bank.

[37] When political independence is measured by comparing the terms of appointments, the relationship with government, and formal responsibilities, the Belgian central bank scores very low and the Dutch central bank very high. Vittorio Grilli, Donato Masciandaro, and Guido Tabellini, "Political and Monetary Institutions and Public Financial Policies in the Industrial Countries," *Economic Policy* 13 (1991): 341–92.

[38] Don Fair, "The Independence of Central Banks," *The Banker*, October 1979, p. 37; Roland Beauvois, "Monetary Policy and Organization," in *Modern Belgium*, ed. Marina Boudart, Michel Boudart, and René Bryssinck (Palo Alto, Calif.: The Society for the Promotion of Science and Scholarship, 1990), 283–84.

In 1973, Parliament approved an amendment to the banking laws that allowed the NBB/BNB to set credit coefficients for the private sector. With this amendment, the Banking Commission also received greater authority to supervise credit institutions. Before this legislation, supervision of the financial sector was full of gaps. Credit institutions were not required to submit annual reports, and each was free to choose its own accounting system.[39]

The new measures also formalized cooperation among the Ministry of Finance, the NBB/BNB, the Banking Commission, and commercial banks on setting liquidity ratios. While no specific legislation obliges Belgian banks to give priority in their lending to the public sector, they are required to keep their legal reserves in the form of securities issued by public authorities.[40] They generally buy treasury bills and raise liquid assets by redeeming them, which the state does on request. The effect of this system is that under no circumstances would the central bank place the Treasury in difficulty by refusing funds it needed to repay commercial banks.[41]

Like the Netherlands, Belgium has no restrictions on the activities of foreign banks or subsidiaries of foreign banks. The only regulations are that foreign banks must be registered with the Banking Commission and that each bank with more than one branch office is required to maintain a separate balance sheet of its operations in Belgium. Practically all banks, whether foreign or national, are members of the Belgian bankers' association, which has no supervisory tasks but maintains close relations with the central bank and the Banking Commission. The association expects to be consulted at an early stage in the formulation of banking laws. (The law explicitly states that the central bank and the Commission can only formulate recommendations on banking ratios and solvency and liquidity ratios after having advised the relevant financial institutions.)[42]

Until the Great Depression, Belgium had so-called mixed banks, which performed the dual role of investor and bearer of general liquidity. During the stock market disaster of 1929, the mixed banks froze their lending facilities, causing a run on their accounts, while deflation reduced the value of the banks' stock portfolios and increased their losses on outstanding credits. Since the passing of the Bank Act of

---

[39] Welch, *The Regulation of Banks in the Member States of the EEC*, 5–8.

[40] Peter Coffey, *The European Monetary System. Past, Present, and Future* (Boston: Nijhoff, 1989), 77; Salvatore Mastropasqua, *The Banking Systems in the Countries of the EEC* (Alphen a/d Rijn, The Netherlands: Sijthoff and Noordhoff, 1978).

[41] Beauvois, "Monetary Policy and Organization," in *Modern Belgium*, ed. Boudart, Boudart, and Bryssinck, 284.

[42] Welch, *The Regulation of Banks in the Member States of the EEC*, 15–17, 29.

1935, commercial banks are prohibited from owning stocks, bonds, or assets in industrial, commercial, or agricultural firms.[43] The law compelled the mixed banks to separate their industrial and banking activities, with the result that from the original Société Générale de Belgique, a holding company was formed, and the Société Générale de Banque became the banking division. Similarly, the Banque de Bruxelles was divided into a holding company, Brufina, and the Banque Bruxelles Lambert. A third significant Belgian bank is the Kredietbank, the merchant bank of the wealthy Flemish bourgeoisie, founded in 1935. While the first two banks hold a variety of interests in manufacturing, the Kredietbank is oriented toward deposits.

Closely trailing the commercial banks in size, public savings banks hold one-fifth of all deposits and own enormous assets. For instance, the Belgian Caisse Générale d'Epargne et de Retraite/Algemene Spaar-en Lijfrentekas CGER/ASLK had a total balance sheet of $16 billion in 1984 and was one of the largest savings banks in the world. It was founded in 1865 to offer workers an opportunity to invest their savings safely and profitably. From the start, the savings banks, of which thirty-five still existed in 1985, collected capital through the time-tested method of passbook savings. Only in 1980 were they allowed to provide full-fledged banking services. Nevertheless, the philosophy behind savings banks remains different from that of private commercial lenders. Savings banks must set aside funds for public housing and are obliged to invest a certain proportion of their capital in government securities. In general, they are supposed to serve the public good and consequently bear a social responsibility that occasionally conflicts with maximizing profits.[44] Institutional investors, whether private or public, are of no significance because they transfer their funds to the savings banks or place them with the holding company.

### Politics and the Statutory Sovereignty of the Belgian Bank

Although the Belgian central bank cannot claim to possess impressive institutional leverage, financial actors and their links to international capital markets endow the bank with more authority than would be expected.

The Bank Act of 1935 followed the calamities of the Great Depression and was instigated by financial groups when they began to fear

[43] J. de Vries, "Benelux, 1720–1970," *Contemporary Economies: Fontana Economic History of Europe*, ed. C. M. Cipolla (New York: Harper and Row, 1977), 6: 20.
[44] "The Transformation of Savings Banks," *Euromoney*, November 1985. Morgan and Harrington, *Capital Markets in the EEC*, 49–51.

increased political meddling in the banking industry. To preempt assignment of a regulator, the mixed banks agreed to regulate themselves and proposed reforms of the banking laws before Parliament was ready to act. By separating banking from industrial activities, the directors of the holding companies managed to escape regulatory supervision; only the banking division was subject to state surveillance while the new industrial holdings remained beyond the reach of supervising authorities.[45] The responsibilities of the Banking Commission, which was formally assigned to implement and control banking and credit legislation, were carefully delimited in order to give the private sector as much freedom as possible and to keep the holding companies out of the clutches of state agencies. The Banking Commission was told to act aggressively only after regular market mechanisms had failed. Many private bankers staffed the Commission, and this hampered its efficient operation by exposing it to considerable manipulation by the private sector.[46]

In the early 1970s, the Socialist party, having seen at short range how difficult it was to steer the holding companies, began to insist on dealing with the regulatory laxness of the existing regime. It was able to introduce tighter supervisory rules, and the new law requested from the holding companies that they regularly publish information on bank solvency and adopt new accounting methods. Party officials also asked for a common format for the publication of annual balance sheets. Nevertheless, the holding companies were still not required to issue annual reports as long as they furnished the public with the required information through other means. The Société Générale de Belgique published its first consolidated balance in 1983.[47]

The enforcement of the prohibition on industrial-financial interlocking was never strict, so the new holding companies continued to own a substantial portion of the equity capital of the divested banks, and the holding companies opened large accounts in the banks they were associated with, thereby becoming their most important customers. Legal separation between financial and industrial firms did not in the slightest way undercut the enormous economic and political influence of the holding corporations.[48]

---

[45] Guy Vanthemsche, "De politiek en economische context van de Belgische bankwetgevingen van 1934 en 1935," in *La Banque en Belgique, 1830–1980* (Brussels: Centre d'Etudes Financières, 1980), 31–50.

[46] René de Preter, *De 200 rijkste families* (Berchum, Belgium: EPO, 1983), 33–34.

[47] Ludo Cuyvers, "Holdings in de schijnwerper," *Vlaams Marxistisch Tijdschrift* 22 (1988): 48–62.

[48] Herman van der Wee and Karel Tavernier, *De Nationale Bank van België en het monetaire gebeuren tussen de twee wereldoorlogen* (Brussels: De Nationale Bank van België, 1975), 295–306.

In the postwar period, the holding companies lost much of their political weight with the rise of Flanders, where comparatively few of their subsidiaries were located. With the ascendance of the Flemish wing in the Social Christian party (which consists of a francophone faction [PSC] and a Flemish faction [CVP] people affiliated with the CVP began to fill critical positions in the financial world. The NBB/BNB was led for years by a Fleming and CVP member. Another career politician of the CVP was director of the largest public investment bank, which transferred hundreds of billions of francs in subsidized loans to Belgian and foreign corporations. The largest public savings bank in the world, CGER/ASLK, which regularly received more than 50 percent of its deposit accounts from Flemish households and corporations but only 30 percent from Wallonia, was headed by a CVP-affiliated technocrat. Finally, the position of chief executive of the Kredietbank, the Flemish bank, was regularly filled by a CVP politician. The process was like a revolving door. Two recent chairmen of the Kredietbank in the 1980s were ex–ministers of finance in a Social-Christian–led coalition; they had worked at the Kredietbank before they entered politics. Such movement back and forth between government functions and the private sector eases coordination and cooperation.

The francophone holding companies entertain close contacts with the francophone branch of the Social Christian party (PCS), which is the junior sister party of the Flemish CVP and always participates with the CVP in government. Francophone financial groups are thus not excluded from the corridors of powers and are kept informed of any plans, measures, or changes that might affect their interests. After 1960, moreover, the francophone holding companies bought into Flemish firms in order to exploit the growth of Flanders.[49]

Against this background of limited regulatory power, the NBB/BNB is not an agency with tremendous institutional capacity or autonomy. Regular central bank activities are handed out to different state agencies, and the bank itself plays a limited role in the supervision of the credit system. Furthermore, every step must be coordinated with the Ministry of Finance. The ministerial departments have regular contact with the private financial world—respected party sympathizers head most financial institutions or corporate groups. One transparent indicator of the bank's subordinate position vis-à-vis government is the unparalleled growth of the public debt, which is, after Ireland, the

[49] Paul Goossens and Paul Koeck, "De financieel-ekonomische bedrijvigheid van de CVP," De CVP-Staat (Berchem, Belgium: EPO, 1979), 43–59; De Preter, De 200 rijkste families, 117–28; CRISP, Morphologie des Groupes Financiers (Brussels: CRISP, 1966), 357–65.

highest in the OECD. A central bank with greater moral suasion and the right to refuse to finance government deficits would have been able, presumably, to stop government from spending beyond its means year after year.

However, although its bureaucratic authority is circumscribed, the NBB/BNB has powerful allies in society. The holding companies have always exercised "undue" influence in economic policy making and political life, and the status of the NBB/BNB ought to be assessed in the light of the concentrated power of this group of economic actors. It should be stressed that the basic character of the Belgian holding company is that of a financial asset holder. Holding companies are classified as financial conglomerates because they do not normally interfere with the technical and commercial decisions of their acquisitions and only aim for a sufficient return on their investments. Furthermore, besides the Société Générale de Belgique (SGB), the other holding companies, including those based in Flanders, specialize primarily in financial mediation, and a relatively large part of their portfolios is derived from financial investments.

In the postwar period, financial holding companies took advantage of the limited capacity of the bank to promote some of their goals, such as superficial regulation of credit institutions and a liberal international investment code. The government also took advantage to obtain finances for social programs and industrial aid to repair the contentious relationship between the two linguistic communities and to mediate between warring unions and management. The NBB/BNB rarely pursued straightforward monetary restrictiveness because it was not in the interests of the key corporate actors nor of the government.[50]

### Internationalization, National Debt, and Exchange Rate Policy

Unstable coalition governments hoped to spend their way out of constitutional, social, and economic crises in the 1970s. Between 1974 and 1981, general government borrowing requirements in relation to the GDP rose substantially in Belgium and went from a manageable 3 to 6 percent of the GDP between 1970 and 1977 to a mind-boggling 9 to 13 percent between 1980 and 1986. In 1986, the gross public debt was the equivalent of 105.6 percent of the GDP. If the deficits in social security and off-budget debt plus local government debt are added together, the gross public debt was in excess of 122 percent of the GDP.

---

[50] Support to firms was 7.3 percent of the GDP in 1984, and total social spending was 38 percent; see R. Boelaert, "Overheid en Bedrijfsleven" *Tijdschrift voor Economie en Management* 33 (1988): 217–44.

The enormous growth in budget deficits emerged in the wake of a slowdown in tax revenues and economic growth after 1979, which required an increase in automatic transfer payments. After 1982, the chief cause for the annual budget deficits was the high level of debt carried from previous years and a resulting sensitivity to interest rate fluctuations. The combination of rising interest rates and a declining GDP automatically increased the debt burden despite a more restrictive fiscal stance. The self-perpetuating impact of interest payments on the debt have made it extremely difficult to reduce the principal in a meaningful way.

Chaotic public finances soon collided with capital market liberalization and international financial integration. Foreign banks established themselves in Brussels in order to serve the multinational clients that had preceded them. To attract foreign banks, the Belgian state created a favorable fiscal system under which interest income received from abroad was considered as already partially taxed even if this was not the case. As a result, foreign banks benefited from tax breaks that allowed them to avoid paying income taxes. In addition, foreign bank subsidiaries received permission to ignore capital ratio requirements for their subsidiary establishments.[51] Belgium, with its central location in Europe, is second only to the United Kingdom as the country with the most internationalized financial sector in the Western world. In 1985, Belgium and Luxembourg accounted for 6.9 percent of the world's foreign bank deposits at domestic banks and 7.5 percent of the world's total share of foreign deposits at domestic banks.[52] Foreign-owned banks represented about 50 percent of the balance sheet total, about 18 percent of customers' deposits, 30 percent of credits to the private sector, and 67 percent of interbank transactions.[53] Transactions with nonresidents represented almost 57 percent of total liabilities and assets of banks operating in Belgium in the late 1980s. Nearly 90 percent of foreign banks' transactions were in foreign currencies or with the foreign sector.

One contrast with Dutch banking is that the internationalization of the financial system has not caused Belgian banks to become authentic transnational institutions. Belgian banks dominate the domestic retail

[51] Alain Saiens, "Financial Services and Markets," in *Modern Belgium*, ed. Boudart, Boudart, and Bryssinck, 254.

[52] Alberto Giovannini, "National Tax Systems versus Euro-Capital Market," *Economic Policy* 9 (1989): 398.

[53] Marc Quintyn, "The Belgian Financial Sector and 1992: Implications and Perspectives," in *European Financial Integration and Monetary Cooperation*, ed. Paul van den Bempt and Marc Quintyn (London: IFR Books, 1989), 68.

network and the domestic currency market. Although the Belgian Kredietbank is the top ECU (the basket of currencies of EC member states) clearing bank in the world, its internationalization represents not an outgrowth of independent penetration and specialization in foreign markets but rather an inflow of capital from non-EC countries (specifically, Japan and the United States), which have taken advantage of the liberal foreign direct investment codes and capital flow regulations to establish banking branches in the European Community. The Belgian banks, like their owners, are in essence averse to risk and conservative, and none of the Belgian financial intermediaries appears on the list of the world's largest transnational banks.

Instead, thanks to the voracious appetite of the central government for liquidity, Belgian banks have bought risk-free treasury certificates with relatively high yields. Government authorities asked all financial institutions to hold a minimum portfolio of securities and public bonds.[54] According to NBB/BNB figures on the structure of the national debt for 1985, more than half the interest on the public debt was accrued by private financial institutions.[55]

Government bonds were a lucrative and stable business; the borrowing requirements of the state practically doubled every four years between 1973 and 1982. In 1973 the government borrowed 3.5 percent of the GDP, 7.0 percent in 1979, and 12.7 percent in 1981.[56] Belgian banks were the nation's chief financiers, holding on average 80 percent of the consolidated public debt; they continued to amass steady, comfortable commissions and profits.

The combination of a high degree of financial openness and the predominance of the public sector as a borrower of funds eventually resulted in an unsustainable situation, with far-reaching political ramifications. The Belgian franc has never been permitted to float freely; interest rate differentials balance financial flows and stabilize the value of the Belgian franc in foreign exchange markets.[57] But the sizable public deficits since the mid-1970s obliged the NBB/BNB to try to lessen the debt service burden as much as possible by keeping interest rates as low as possible. Yet low interest rates were inflationary, discouraged capital inflows, and undermined confidence in the franc.

Compared with officials of the Dutch central bank, Belgian bank officials took a more flexible or pragmatic view of an exchange rate

---

[54] OECD, *Economic Surveys. BLEU 1981/82* (Paris: OECD, 1982), 27.
[55] OECD, *Economic Surveys. BLEU 1987/88* (Paris: OECD, 1982), 44, 80 n.11.
[56] OECD, *Economic Surveys. BLEU 1981/82*, 21.
[57] B. Naudts and E. Schokhaert, "Government Debt and Interest Rates in Belgium, 1974–1986," *Tijdschrift voor Economie en Management* 33 (1988): 339–54.

system of fixed parity. To them, the purpose of the system was to guarantee the stability of the rate at which the franc was exchanged but not to discipline domestic actors or to enforce greater monetary restrictiveness. This has meant that the definition of stability has varied over time from average stability, to stability of the weighted average rate to nominal stability against a dominant partner.[58] In 1972, Belgium signed the Basel Agreement, the objective of which was to establish a stable exchange rate system among the currencies of the member states of the European Community. Belgium also joined the European Monetary System in 1979 to counter inflation and support trade. But the escalating interest rates that resulted from Belgium's high borrowing threatened the exchange policy, monetary stability, and everything else in which the monetary authorities believed. This situation provoked a major political standoff between the bank and the center-left coalition of Socialists and Christian Democrats in 1981.

For the new coalition of Socialists and Christian Democrats in 1977, the economic crisis had been essentially a product of sluggish demand resulting from the restrictive center-right government of 1974–77. The new government's fiscal policy was therefore moderately expansionary to boost household incomes, though its timing had been frequently off and possibly had procyclical effects.[59] Because of the commitment to a fixed exchange rate, the moderately expansionary program began to backfire, and the current account started to register substantial deficits. Because the real weakness of the Belgian economy was its uncompetitive industrial structure, the current account deteriorated precipitously, declining from a surplus of 3.5 percent of the GDP in 1972 to a deficit of 4.5 percent in 1980 and 1981. The central bank, to defend the franc in the foreign exchange market, raised the discount rate continuously. Real interest rates were set well above those of Germany and at the end of 1981 were among the highest in the OECD at 5.5 percent for long-term rates and 7 percent for short-term rates. The annual rate of growth of interest payments on government debt was an astonishing 30 percent between 1979 and 1981. There was no doubt in anybody's mind that something had to be done immediately.[60] For one, the high interest rates undermined industrial restructuring

[58] Jean-Jacques Rey, "The Implications of Financial Integration for Belgium's Monetary Policy," in *European Financial Integration and Monetary Cooperation*, ed. van den Bempt and Quintyn, 180–83.
[59] W. D. McClam and P. S. Andersen, "Adjustment Performance of Small, Open Economies: Some International Comparisons," in *Inflation and Unemployment: Theory, Experience and Policy-Making*, ed. V. E. Argy and J. W. Nevile (Boston: Allen and Unwin, 1985), 253. André Mommen, *Een tunnel zonder einde: Het neo-liberalism van Martens V en VI* (Deventer, Netherlands: Kluwer, 1987), 22–28.
[60] OECD, *Economic Surveys. BLEU 1981/82*, 28.

programs. Second, exchange rate parity would only widen the gap between interest rates at home and abroad. In addition, the overappreciated franc hurt exporting firms as well as import-competing sectors.

For the first three months of 1981, the bank had spent BF 96 billion to defend the franc. In five days alone, at the end of March, the bank lost BF 28 billion in an attempt to shore up the franc in international markets.[61] One report after another by the research division of the NBB/BNB faulted the comprehensive system of wage and salary indexation in the private and public sectors for the rigidity of the labor market, unemployment, government expenditures, and excessively high labor costs. Since the central bank believed that indexation was the chief culprit because it prevented the government from reducing social expenditures in order to restore sanity to public finance, the bank wanted to abolish it. The NBB/BNB urged the suspension of the indexation system for a year or two at the very least. To expedite the matter, the governor of the bank drafted an emergency plan and presented it to the Social Christian prime minister Martens. The plan called for an immediate pay reduction of 5 percent for all income groups and welfare beneficiaries. It also proposed a suspension of the index and the reduction of family allowances and vacation money.

The prime minister adopted the bank's plan as his own and brought it for discussion to a cabinet meeting. His Socialist coalition partners, who were not privy to the first secretive discussions between the governor and a small group of Social Christian (CVP/PSC) leaders, could not accept the bank's ultimatum because the party's member unions absolutely insisted on a fair distribution of the burden of adjustment.[62] For the trade union federation leadership, the weakness of the plan was that unions were asked to make sacrifices while business was not asked for comparable concessions. Union leaders had held a round table conference with employers in February 1981 and reached an agreement on income ceilings. Events had clearly nullified the outcome of this central accord—the first after six years of deadlock—and the unions wanted to see some proof that their standard of living and jobs would be safe. With the cabinet divided and undecided, the prime minister resigned. Elections in November 1981 brought the Liberal party back to power. In February 1982, the Belgian franc was devalued by 8.5 percent after the government had suspended the cost-of-living index, cut welfare payments, frozen wages and salaries, and begun to introduce smaller savings measures in the public sector.

[61] Hugo de Ridder, *Geen winnaars in de wetstraat* (Louvain: Davidsfonds, 1986), 51, 67.
[62] Mommen, *Een tunnel zonder einde*, 32; De Ridder, *Geen Winnaars in de Wetstraat*, 45–75; M. Deweerdt, "Overzicht van het Belgische politiek gebeuren in 1981," *Res Publica* 24 (1982): 221–60.

This episode demonstrates that it is impossible to reconcile a liberal approach to financial integration and capital flows with a sizable public debt caused by substantial transfer payments and public spending programs. The internationalization of the Belgian financial system and the inflow of foreign banks put extra pressure on the NBB/BNB to pursue a "credible" exchange rate policy. But a fixed exchange rate was preserved at a high price; real interest rates and public debt burdened the economy considerably. Before the devaluation, the distressing debt payments and public deficits undermined the confidence of investors, who were more attracted by financial investments with a high and steady return than by capital or productive investments with their long-term uncertainty and slow return. An earlier devaluation might have prevented several years of futile struggle to keep the exchange rate unaltered and might have bolstered the export competitiveness of some components of the manufacturing industry. However, from the end of 1970s until February 1982, the central bank insisted on fiscal adjustments and incomes policies first and only later acknowledged that a devaluation was needed because domestic adaptation was not sufficient to arrest the run on currency and capital outflows. The bank pressed for a stable exchange rate because the financial community expected the central bank to safeguard the external value of the currency.

The deep distrust between labor and business was the main reason for the combativeness and unwillingness of the unions to let go of the indexation system. For them, the choice was either to resist and preserve social welfare gains and bargaining power or to capitulate and lose everything. The currency devaluation and the end of a contractual system of wage determination were radical economic policy decisions, the undeniable aim of which was to transfer a major share of household income to the corporate sector and then to the public sector. Corporate profits were boosted, and the current account recorded a small surplus in 1986. However, this surplus was attributed to a decline in consumer demand and terms-of-trade amelioration. The improvement in price competitiveness, however, had an extremely modest impact on foreign trade volume; the productive system was still hampered by mismatched technology and specialization. Corporate investment ratios, moreover, did not rise even though the corporate sector's share of national income more or less doubled in five years (1982–87). Similarly, confidence in the Belgian franc did not fully recover until the late 1980s because the interest rate differential remained large and the bank needed to intervene regularly on behalf of the franc until late 1985.

Monetary authorities did not propagate a rigid monetary doctrine in

Belgium, although the maintenance of a stable exchange rate ranked high on the list of priorities. A stable and strong franc attracted foreign capital and made Brussels a center for international banking. Public expenditures rose rapidly after the deterioration in industrial manufacturing and the turbulence in international markets. Growing government budget deficits led by a growing appetite for borrowing clashed with the objective of maintaining a stable exchange rate. International financial interpenetration and inflationary spending habits exposed the economy to recurrent speculative attacks against the Belgian franc. Gradually, monetary and fiscal authorities came to focus more on appeasing or fulfilling the needs of banking and of their international allies than on meeting the demands of labor or tripartite exchanges.

In both Belgium and the Netherlands, monetary policy and central bank actions undermined repeated attempts by politicians to resurrect social concertation and to revive industrial investments. Economic recovery strategies were largely checked by restrictive monetarism while economic management at home in turn propelled industrial and non-industrial corporations to export capital and investments. It is no surprise that tripartism ceased to exist as a system for policy deliberation and action.

CHAPTER SEVEN

# Dependent Central Banks
# in Austria and Sweden

Quantitative studies that compare and test central bank independence neglect the context of banking politics.[1] An interpretive assessment of central bank independence, one that is sensitive to historical and political nuances, does not easily lend itself to econometric analyses and therefore is not useful to many scholars who prefer rigorous statistical testing.

Econometric investigations, however, fail to define whether the Oesterreichische Nationalbank, the Austrian central bank, is independent or dependent. From a distance, this bank appears to enjoy the same kind of leverage and prestige as the Dutch central bank. Inflation rates are persistently below the European average, and the exchange rate is firmly pegged to the German mark, dictating a restrictive monetary regime and resulting in continuous upward pressure on the Austrian schilling. Nevertheless, in the absence of internationally oriented financial institutions, the central bank is vulnerable to political meddling, and its board members are appointed by government and the social partners. Monetary stability and corresponding low inflation is regarded by the literature on central bank independence as an affirmation of the independence of monetary authorities, but in the case of Austria, they are no proof at all of central bank sovereignty. Fifty percent of the shares of the Nationalbank are owned by the main interest groups, including the trade union confederation, and these groups are also on the governing board of the bank. Price stability was demanded by the trade union

[1] For example, see King Banaian, Leroy O. Laney, and Thomas D. Willett, "Central Bank Independence: An International Comparison," *Federal Reserve Bank of Dallas Economic Review* (March 1983); 1–13. Richard C. K. Burdekin and Mark E. Wohar, "Monetary Institutions, Budget Deficits, and Inflation: Empirical Results for Eight Countries," *European Journal of Political Economy* 6 (1990): 531–53.

confederation in the 1950s as a tool for calibrating pay compensation and as a way to stay in control of collective wage contracts.

Like the Nationalbank, the Swedish Riksbank is incorporated in the tripartite social arrangements and lacks the persuasive power enjoyed by central banks with links to a financial community active in international transactions. Commercial banks in both countries focus on retailing and have been aligned with domestic manufacturing.

Sweden's Riksbank is a prototypical dependent bank in that its directors are appointed by the governing political party and can be dismissed by the prime minister. Fixing interest rates and other monetary or exchange rate decisions frequently reflected government biases for credit allocation to electorally popular areas and for countering financial speculation. Commercial banks were not allowed to construct their own sphere of activities in international markets and remained subject to regulations and prohibitions until the mid-1980s. Since then, with the abolishment of many barriers to banking and financial transactions, Sweden has been drawn closer to international financial markets and is less able to withstand volatile capital flows. Subsequently, the central bank has been given more decision-making power to react as quickly and effectively as possible to the harmful reverberations of more integrated financial and capital markets. In particular, with the removal of exchange and capital controls, maintaining confidence in the currency displaced other objectives that the Social Democratic government and monetary authorities formerly pursued.

## THE OESTERREICHISCHE NATIONALBANK

Paragraph 2 of the central bank law of 1955 states that the Austrian National Bank, Oesterreichische Nationalbank (OeNB) is required to maintain the domestic and external values of the Austrian schilling and to monitor credit expansion. Paragraph 4 admonishes the bank to be consistent with the economic policy of the federal government, which has been geared to economic growth and full employment. The central bank act of 1955 does not specify how the Nationalbank must incorporate national economic policy goals. But the state owns 50 percent of the shares of the bank, and the remaining shares are held by the organized interest groups of the social partnership.[2] All shareholders ap-

---

[2] Georg Winckler, "Geld und Währung," in *Handbuch der österreichischen Wirtschaftspolitik*, ed. Hanns Abele et al. (Vienna: Manzsche Verlags- und Universitätsbuchhandlung, 1989), 252; Karl Socher, "Monetary Policy in Austria," in *Monetary Policy in Twelve Industrial Countries*, ed. Karel Holbik (Boston: Federal Reserve Bank of Boston, 1973), 2–5. Besides the trade union confederation and Chamber of Commerce, private banks, agricultural cooperative banks, and insurance institutions also own equal parts of the central bank.

point directors to the governing board and have direct influence over banking decisions.

Credit institutions, whose influence exceed their proportional representation (four out of fourteen board members), are also in a favorable position to lobby the bank.[3] According to insiders, the real powers in the financial area are not the central bank, which has not been able to shake off its political shackles, but the joint-stock commercial banks. The OeNB is but a junior partner of the commercial banks.[4] Austrian commercial banks are of the universal type. They carry out not only standard deposit and lending activities but also many other functions, such as portfolio management, investment advice, securities brokerage, bond issues, and all other kinds of financial transactions and services. The joint-stocks banks—Creditanstalt Bankverein, Österreichische Länderbank, and the much smaller Österreichische Kontrollbank— accounted for 37 percent of the balance sheet total of the banking sector in 1986. Compared with the Netherlands, Sweden, and Belgium, the concentration of all-purpose banks is low. Austria has many different types of credit institutions, with specialized clienteles, although the divisions among these institutions are increasingly blurred. Along with the joint-stock banks, private and savings banks accounted for 26 percent of the balance sheet total, and the rural credit cooperatives, which are mainly involved in agriculture, had 17 percent. Most of the country's international financial activities are performed by the commercial banks. During the 1980s, the banking sector has witnessed greater concentration, but not to an especially high degree compared with other countries. For example, in 1986 the assets of the ten largest Austrian banks amounted to 51 percent of the balance sheet total.[5] In the Netherlands, one merged bank alone claimed 60 percent of the balance sheet total of Dutch banking in the mid-1980s.

The Nationalbank retained a low profile and delegated the responsibility of monetary policy making to the Ministry of Finance until the early 1960s. The atmosphere in the board of governors was highly charged; the two political blocs mistrusted each other's proposals. The Ministry of Finance, with the help of credit control agreements with the commercial banks, was forced to formulate money and banking policies because the representatives of the two coalition partners (Socialists and the conservative People's party) in the central bank were afraid of

[3] Ewald Nowotny, "Institutionen und Entscheidungsstrukturen in der österreichischen Wirtschaftspolitik," in *Handbuch der österreichischen Wirtschaftspolitik*, ed. Hanns Abele et al. (Vienna: Manzsche Verlags- und Universitätsbuchhandlung, 1982), 120.

[4] Ibid., 120. See also Socher, "Monetary Policy in Austria," in *Monetary Policy in Twelve Industrial Countries*, ed. Holbik, 31.

[5] OECD, *Economic Surveys. Austria 1985/86* (Paris: OECD, 1986), 37–38.

igniting a political controversy by doing something that the other condemned. Finally, in 1960 the OeNB board raised the minimum reserves, thus reasserting its sovereignty over its decision-making sphere.[6]

Once the OeNB resumed its original mission, party bosses still had a voice in monetary policy through their delegates on the bank board and among the shareholders. This has created a situation where the Nationalbank has become adept at using a variety of instruments, such as discount setting, cash reserve ratios, open market intervention, and foreign currency regulation, to influence monetary, interest, and exchange rate policies. Yet the Ministry of Finance continues to issue government loans and can also impose direct credit ceilings after reaching an agreement with the banks.

## Institutional Independence of the OeNB and the Social Partnership

Central banks need political allies to persuade politicians to place a premium on price stability and balance-of-payments equilibrium. In Austria, the largest credit institutions were state-owned and themselves owned substantial shares in industry. The Nationalbank's clientele was composed of partially nationalized commercial banks, which held diverse interests in manufacturing industry.

The three largest banks—Creditanstalt, Länderbank, and Mortgage and Credit Institute—were nationalized after World War II. The state controlled over 60 percent of the deposit activities of all credit institutions, 75 percent of securities issuance, and 90 percent of foreign exchange transactions. In 1955, the Socialists agreed to sell 40 percent of the stock holdings of the banks to the public, retaining the majority share and control. In the early 1960s, the three banks held majority interests in about ninety industrial corporations accounting for nearly 10 percent of the total capital assets of joint-stock companies. Eleven percent of the industrial labor force was employed by industrial enterprises controlled by the banks. The Creditanstalt owned the largest number of firms. Industrial firms benefited from their association with the Creditanstalt, for they were able to borrow at very favorable terms, and the banks were inclined to finance their modernization in order to counterbalance the dominance of the SPÖ in the state-owned industries.[7] Nonetheless, the total amount of credit made available to the banks' firms was comparatively small and did not harm the ability of

---

[6] Eduard März, *Österreichs Wirtschaft zwischen Ost und West: Eine sozialistische Analyse* (Vienna: Europa, 1965), 157–58.

[7] Elisabeth Beer and Brigitte Ederer, "Industriepolitik der österreichische Banken," *Wirtschaft und Gesellschaft* 13 (1987): 361.

private firms to obtain investment capital from the banks. As time went by, the Creditanstalt became increasingly less interested in managing its industrial assets expertly, and it sold many firms to the German Federal Republic during the early phase of the privatization in the 1980s.[8]

Every nationalized enterprise was managed by a team of Socialist and Conservative appointees in accordance with the system of distributing political offices equally among the two main parties. Political patronage in the credit sector, however, followed a less rigid symmetry, and interference in the running of the banks was correspondingly diminished. The Creditanstalt was "black," or conservative, while the Länderbank was "red," or socialist. Through the banks, the state owned equity in many industrial corporations. In the 1980s, the Creditanstalt sold many of its industrial enterprises, and its holdings have been more than halved since 1946. The Länderbank owned less property and fewer industrial interests, while the third bank was substantially smaller and was allowed to be 100 percent state-owned.[9]

Thus, until the late 1980s, the nature of Austria's financial sector was quite different from that of the Netherlands or Belgium. Neither commercial banks nor specialized credit institutions were driven by international ambitions, nor were they at the forefront of financial innovations. The institutional clout of the OeNB and its ability to ignore government wishes were limited by several factors. First, delegates of the Socialist and People's parties and two interest group organizations (the trade union confederation and the Chamber of Commerce) sat on the board of directors of the OeNB and controlled the list of top appointments. Second, the central bank could not draw on the private sector or the financial community, which itself was absorbed in the social partnership, to lessen the political meddling of the politicized staff or to bolster its own independent professional standing. Third, the financial sector was closely aligned with manufacturing industry and shared a community of interests with other key players in postwar economic policy design. It was not likely to criticize or amend existing procedures and objectives of the social partnership. Fourth, the bank's administrative scope was at times greatly enhanced, when a forceful

---

[8] Inge Morawetz, "Schwellenland Österreich? Aktuelle Veränderungen der österreichischen Eigentumsstruktur im Sog der Internationalisierungsstrategien der Bundesrepublik Deutschland," in *In deutscher Hand: Österreich und sein grosser Nachbar?* ed. Margrit Scherb and Inge Morawetz (Vienna: Verlag für Gesellschaftskritik, 1990), 91–95. The Creditanstalt sold its largest holding, Steyr-Daimler Puch, to German interests and thereby shifted seventeen thousand jobs from Austrian to German foreign control.

[9] Alexander Vodopivec, *Die Balkanisierung Österreichs: Folgen einer grossen Koalition* (Vienna: Fritz Molden, 1966), 172–75; Karl Socher, "Die öffentlichen Unternehmen im österreichischen Banken- und Versicherungssystem," in *Die Verstaatlichung in Österreich,* ed. Wilhelm Weber (Berlin: Duncker und Humblot, 1964), 403, 406–9.

personality with ties to the right people governed the OeNB. (But politicians were not always in the mood for a "forceful" individual and occasionally preferred a more pliable personality at the head of the Austrian central bank. In any event, not even a devoted technocrat could liberate the bank from party patronage.) Finally, the joint-stock banks did not object to the fact that the OeNB was a loyal partner in the Byzantine world of Austrian politics because it did not hurt their own interests.

All these points are significant for understanding why monetary stability—low inflation and a strong currency—produced very different economic outcomes in the Netherlands and Austria.

Both the Austrian and Dutch central banks interpreted price stability in narrow terms, and both pursued a hard currency option by pegging their currencies to the German mark (DM). But the context in which this policy was pursued differed. In the Netherlands, it is difficult to deny that the DM-guilder parity was also meant to support the international expansion of transnational corporations and to promote the use of the guilder in international transactions.

In Austria, by contrast, the prevailing attitude in the OeNB and among government officials was to inhibit as much as possible the international use of the Austrian schilling. The government pledged to remove all remaining restrictions to capital movements by 1990, but it has moved cautiously, and the liberalization of capital movements has proceeded in a piecemeal fashion.[10] Policymakers' great reticence in liberalizing capital flows is justifiable—such flows would allow foreign exchange movements to disrupt national economic strategies and planning. The bank tried to discourage the trading of the Austrian schilling as an investment currency on the international markets, but the issuing of schilling bonds abroad was allowed as long as the issue did not deplete the foreign exchange reserves of the central bank, inhibit domestic monetary capital formation, or undercut the fixed parity with the German mark. Permission was granted if the action was neutralized by simultaneously raising loans abroad or by seeking currency swaps. In the 1980s, the monetary authorities did not adhere strictly to the existing restrictions on international capital movements; domestic banks have been able to increase their foreign activities. In the early 1970s, the share of foreign assets or liabilities in their balance sheet total was 10 percent, but it rose to 23 percent in 1985.[11] Nevertheless,

---

[10] For a list of barriers, see Kurt Pribil, "Möglichkeiten einer stärkeren Orientierung an der EG bei der Liberalisierung des Kapitalverkehrs," *Wirtschaftspolitische Blätter* 34 (1987): 351–56.
[11] OECD, *Economic Surveys. Austria 1985/86* (Paris: OECD, 1986), 52.

*Table 11.* Current account surplus/deficit
as percentage of GDP

|  | 1974–79 | 1980–88 | 1960–88 |
|---|---|---|---|
| Austria | −1.4 | −0.4 | −0.4 |
| Netherlands | 1.2 | 2.4 | 1.3 |

*Source:* OECD, *Historical Statistics, 1960–1988*, 73.

there is no such thing as a "Euroschilling," while the "Euroguilder" flourishes.

In the Netherlands, the emphasis on domestic prices and output, coupled with banking internationalization, led the Netherlands Bank to issue alarming reports as soon as the current account registered a small deficit. Austrian monetary officials were more casual about chronic current account deficits. The current account recorded a small deficit from 1973 until the late 1980s (see Table 11), yet the chronic deficit neither spread waves of panic nor resulted in restrictive budgetary policies. Nor was the Austrian government prohibited from financing its budget deficits through borrowing abroad.[12] So long as it did not seem to interfere with the DM-schilling parity, the OeNB raised the discount rate and encouraged the Treasury to borrow capital abroad. Of course, neither fiscal nor monetary policies could be consistently different from German patterns, since that would cause higher inflation rates, a larger deficit, and ever-higher interest rates. But the external balance was neglected unless it harmed the pegging to the deutsche mark.

### The Hard Currency Option

The Austrian establishment opted for a pegged exchange rate after the first oil price rise to combat inflation. If the schilling floated upward, it would depress the costs of imported raw materials and goods. Another consequence, the squeeze on price competitiveness of export goods, would be balanced by the lower costs of imported goods. The president of the OeNB, Stephan Koren, also advocated the hard currency policy as a way to secure incomes policy in the future, as it would curb inflationary expectations. He added that a revaluation would also minimize a misallocation of resources by business and thus encourage

[12] Peter J. Katzenstein, *Corporatism and Change: Austria, Switzerland, and the Politics of Industry* (Ithaca: Cornell University Press, 1984), 43.

greater efficiency, since short-term miscalculations would be horrendously costly.[13] Above all, the bank saw the hard currency policy as a way of firming the bargaining position of employers because generous pay settlements would hurt them considerably.

Between 1971, when the Bretton Woods fixed exchange rate regime ended, and 1976, the schilling was pegged to the combined currencies of nine trading partners, and then to six currencies after the depreciating French franc, Italian lira, and British pound were withdrawn. In 1976, the authorities turned to a more transparent policy of linking the schilling to the German mark but allowed it to fluctuate within narrow margins to reflect the different developments and strengths of the two economies. The result was an appreciation of 106 percent, from 1971 until 1986, according to an International Monetary Fund (IMF) index.[14]

In the fall of 1977, the government presented a package of economic measures to arrest the growing budget deficits and the deterioration of Austria's competitiveness. The debate centered on how to reduce the current account deficit—whether to devalue the currency or to rein in consumer spending and wage growth. Not surprisingly, pegging the schilling to the DM, rather than secure pay earnings, was considered the cornerstone of economic policy, and it was agreed to decrease fiscal spending. In 1979, the fixed exchange rate to the DM helped stabilize prices, but interest rates, following international patterns, jumped to heights unseen before. The OeNB tried to break through the international pattern by aiming for lower domestic rates. Toward the end of 1979, the bank admitted defeat; lower interest rates at home had spurred an enormous outflow of capital, and the bank lost more than a third of its foreign exchange reserves.[15] Since then, interest rate policy has no longer been an independent instrument or target and do not complement demand management. Rates are set a little above the interest rates of the German Bundesbank and are unrelated to the supply of

[13] Stephan Koren, "Die österreichische Hartwährungspolitik" *Wirtschaftspolitische Blätter*, 35 (1988): 21. See also Fritz W. Scharpf, *Crisis and Choice in European Social Democracy* (Ithaca: Cornell University Press, 1991), 63.

[14] Gunther Tichy, "Hartwährungspolitik—ein irreführendes Schlagwort zur Maskierung einer überholten Politik," *Wirtschaftspolitische Blätter* 35 (1988): 38. An OECD index estimates a revaluation of 41 percent, and the Austrian Institute of Economic Research estimates 70 percent for the period 1970–86. See also Kurt Bayer, "Evaluierung der Effizienz der staatlichen Instrumente zur Investitionsförderung," in *Stahl und Eisen bricht: Industrie und staatliche Politik in Österreich*, ed. Margit Scherb and Inge Morawetz (Vienna: Verlag für Gesellschaftskritik, 1986), 35.

[15] Stephan Koren, "Austrian Monetary and Exchange Rate Policies," in *The Political Economy of Austria*, ed. Sven Arndt (Washington, D.C.: American Enterprise Institute, 1982), 29–30. See also Scharpf, *Crisis and Choice*, 66–67.

liquidity. Since about 1982, inflation, budget deficits, and current account deficits, which are all higher than in Germany, resulted in a stricter mix of monetary and fiscal policy and have helped raise the value of the schilling.[16] Since 1982, the economic theme of government stresses budget cuts, tax reform, and privatization to bring Austria closer in line with German developments. While Keynesian demand management clashes with an exchange rate pegged to the DM, the hard currency option nonetheless enjoys wide appeal and the full support of the social partners, including the trade union federation.

There is no question that fixing the schilling to the German mark has won many adherents. The ÖGB top leadership feels that a strong and stable currency has forced business to seek general centralized wage accords and has dissuaded profitable export-oriented firms from defecting from the peak-level coordinated incomes policy. The possibility of sudden price rises in the 1970s induced unions to act independently of the Parity Committee of Wages and Prices and threatened the central accords signed by the top leadership. The constraints imposed by the hard currency policy obliged workers to moderate their wage demands and thus to pledge their solidarity in an effort to maintain the international competitiveness of Austrian goods. Moreover, the promise of lower import prices represented a slight improvement in real income for wage earners.[17]

The revaluation of the schilling also motivated employers to stay within the centrally coordinated parameters and to request wage moderation in the light of deteriorating terms for trade for exporters. The Chamber of Commerce supported the hard currency option because it offered price stability and because small firms, which dominated the Chamber, did not export more than 10 percent of their turnover.[18] Similarly, neither the sheltered (nontradable) sector nor import-competing firms were hindered by the strong exchange rate. Although imported consumer goods would be competing with domestic industry, relatively high tariffs of 16.8 percent, or about twice the rate prevalent in the EC member states, gave some protection to the small business

[16] Tichy, "Hartwährungspolitik—ein irreführendes Schlagwort zur Maskierung einer überholten Politik," 36; Winckler, "Geld und Währung," in *Handbuch der österreichischen Wirtschaftspolitik*, ed. Abele et al., 262–63.

[17] Winckler, "Geld und Währung," in *Handbuch der österreichischen Wirtschaftspolitik*, ed. Abele et al., 265. See also his "Hartwährungspolitik und Sozialpartnerschaft," *Wirtschaftspolitische Blätter* 35 (1988): 63. According to Scharpf (*Crisis and Choice*, 63), the OeNB pulled off a strategic masterpiece because it practices monetarism yet is free from all political controversy.

[18] Josef Richter, "Exportquoten nach Unternehmens grössen, 1976–1982," *Wirtschaftpolitische Blätter* 33 (1986): 44–54.

sector.[19] Further regulations such as the *Gewerbeordnung* (trade and professional regulations) sheltered domestic goods, services, and the independent professions from cheaper competitors.[20] The only dissenting voice came from the association of Austrian industry (VÖI) because its members were usually price-takers and chiefly export-oriented.[21] While the export-dependent firms criticized the exchange rate policy, they were not directly hurt from the price distortions caused by an appreciating exchange rate.

As evidence for this last statement it suffices to point out that Austrian business did not undergo a lengthy phase of squeezed profit margins, lost market shares, increased import penetration, and job losses. This is all the more surprising because Austrian industry did not launch a structural transformation in order to overcome the handicap of creeping appreciation or prohibitive export prices. If anything, it appeared to lag behind in research and development spending, in high-technology–intensive production, and new specialization.[22] Yet unemployment and de-industrialization, which were symptomatic of the decline in export competitiveness in Belgium and the Netherlands, did not cause economic carnage in Austria.

Why did Austria escape the constraints of an appreciating currency and monetary restrictiveness when comparable monetary policy decisions brought economic disaster to other countries? One reason is that the most export-intensive companies were state-owned; the state absorbed the export losses. State-owned industries received 16.5 billion schillings in aid in 1983 on the condition that they would return to profitability by 1986. The target was not met and more aid was handed out.[23] Chapter 4 described the vast support system for the corporate sector and the multiple grants, subsidized interest rates, tax reliefs, and

[19] Fritz Breuss, *Österreichs Aussenwirtschaft, 1945–1982* (Vienna: Signum, 1983), 77.
[20] Peter Szopo, "Deregulierung in Österreich: Problematik und Ansätze," *Wirtschaft und Gesellschaft* 12 (1986): 43–61.
[21] Winckler, "Hartwährungspolitik und Sozialpartnerschaft," 63.
[22] An exception to this view is in Dalia Marin, "Assessing Structural Change: The Case of Austria," *International Review of Applied Economics* 3 (1989): 89–106, 465–81. Her series of indicators does not go beyond 1981/82 and does not take into account the developments after the second oil price rise in 1979. This might also account for the different perceptions of the positive effects of the hard currency option. Winckler, "Geld und Währung," in *Handbuch der österreichischen Wirtschaftspolitik*, ed. Abele et al., 266. Other authors disagree: Tichy, "Hartwährungspolitik—ein irreführendes Schlagwort zur Maskierung einer überholten Politik," 35–46; Alois Guger, "Coping with Crisis: Lessons from Corporatist Experiments," in *Social Corporatism—A Superior Economic System?* ed. Jukka Pekkarinen, Matti Pohkjokla, and Rob Rowthorn (New York: Oxford University Press, 1992).
[23] OECD, *Economic Surveys. Austria 1985/86*, 55.

direct transfers. When public spending was no longer popular in 1985, business could still count on financial transfers of 4.5 percent of the GDP, or 9 percent including off-budget financing. Supply-side generosity has lessened the inconvenience of a strong currency and relatively high unit labor cost.[24]

Government support for industrial firms has also been a windfall for the financial sector. A large majority of tax concessions, loans, grants, and preferential interest rates for the private and nationalized sectors are distributed through the commercial banks.[25] The financial sector, therefore, has a stake in the perpetuation of capital transfers because they earn steady commissions from the many government subsidy programs. Accordingly, their criticism of the inconsistency between the government's rhetoric and its actions is muted. Nor do banks object to the steady flow of unofficial subsidies that they dispense—banks are sheltered from bad loans to industry. Preferential credits to industry are guaranteed by the government and are essentially risk-free. In addition, loans to numerous small businesses help spread the risk of loan failures for the creditors.[26] This is why the OeNB, which consults with the commercial banks, has only mildly objected to a practice that so clearly conflicts with the original purpose of a hard currency.

The union leadership has also undermined the original purpose of a fixed exchange rate. Unions have accepted a continual loss of purchase power in order to conserve international competitiveness. Were it not for their conviction that centralized wage bargaining is more important than incomes compression or pay solidarity, labor demands would have put extra pressure on firms to compensate for relatively high export prices by excelling in packaging or presentation quality, high technology, or advanced marketing skills. The ÖGB has repeatedly and persistently moderated its pay claims because of its concern for the health of the state-owned industries, the absolute primacy accorded to full employment, and a deep-seated fear of internal conflicts.

There are natural limits to this mix of policies. The structural budget deficits and growing national debt after 1979 compelled government coalitions to rethink their customary subsidization efforts. Selective

[24] Ibid., 54. See also Kurt Bayer, "Evaluierung der Effizienz der staatlichen Instrumente zur Investitionsförderung," in *Stahl und Eisen bricht*, ed. Scherb and Morawetz, 34. According to an EFTA study, support to manufacturing as a percent of the GDP was 1.9 percent in Sweden and 3.6 percent in Austria. OECD, *Economic Surveys. Sweden 1990/91* (Paris: OECD, 1990), 91.

[25] OECD, *Economic Surveys. Austria 1985/86*, 56.

[26] Ibid., 48. In 1990, 40 percent of all bank credits to the private nonfinancial sector was still subsidized. OECD, *Economic Surveys. Austria 1990/91* (Paris: OECD, 1990), 92 n. 47.

protectionism has given way to privatization of the nationalized industries, which, though it is far from complete, will nonetheless interfere
with the ability of the governments to soften the impact of the hard
currency option for the most trade-sensitive sector. As soon as firms
must cope with the consequences of a strong schilling, opposition to
pegging it to the DM might finally be aroused.

The Austrian National Bank is obliged to support government policy
and cannot pursue a monetary regime inconsistent with the requests of
the social partners. However, the withdrawal of state intervention on
behalf of exporters and small business will endow the OeNB with a new
identity, one separate from the social partnership. Of course, the
OeNB actually has no room for a genuine independent monetary policy course since the link to the German mark dictates broad harmonization. But if the consensus on restrictive monetarism breaks down, the
bank can cast policy measures and outcomes on its own terms and
articulate a viewpoint against the social partners and government. It
might seek allies among those who continue to support a fixed and
appreciating exchange rate, even after the compensatory mechanisms
introduced by successive cabinets are withdrawn. This stage has not yet
been reached, but there is no reason to doubt that the hard currency
policy will eventually begin to undermine the international competitiveness of the Austrian political economy. Increased exposure to external pressures could produce economic and political rifts not seen
before and result in new alliances that could augment the decision-
making capacity of the central bank.

## SVERIGES RIKSBANK

Unlike other central banks, the Riksbank's role is described in the
Constitution of Sweden, and the Riksbank is directly responsible to
Parliament. The purpose of the banking legislation was to draw a clear
line between the legislative and executive branches of government and
to safeguard the independence of the bank from the Crown. Formally,
the Riksbank was supposed to be independent from government as the
bank's activities were controlled and supervised by the banking committee of Parliament. After World War II, the distinction between executive and legislative branches of the state blurred, and the Riksbank
functioned as an agency affiliated with the Ministry of Finance. It has
no special duties except to carry out monetary and financial policies
within the framework of the Riksdag's general economic management.

The National Debt Office occupies a similar position and is also accountable to Parliament.[27]

The central bank is governed by a board of seven directors. The party with a majority in parliament and in office is authorized to appoint the chairperson of the board of directors for a three-year term that can be ended at any time by the government. The chairperson may also be reelected. Parliament elects the other five or six directors. The governor of the bank is elected by the board of directors from among themselves. The chairperson of the board may not be the governor, and the board of directors may not accept instructions from anyone but the Riksdag or its special banking committee. Parliamentary deputies also appoint an auditing team to supervise the internal administration of the bank.[28]

Broad political coordination of monetary and budgetary policy is guaranteed because the composition of the board of directors mirrors the outcome of partisan parliamentary elections. Since for most of Sweden's modern history the Social Democrats have led the country, they have also run the central bank. Swedish Socialists, echoing the wisdom of Keynesian thinking, were deeply suspicious of financial agents and transactions.[29] Stabilization policy, according to the conventional leftist thinking after World War II, was only viable if financial speculation and capital flows were unequivocally restricted. Politicians endowed the central bank with a wide range of policy instruments and intervention mechanisms to deal with financial disturbances. Liquidity ratios, cash ratios, credit ceilings, investment ratios, bond issue control, and interest rate regulations were all actively administered by the bank until recently. Social Democratic politicians have also used their presence in the central bank to engage in selective credit allocation. The aim of the Swedish Social Democratic party (SAP) was twofold: to detach the domestic financial system from international entanglements while routing subsidized credit to those sectors favored by the government. The steering and manipulation of credit was facilitated by exten-

[27] Jukka Pekkarinen, "Keynesianism and the Scandinavian Models of Economic Policy," in *The Political Power of Economic Ideas: Keynesianism across Nations*, ed. Peter Hall (Princeton, N.J.: Princeton University Press, 1989), 311–46. For a historical account of the Swedish central bank, see C. A. E. Goodhart, *The Evolution of Central Banks* (Cambridge, Mass.: MIT Press, 1988), 122–28.

[28] Bank for International Settlements (BIS), *Eight European Central Banks* (London: Allen and Unwin, 1963), 308–13; P. Uusitalo, "Monetarism, Keynesianism, and the Institutional Status of Central Banks," *Acta Sociologica* 27 (1984): 31–50. See also John T. Woolley, "Monetary Policy Instrumentation and the Relationship of Central Bank and Government," *Annals of the Political and Social Sciences* 434 (1977): 151–73.

[29] James R. Crotty, "On Keynes and Capital Flight," *Journal of Economic Literature* 21 (1983): 59–65.

sive foreign exchange controls that divorced the domestic capital market from international trends.

For most of the period after 1945, the central bank had informal, voluntary agreements with the commercial banks, whereby the latter promised to adhere to the liquidity ratios and loan ceilings. In regular monthly meetings, the Riksbank elicited verbal agreements concerning the amount and allocation of credit extended by the commercial banks.[30] The Riksbank could punish offending banks by limiting their access to discount borrowing or by making their lives, in general, unpleasant.[31]

Commercial banks hold about 60 percent of total bank deposits. There are some fourteen commercial banks, but Skandinaviska Enskilda Banken, Svenska Handelsbanken, and PK-Banken clearly dominate. Cooperative banks are much smaller than commercial or savings banks, and about a hundred still exist. The largest commercial banks have progressively expanded their foreign business. In the mid-1980s approximately one-third of their total liabilities consisted of liabilities to nonresidents.[32]

National Pension Insurance Fund, several other institutional insurance companies, and capital market institutions (including the state-owned Swedish Investment Bank, mortgage institutions, export credit, and long-term credit institutions for manufacturers, farmers, and local authorities) procure capital by borrowing on the long-term capital market. They are important financial intermediaries.[33]

The National Pension Insurance Fund (AP fund) is especially noteworthy because of its huge assets totaling, in 1989, Skr 315 billion, of which 26 percent was in the form of government bonds, 53 percent in mortgages, 15 percent in industrial and business loans, and 3 percent in local government loans.[34] Established in 1960, the fund receives its

[30] Andrew Martin ("Economic Stagnation and Social Stalemate in Sweden," in *Monetary Policy, Selective Credit Policy, and Industrial Policy in France, Britain, West Germany, and Sweden*, ed. U.S. Congress Joint Economic Committee [Washington, D.C.: Government Printing Office, 1981]) discusses the monetary framework and credit allocation system in Sweden before the reforms were legislated. See also Lars Jonung, "Financial Deregulation in Sweden," *Skandinaviska Enskilda Banken (SEB) Quarterly Review*, no. 4 (1986): 110.

[31] Lars Hörngren, *On Monetary Policy and Interest Rate Determination in an Open Economy* (Stockholm: EFI, 1986), 7. See also Sid Mittra, *Central Bank versus Treasury: An International Study* (Washington, D.C.: University Press of America, 1978).

[32] Lars Hannson and Mats Josefsson, "Financial Innovation and Monetary Policy in Sweden," in *Financial Innovation and Monetary Policy*, ed. M. A. Akhtar (Basel: Bank for International Settlements, 1984), 195.

[33] *Growth Policies in Nordic Perspective* (Helsinki/Copenhagen/Stockholm/Bergen: ETLA/IFF/IUI/IOI, 1987), 263–64.

[34] The Economist Intelligence Unit, *Country Profile. Sweden 1990–91* (London: The Economist Intelligence Unit, 1990), 29.

capital through payroll taxes and invests in bonds. In 1974, a special fund (Fourth Fund) was begun to enable the pension fund to invest in shares as well. Had the SAP failed to establish a national pension system in the late 1950s, private institutions would have filled the need and would have thwarted the SAP's efforts to fix credit ceilings and allocations.

Starting in the mid-1970s, finance companies emerged that soaked up excess corporate savings and lent them at market rates to corporate customers. The growth of nontraditional financial intermediaries was rapid. For example, in 1975 seventy-nine finance companies released Skr 8 billion, the equivalent of 7 percent of all bank lending. Ten years later, no less than 208 firms advanced Skr 53 billion, a quarter of all nonpriority lending.[35] They engaged in activities other than normal banking and were therefore not subject to the banking restrictions of the Riksbank. They refinanced contracts and engaged in factoring and leasing, credit card issuance, and regular lending. Because of their rapid expansion, the finance companies were finally reclassified as banks and brought under the supervision of the Bank Inspection Board. However, many finance companies escaped regulation because they were wholly owned by large Swedish firms such as Volvo and Saab-Scania. Despite their size—Volvofinans matched the assets of Sweden's sixth largest bank in 1985—such finance companies belong to a manufacturing corporation and only finance sales of the parent company's products.[36] Finance companies have brought opportunities and strains to the financial system.

*Credit and Monetary Policy*

Social Democratic governments, through the Riksbank, have had an immoderate influence on the credit system and capitalized on monetary policy to achieve certain distributive goals.[37] Much has changed since the glory days of the Swedish model in the 1960s because of internal contradictions and international pressures. But before the major move toward financial liberalization and credit deregulation in the mid-1980s, though smaller steps had been taken already in 1978 with the abolition of interest rate setting on household deposits at commercial banks, savings and commercial banks struggled against formidable restrictions on their activities. Like the ruling party, the Riksbank did

[35] Sveriges Riksbank, *Riksbank Quarterly Review*, no. 1 (1985): 23.

[36] "Nordic Finance," *Euromoney*, September 1985, supplement, p. 72.

[37] Andrew Martin, "The Politics of Employment and Welfare: National Policy and International Independence," in *The State and Economic Interests*, ed. Keith Banting (Toronto: University of Toronto Press, 1986), 157–241.

not apply traditional measures to direct market outcomes but inter-fered in the market before market forces gave rise to unmanageable outcomes. Examples include interest rate policy, liquidity ratios, and capital movement controls.

From 1952 to 1983, the Riksbank set liquidity ratios to compel banks to hold a certain minimum proportion of their liabilities in "priority assets"—chiefly government securities, housing bonds with below mar-ket interest rates, and net claims on the central bank.[38] It also pursued a policy of low interest rates where banks' deposit rates were linked to the discount rate of the central bank. Insurance companies and pen-sion funds also operated under restrictions and had to invest a certain proportion of their funds in housing and government bonds.[39] In the long run, priority lending, that is, compelling institutional investors and commercial banks to lend at favorable rates to government and housing construction, was unsustainable since it tended to fuel demand for credit. By the 1960s, the monetary authorities were forced to intro-duce quantitative restrictions on credit to offset the availability of cheap capital and the favorable treatment of interest payments ac-corded by the tax system, which allowed interest rate payments to be fully deducted. Wealthy or profitable companies borrowed extensively simply to bring down their taxable incomes.[40] Thus, the Riksbank re-lied on quantitative controls on the volume of commercial bank lend-ing to the public.

In the 1950s and 1960s, the Riksbank depended on moral suasion to reach verbal agreement with the commercial banks concerning the amount and allocation of credit extended by the banks. The number of commercial banks was small (four, to be exact), and the Riksbank could easily intimidate offenders. In the mid-1970s, the monetary authorities widened the scope of their regulatory policy instruments to compen-sate for greater external volatility. In 1974, the Monetary Policy Mea-sures Act was passed to replace conventions and verbal understandings with formal rules and codes of conduct. The law enjoined the central bank to consult the government about proposed actions but did not compel it to reach similar agreements with the banking industry as a whole. (In contrast, other countries have explicitly written into their monetary legislation that the central bank must consult with the private

---

[38] Hannson and Josefsson, "Financial Innovation and Monetary Policy in Sweden," in *Financial Innovation and Monetary Policy*, ed. M. A. Akhtar, 200; Hörngren, *On Monetary Policy and Interest Rate Determination in an Open Economy*, 6.

[39] Jonung, "Financial Deregulation in Sweden," 111; Inge Vikbladh, "Monetary Policy in Sweden," in *Monetary Policy in Twelve Industrial Countries*, ed. Karel Holbik (Boston: Federal Reserve Bank of Boston, 1973), 414–18.

[40] Hörngren, *On Monetary Policy and Interest Rate Determination in an Open Economy*, 6.

sector.) Since the government and the central bank worked closely together, banks could not escape another round of regulations.[41]

The further tightening of regulations was, in retrospect, a futile attempt to cope with rising difficulties stemming from higher inflation, greater exchange rate fluctuations, and the uncontrolled expansion of new types of nonbank financial institutions. After the breakdown of Bretton Woods, the krona suffered greater fluctuations, and the sudden explosion in worldwide inflation rates also engendered greater price instability in Sweden. Increased prices and exchange rate instability prompted financial institutions and manufacturing businesses to design new financial instruments and to seek more sophisticated ways of managing their financial needs to neutralize the costs of monetary turmoil.

Much of the tightening of restrictions in the 1970s was meant to curb the money-creating impact of the budget deficit, not to deal with the unprecedented changes in financial management. The Riksbank compelled insurance funds and commercial banks to purchase more government securities, and in 1982 commercial banks' holdings of government and housing bonds equaled about 60 percent of their deposits and liabilities to the public.[42] Since the government did not want to squeeze the corporate sector totally and was still committed to a policy of low interest rates, it also imported capital to finance the budget deficits.[43]

Direct credit restrictions on banks left the growing demand for credit unmet. Finance companies moved into the profitable niches of interfirm trade lending and regular lending to close the gap between supply and demand for credit. As stated, after their early years of explosive growth, finance companies were redefined as banking institutions and fell under the 1980 Monetary Policy Act. The reaction of many corporations to the new classification was to create internal finance divisions and to seek markets for their own bonds. One result was that the traditional strong role of the "house bank" has been weakened as interfirm lending grew and finance companies began to trade funds.[44]

Greater external volatility coupled with the uncontrolled growth of nontraditional financial institutions convinced the authorities to relax their control over financial agents and markets. Financial deregulation

---

[41] Ibid., 9.

[42] Hannson and Josefsson, "Financial Innovation and Monetary Policy in Sweden," in *Financial Innovation and Monetary Policy*, ed. M. A. Akhtar, 203.

[43] Hörngren, *On Monetary Policy and Interest Rate Determination in an Open Economy*, 10.

[44] OECD, *Economic Surveys. Sweden 1986/87* (Paris: OECD, 1987), 38. *Growth Policies in Nordic Perspective*, 270.

and innovation, begun in the late 1970s, quickened in the 1980s. Deregulation had domestic and international origins. Regulation of credit created an unmet demand for credit that was filled by finance houses. The Swedish authorities were contemplating a further tightening of credit restrictions, but higher inflation and exchange rate volatility drove up the costs and complexity of re-regulation. For example, corporations flushed with profits after the steep devaluation of 1982 used their cash reserves to set up their own finance departments. How could current rules be extended to cover the activities of industrial firms engaged in intrafirm lending? One major result of the process of deregulation was that it stimulated the expansion of the financial sector because profit margins of financial activities improved.[45]

In 1983, the Riksbank abolished liquidity ratios. It was certainly not SAP's design to turn commercial banks and private insurance companies into parastatal institutions whose purpose was to store government bonds. The large proportion of low-yield housing and government bonds held by these institutions distorted the functioning of the financial system. The banking system was needlessly exposed to increased risks—its liabilities mainly consisted of short-term prime rate accounts and household savings deposits, while its assets were frozen in long-term low-interest–bearing securities.[46] The monetary authorities decided to remove some restrictions.

Deregulation has accelerated since 1985. With the first major reforms—the abolishment of liquidity quotas for banks and liberalization of bond issues whose timing, yield, and amount had been determined by the authorities—the principal tools for credit rationing and allocation were withdrawn. Once the government stopped setting interest rates and credit ceilings, banks and finance companies were suddenly able to set their own volume and interest rates. Since 1987, insurance institutions have no longer been obligated to meet quantitative limits for priority bonds. Along with deregulation have come financial innovations, of which the most important is the development of a money market in the early 1980s. The emergence of certificates of deposit and tradable treasury discount notes shifted the government's reliance from priority bonds to marketable debt instruments. It also led to the establishment of an interest rate auction for government discount bills and bonds. New financial instruments and greater room for market

[45] Jonung, "Financial Deregulation in Sweden," 118. Cf. Michael Loriaux, *France after Hegemony: International Change and Financial Reform* (Ithaca: Cornell University Press, 1991).

[46] OECD, *Economic Surveys. Sweden 1986/87*, 41. Jonung, "Financial Deregulation in Sweden," 115.

mechanisms brought about the liberalization of the gray market in 1985.[47] In brief, the financial system has undergone revolutionary changes, and neither the Riksbank nor the socialists can expect to control credit and monetary developments as tightly as before.

## Social Democracy and the Pension System

Swedish workers never wrested the allocation of profits from capital. But government—and essentially Sweden has had only one kind from the 1930s until 1991, with a short interruption between 1976 and 1982—established various schemes that allowed for some credit steering and control over investment allocation. Examples include the public pension system. The primary objective in pension reform was to eliminate inequalities in pension payment plans among wage earners. The result after many deliberations was the creation of three different funds, each of which collected savings from a different sector of the economy.[48] The first fund administered the fees collected from public employers, the second from private employers, and the third from the self-employed. The board of directors of each fund is composed of government, unions, and employers. The AP funds primarily lent to the public sector and could only issue bonds (promissory-note loans to intermediary credit institutions) and re-lend a portion of the fees to employers that deposited them.

Low credit costs stimulated housing construction and fulfilled the SAP's campaign promise to limit housing costs to about 20 percent of the average household's income in the 1960s. A market solution to the housing problem was firmly rejected. The Social Democrats organized building associations that had access to capital on more favorable terms than private companies enjoyed. In 1964, the SAP announced its most ambitious social program: to construct one million new dwellings in the next decade through the building associations. They met their target; Swedish housing is eminently affordable, with rent or mortgage payments at about 15 percent of income before taxes.[49] Through housing, the SAP has achieved its redistributive goals, and this has had long-term ramifications for cementing an alliance with middle-class voters. Housing legislation has created new constituencies, such as tenants'

[47] OECD, *Economic Surveys. Sweden 1986/87*, 44. L. E. Thunholm, "Sverige," in *Penningpolitik i Norden*, ed. Marianne Stenius (Lund, Sweden: Nordic Economic Research Council, 1987), 88–96.

[48] H. G. Jones, *Planning and Productivity in Sweden* (London: Croom Helm, 1976), 182–88.

[49] For a discussion of housing, see Hugh Heclo and Henrik Madsen, *Policy and Politics in Sweden: Principled Pragmatism* (Philadelphia: Temple University Press, 1987), 207–32.

movements and building cooperatives, with vested interests in the electoral survival of the SAP. Had it not been for the government's ability to
route subsidized credit to construction, it never could have formulated,
let alone realized, its ambitions for a de-commodified housing market.

The AP funds greatly helped consolidate the SAP's influence over
the financial system, and they furnished inexpensive public sector finances. They did not do much for business because most of their
capital was channeled back to central or local governments. Each year,
the public pension funds earmarked 60 to 67 percent of their capital
for public-sector priority bonds. In the 1970s, when budget deficits
rose, one-fourth of the assets of the AP funds were central government
bonds.[50]

The remainder of the capital assets of the AP funds went to agriculture and business. Pension fund managers, recruited from the two
labor market organizations, stressed industry financing because the
yields on corporate bonds and loans were higher than yields on government and housing securities, and also because subsidized lending to
industry would return a steady flow of pension fees from employers.
The 1960 law had made provisions for the pension funds to supply
long-term credit to business. Although not much capital was involved—
the total volume of business lending was about 7 percent of the combined assets of the AP funds—this supply of credit accounted for 20
percent of corporate lending in the early 1980s.[51]

Not surprisingly, business lending by the AP funds exhibited the
same biases as other corporate measures enacted by the Social Democrats. Firms can reborrow up to 50 percent of their pension fee contributions for up to ten years. A loan application is automatically granted
as long as a commercial bank covers the risk of the loan. It is the
commercial bank that submits the application, and neither the pension
fund nor the Riksbank exercises any control over the use of the money.
The law stipulates that the AP funds must charge an interest rate half a
point higher than the rate on deposit accounts. Since reborrowing is
arranged through regular financial intermediaries, the two largest
commercial banks—Skandinaviska Enskilda Banken and Svenska
Handelsbanken—processed nearly 90 percent of the refinancing options for their largest customers, the international corporations. One
percent of small firms and 5 percent of medium-sized firms (those with
up to two hundred employees) took advantage of the pension credit,

[50] Jonas Pontusson, *Public Pension Funds and the Politics of Capital Formation in Sweden* (Stockholm: Arbetslivscentrum, 1984), 51–53.
[51] Ibid., 66. For an earlier period, see Vikbladh, "Monetary Policy in Sweden," in *Monetary Policy in Twelve Industrial Countries*, ed. Holbik, 381–82.

while savings and cooperative banks accounted for 2 percent of the retroverse loans.[52] In other words, a commonality of interests between big business and big labor was forged by piping back pension-fund capital to private capital. This phenomenon highlights the fact that the Social Democrats and their union partners had not tried to disrupt the process of private capital accumulation and had no intention of abusing their influence over credit policy for the sake of some quixotic socialist principle.

The Fourth Fund was established in 1974 in reaction to the scarcity of equity capital and the growing sense among the trade union confederation (LO) that it needed more power over the destination of collective savings. The Fourth Fund was authorized to purchase industrial shares. The legislation that established the Fourth Fund followed a well-worn path of providing business with some interesting fiscal incentives but refrained from interfering in managerial prerogatives. Although limited to about 5 percent of the pension fees collected, during the year, this amount was almost as large as the average annual equity capital raised in Stockholm's small stock market during the 1960s. The limit was doubled in 1976, by which time the Fourth Fund held shares in twenty-six firms, including Volvo. In 1979, the fund's limit was raised again, although its holdings in any one company were restricted to 10 percent.[53] In the 1980s, the Fourth AP Fund was the third or fourth largest owner of corporate shares, although its total assets are about 1 percent of the combined assets of the three older pension funds.

Despite the advantages for commercial banks that were built into the pension fund system, this restrictive credit allocation undermined the partnership between finance and industry. In the 1970s, the rate of return on investments exceeded the real interest rate on loans by a considerable margin. Borrowing from banks was highly profitable because the artificially low interest rates made capital cheap. Hence, businesses borrowed funds for investments as a norm until the early 1980s, when the differential between their rate of return on physical capital and the real interest rate narrowed. Since then, corporate ties between banks and manufacturers have been noticeably weakened.[54]

[52] Pontusson, *Public Pension Funds*, 70.

[53] Andrew Martin, "Wages, Profits, and Investment in Sweden," in *Politics of Inflation and Economic Stagnation*, ed. Leon Lindberg and Charles S. Maier (Washington, D.C.: Brookings Institution, 1985), 448.

[54] OECD, *Economic Surveys. Sweden 1986/87*, 50. Jonung, "Financial Deregulation in Sweden," 112. Jan Södersten, "Profitability of Swedish Industry," *SEB Quarterly Review*, no. 2 (1986): 40–44. Between 1980 and 1983, the real return on physical capital decreased in relation to real interest.

*Devaluations and Financial Openness*

The principal objective of exchange restrictions on capital transactions, which were in force from 1939 until the late 1980s, was to facilitate the implementation of domestic monetary policy. Foreign exchange transactions were formally prohibited, with the large exception of payments or credits related to trade in goods and services. The idea was to shield the domestic financial system from international developments as much as possible. Exchange controls also made it possible to keep interest rates low in order to secure adequate financing for the priority sectors (housing and government).[55] Repeated devaluations after the first oil price rise were part of the package of monetary policy instruments to improve the export competitiveness and profit margins of business and to secure reinvestments and jobs. It was only because the domestic financial market was uncoupled from international markets that devaluation strategies could work.

The bourgeois coalition, governing from 1976 to 1982, began its rule by declaring a small devaluation of the krona in October 1976, followed by two larger ones in April and August 1977. It also unpegged the krona from the German mark and firmed the currency against the basket of fifteen currencies of Sweden's most important trading partners. One little trick was to increase the weight of the dollar to 22 percent, though the U.S. share in Swedish foreign trade was half that. The effective exchange rate of the krona moved up or down with the dollar and counter to the German mark.[56]

In 1982, when the SAP returned to office, the currency was devalued by another 16 percent to arrest the deterioration of the current account quickly. The devaluation was accompanied by a variety of economic programs to address the wide cost discrepancies between Sweden and its trading partners.[57] The government also tried to preserve the effect of the devaluation long enough to provide business with a true boost. These efforts focused on wage concessions from unions. For labor, wage restraints underline the hazards and uncertainties of not knowing whether its current sacrifices go to investments and an improved future standard of living. Past experience made the top LO leadership acutely

[55] L. E. Thunholm, "Sverige," in *Penningpolitik i Norden*, ed. Stenius, 99–103; OECD, *Economic Surveys. Sweden 1986/87*, 57.

[56] OECD, *Economic Surveys. Sweden 1986/87*, 61 n. 7.

[57] By the end of 1982, the series of devaluations improved Sweden's export price by about 25 percent in local currency from the 1973 level. In common currency, Sweden's export prices were between 85 to 90 percent of the 1973 level. Johan A. Lybeck, *Devalveringar: ett inslag i de nordiska ländernas stabiliseringspolitik* (Malmö: Liber, 1985), 148, 157.

aware that promoting wage restraint endangered organizational unity. Defection by workers in highly profitable industries was likely, and a corresponding breakdown in centralized wage bargaining stimulated further interunion rivalry and undermined wage solidarity. In the end, unions bargained for less, but the wage negotiation system was under considerable stress, and the government intervened several times in the 1980s on behalf of central accords. Profits, however, rose to unparalleled heights in fiscal year 1983–84 but were not redistributed to workers or consumers. In 1986, though the benefits of the 1982 devaluation had been exhausted and wage settlements were generous, Sweden recorded nonetheless a slight improvement in competitiveness thanks to the pegging of the exchange rate to a basket of currencies in which the dollar was assigned disproportionate weight.[58]

To conclude, the combination of a flexible approach to exchange rate decisions and the rationing of credit gave the Swedish political establishment extra room to achieve certain programmatic goals. It underpinned the electoral endurance of the SAP and provided firms, labor, and the economy with additional stimulus at critical moments. In addition, the politicization of the Riksbank and the subordination of banks and other financial institutions created a protective barrier against speculative capital movements.

Even after the 1983 wave of domestic banking deregulation, significant controls on international capital movements had been retained.[59] For example, firms could not issue domestic securities that matured in less than a year and were denominated in Swedish currency in foreign capital markets. Nonresidents could not purchase bonds on the Swedish market, and borrowing by foreigners in the Swedish krona was restricted. Foreign securities could not be issued or sold on the Swedish market, and the purchase by residents of foreign securities was restricted. Residents were not permitted to grant credits to nonresidents, except for credits related to trade.

But higher inflation, greater exchange rate volatility, and larger capital imports to finance government deficits resulted in the incremental liberalization of capital and financial flows. Among the new measures was the 1986 law allowing foreign banks to open branches in Sweden.[60] Further lifting of restrictions took place in 1989. The Riksbank re-

[58] OECD, *Economic Surveys. Sweden 1986/87*, 15.

[59] Professional economists and the economic research divisions of the commercial banks lobbied strongly against the existence of exchange controls. See Lars Calmfors, "Exchange Controls can be Abolished," *SEB Quarterly Review*, no. 4 (1985): 90–95; Magnus Henrekson, "Exchange Controls and Liberalized Forward Trading," *SEB Quarterly Review*, No. 4 (1987): 100–105.

[60] "Foreign Banks in Sweden," *SEB Quarterly Review*, no. 1 (1986): 4–20.

moved all restrictions on selling Swedish shares abroad, on the purchase of real estate abroad, on direct purchase of foreign shares from nonresidents, and on investments in foreign bonds. Moreover, Swedish residents are permitted to buy foreign currencies and take all means of payments and security in and out of the country.[61]

By 1990, the closer ties between domestic and international financial markets have irrevocably diminished the ability of Swedish authorities to pursue monetary policies contrary to the framework of its most important trading partners. Deeper penetration by international financial institutions also contradicts Sweden's reliance on exchange rate adjustments to correct domestic imbalances and improve international competitiveness. Unless the domestic capital market is shielded from external exposure, governments cannot use exchange rate adjustments to bring relief to the export sector and bridge labor cost gaps. Once the economy is drawn into international financial markets, it becomes imperative to maintain confidence in the currency and forswear devaluations.

*The End of an Era*

Administrative credit allocation in Sweden served two goals. The first was to cement an electoral alliance with the middle class by singling out housing as a critical target for reform. The second objective was to guarantee the adequate supply of long-term investment funds for productive economic agents. This second goal was only halfheartedly pursued; the temptation to use pension reserves for budget financing and social programs was too powerful. Once the public sector had claimed its share, not much was left for corporations. Swedish firms, however, did benefit from government intervention in the monetary arena in another fashion. Competitive devaluations boosted the profits of export firms by closing emerging labor cost discrepancies. Taxation was also tailored to reward reinvestment and profitability.

This comfortable situation came to an abrupt end in the late 1980s. The system of credit control became so unwieldy that deregulation and liberalization were the only solution. From the beginning there was an inherent contradiction between credit flow regulation and low interest rates—the growing demand for affordable capital was unmet. This demand created a market, outside the jurisdiction of the central bank, and new financial instruments emerged to circumvent government regulations. They defeated the entire purpose of the credit regime and decreased the regulatory power of the central bank over the banking

---

[61] OECD, *Economic Surveys. Sweden 1990/91* (OECD: Paris, 1990), 25.

industry as the volume of credit was increasingly determined by unregulated actions and actors. Other changes in international securities markets forced adaptations; currency regulations and low interest rates were finally discarded. Liberalization and deregulation moved the financial system beyond administrative manipulation.[62]

Similarly, repeated devaluations, which lowered the effective exchange rate by 26 percent after 1970,[63] have not constituted a long-term cure for industrial adjustment. Real resources were not permanently transferred from the sheltered sectors of the economy to those in international competition. From 1986 to 1988, the consequences of the lack of a permanent shift in resources were hidden by a combination of circumstances. In this period, Sweden's terms of trade improved because oil prices fell by half and wood pulp prices doubled. At the same time, competitive strength was preserved; the krona accompanied the dollar on its downward course in relation to the German mark. But in early 1989, inflation surged after public-sector employees received substantial pay raises and after financial deregulation increased profits on short-term financial investments. The competitive strength of Swedish industry declined steadily; the balance on the current account moved back toward deficits as large as those recorded in 1982. Inflation had obliterated the competitive advantage conferred by devaluation. And the central bank had to raise interest rates to defend the krona.[64] The economy was in deep trouble.

Lack of confidence in the currency, indicating a lack of confidence in the government, was fed by an inflation rate in Sweden higher than that of its trading partners. Inflation averaged 7.5 percent between 1988 and 1990. Financial asset holders predicted a further rise in inflation with the breakdown in central bargaining. In 1990, the financial community made a run on the krona and caused panic on the foreign exchange market. The Riksbank raised the interest rates to 17 percent to quell the apprehensions of international finance. But the international community and domestic investors were not convinced that Sweden's financial and monetary equilibrium would be restored, and so they continued to avoid the krona.

[62] A telling development is the creation of larger Nordic banking and financial service groups to prepare for internationalization and entry into the EC. Thus, Sweden's fourth largest banking group, Gota Group, and the leading bank of Finland created a new holding company in 1990 to establish a further presence in international financial markets. See Sara Webb and Olli Virtanen, "Scandinavian Banks Plan to Form New Finance Group," *Financial Times*, 1 June 1990, p. 1.

[63] Barry P. Bosworth and Alice M. Rivlin, *The Swedish Economy* (Washington, D.C.: Brookings Institution, 1987), 57. Depending on which years are used, the actual gains in cost price competitiveness vary. There is no doubt that the devaluations were effective until around 1985.

[64] Hans Bergström, "Sweden's Politics and Party System at the Crossroads," *West European Politics* 14 (1991): 15–17.

Out of despair, former Prime Minister Ingvar Carlsson announced in spring of 1991 that the Swedish krona would be pegged to the ECU (and the German mark) to enhance policy credibility and to counter currency speculation. A neoliberal austerity package, passed in 1990, would also send a positive signal to the international financial community. While fighting off repeated attacks on the krona, the Riksbank has become a more important player in Sweden's domestic policy debates. It needs to be a stronger player in order to signal to jittery foreign and national financial agents that Sweden's budget deficits and inflation rates will converge toward the EC average. If the central bank fails to convey this message, Swedish politicians will be hostage to the anonymous actions of countless speculators and currency traders and will have to set interest rates at excessively high levels. High real interest rates are damaging to productive investment and labor market developments and it makes more sense in the long run to bring down inflation at all cost, even at the expense of full employment.

The two chapters on central bank behavior provide the most arresting example of how politicians and technocrats from different small open economies place different values on maintaining confidence in the currency. Dutch elected officials and administrators aimed for a durable exchange rate to advertise the reliability of the guilder as an extremely secure investment. Belgian authorities purposefully sought international financiers and investors because they complemented the normal specialization of financial groups and brought transnational corporations to Belgium.

Values and policy strategies of Swedish officials differ from those in either Belgium or the Netherlands. In Sweden, the government opted for improved use of production and job growth, at the expense of a relatively high inflation rate (about 9.7 and 6.9 percent in 1983 and 1985). Unions supported this choice; they moderated their wage demands and did not fully exploit their bargaining leverage. Such voluntary wage restraints, as well as the distributive burden of the devaluations, were blunted by public funding for social programs for vulnerable groups.

In the Netherlands and Belgium, the concerns of financial agents (and their fear of inflation) induced, despite high unemployment and foreign trade dependence, monetary restrictiveness and an appreciated exchange rate. In Belgium, the central bank made frantic efforts to maintain the franc's value in foreign exchange markets, despite current account deficits, large public sector debt, and export decline. To achieve this goal, interest rates rose to unprecedented levels with the concomitant burden on the public-sector deficit and investments. In the Netherlands, the combination of natural gas exports and restrictive monetary policies drove up the guilder, hurting nonenergy-related trade sectors and contributing to de-industrialization with the result of high unemployment.

Compared with those in Sweden, banks in the Netherlands are not only significant but also internationally oriented and at the forefront of financial innovations. Belgian banks are deeply involved in international capital market mediation. But commercial banks in Sweden never crafted an independent identity, and their natural growth was also strangled by Social Democratic administrative rulings. Nonpriority lending is the bread and butter of commercial banks because this lending earns commissions. Yet for years Swedish banks were forced to cut down on their normal activities in order to meet government quotas. In the meantime, the bank's more profitable customers, such as industrial corporations, tapped new funding sources. Bank credits to business perceptibly declined after governments set up subsidized credit facilities and the demand for credit was low. Recovery during the early 1980s coincided with the growth of unregulated finance companies; the banks did not bounce back but instead lost more customers.[65]

The Austrian central bank, like its Swedish counterpart, was politically subservient and executed monetary policies consistent with the objectives of government. As in Sweden, interest rate policies complemented the economic recovery strategies or compensation programs of governments. Generally, in contrast to Belgium and the Netherlands, all facets of central banking in Austria and Sweden fed into the incentive system built for business and for conserving tripartite exchanges.[66]

Pegging the schilling to the German mark, I argue, is not comparable to the anti-inflationary and restrictive monetary policies of the Netherlands or Belgium. The constraints arising from the hard currency policy did not generate serious trade-offs between economic welfare and price stability, thanks to the availability of numerous direct forms of compensation and subsidized interest rates. The Austrian establishment could get away with this contradictory arrangement because the financial integration of the Austrian economy into the world economy was moderate. Cabinets and unions could ignore how international markets, the banking industry, and manufacturing would perceive

[65] Private banks in the 1970s were annoyed that they could not lend money to Latin America! Interview with the author. See also Curt G. Olsson, "Banks as Suppliers of Credit," *SEB Quarterly Review*, No. 4 (1984): 112–18; Peter Wallenberg, "Abolish Exchange Control!" *SEB Quarterly Review*, No. 2 (1988): 27–29. Peter Wallenberg, "Effects of Exchange Control on Trade and Industry in Sweden," *SEB Quarterly Review*, No. 3 (1985): 72–75.
[66] For a similar conclusion, see Scharpf, *Crisis and Choice in European Social Democracy*, 202–9.

measures that challenged the essential objectives of a hard currency policy. Furthermore, the fixed exchange rate, although it eliminated an independent interest rate setting, did not enlarge the bureaucratic visibility and influence of the central bank. Rather, the exchange rate regime drew the bank into the bargaining games of the social partnership.

Change is under way, as this chapter suggests. The central banks of both Austria and Sweden began the 1990s with more influence on economic decisions just as the world economy started to intrude on the policy-making sphere. In Sweden, gradual financial liberalization—in particular the removal of capital flow restrictions—caused government programs or budget plans to be vulnerable to waves of speculative capital outflows.

In Austria, more subtle changes will, in all likelihood, widen the central bank's influence in the 1990s. Deregulation of financial services and privatization of manufacturing go hand in hand with the idea of strengthening the connections of national companies with the international economy. The central bank's original plan to spur greater efficiency in Austria's pampered manufacturing companies is now viable and likely to be achieved. With the opening of the domestic market to more foreign competition, private and public capital must become more self-sufficient. Once this plan is in place, an exchange rate pegged to the German mark can achieve its goals; the federal budget will not cover strategic mistakes and corporate lethargy. A strong schilling and the reduction of state aid will force private and public companies to be more sophisticated international actors. The central bank will then emphasize the need to control inflation, budget expenditures, and current account deficits. Social accords will be endangered— neither government nor organized labor will have anything special to offer to business, and neither can be sure how business would use their proffered assistance.

PART III

# THE INTERNATIONAL DIMENSION

CHAPTER EIGHT

# The Question of
# Community Membership

Deepening financial integration and business multinationalization, two trends that changed the environment for social democratic electoral victories and for durable class compromises, would not have gotten far had it not been for European integration. Even before the launching of the Internal Market (1992) project and the reforms of voting procedures in the European Council (Single European Act), membership in the European Community hindered the survival or the resumption of old-style Keynesian intervention and income redistribution. Analogously, nonmembership gave countries breathing space before the impact of financial innovations and volatile capital movements undermined independent policy action and tripartite exchanges. Of our four countries, Belgium and the Netherlands were founding members of the European Community. Austria and Sweden, after three decades of questions and doubts, rushed to submit applications for membership in 1989 and 1991, respectively.

In this chapter I explore the reasons why in 1957 Austria and Sweden declined EC membership and Belgium and the Netherlands joined. In most of this chapter I examine the political gyrations and debates in Austria and Sweden in the 1960s and comment only briefly on the foreign economic policy of Belgium and the Netherlands. For Austria and Sweden, genuine apprehensions about how to reconcile nonalignment with the objectives and obligations contained in the Treaty of Rome colored the decision not to join the European Community. Yet Swedish and Austrian cabinets debated repeatedly how or when to enter the EC in the 1960s because they were reluctant to reject institutional linkage outright. In the 1970s, EC membership was no longer of great concern, because the 1972 free trade treaty allayed the deepest worries about economic discrimination and because national economies inside the Community stagnated. Thus, it was not until Gorbachev's rise to power and strains in the Swedish model and Austrian partnership sharpened that the political establishment in each country reviewed its relationship with the reinvigorated Community.

I attribute the final decision of Austria and Sweden not to seek associate membership to a combination of factors that reflected their concerns about maintaining a policy of neutrality or nonalignment and that mirrored the lukewarm support of business and finance for membership. Notwithstanding the potential rewards of EC membership, business and finance in the two countries did not fight very hard for accession. They viewed the range of free trade treaties that were signed in the early 1970s as a sufficiently attractive substitute to Community membership. Surely, leaders and spokespersons for the economic establishment complained quietly about discrimination and trade barriers, but in fact, nonmembership meshed well with their belief in neutrality and with their economic orientation.

Business and financial agents set the general tone for foreign economic strategies because the stakes are greatest for them. They function as the transmission belt between the domestic market and the international system; they are the first to define the meaning of foreign competition in international markets. Since their first experiences in international competition took place decades ago, business and finance have molded the more general vision through which the external world is perceived. Why else would every single political party in Belgium and the Netherlands be for free trade, customs unions, and economic integration while very few politicians in Sweden and Austria were unequivocally fond of institutionalized international cooperation, economic harmonization, the removal of capital and exchange controls, and the disappearance of economic frontiers? This question cannot be reduced to concerns about maintaining confidence in neutrality. In preceding chapters I highlighted the distinctive nature of business and finance in the two pairs of countries—Austria and Sweden, and Belgium and the Netherlands. In this chapter I build on that evidence to examine how the variations in financial and business interests help explain how each of the four countries made its most important foreign economic policy decision of the late 1950s and 1960s.

*The Low Countries*

The business groups that are most internationally oriented and committed to free trade are found in the Netherlands, where commercial capitalism gave way to manufacturing only in the second half of the twentieth century.

*196*

Since the seventeenth century the Dutch bourgeoisie has preached a moralistic worldview in which peace and the promotion of trade are mutually beneficial: trade would increase wealth, and increased wealth would create a community of interests among peoples of different nations. Putting this belief into action, Dutch universities trained an impressive number of international law experts, and Dutch governments abolished preferential trade treaties during the 1840s. Once the Dutch monarchy abstained from great power competitions and quietly accepted its diminished territory after the secession of Belgium in 1830–31, free trade became sacred. Foreign policy was a tool for strengthening Dutch commerce and opening markets—not markets for manufactured goods, but markets for shipping, colonial trade, or business services. The new Dutch neutralism and pacifism were wedded to internationalism. Dutch political leaders in the nineteenth century, with their mercantile interests in international peace, deplored the despicable behavior of great powers and attempted to instruct them in the finer points of humanitarian universalism and supranationalism.[1] After 1945, for example, the Dutch felt that commercial liberalization ought to extend beyond the Europe of the Six.[2] The Dutch insisted on the inclusion of Britain in the Community, when Britain itself was ambivalent about EC membership.

In 1955–56, during the preliminary rounds of discussion on the European Economic Community, the Netherlands had one objective: to extend free trade to include agriculture. Agriculture was excluded in the first version of the draft treaty, and farmers' associations and cooperatives persuaded the Dutch ministry of agriculture and the cabinet to fight for the inclusion of free agricultural trade. Dutch farmers were highly competitive because they imported fodder and cheap grain but exported value-added dairy and meat products. In 1957, agriculture accounted for one-third of Dutch merchandise exports and one-quarter of imports.[3]

[1] On the historical foundations of Dutch foreign policy, see, for example, J. H. van Stuivenberg, ed., *De economische geschiedenis van Nederland* (Groningen, Netherlands: Wolters-Noordhoff, 1977). For works in English, see J. C. Boogman, "The Netherlands in the European Scene 1813–1914," in J. S. Bromley and E. H. Kossmann, eds., *Britain and the Netherlands in Europe and Asia* (New York: Macmillan, 1968); C. B. Wels, *Aloofness and Neutrality: Studies on Dutch Foreign Relations and Policy-Making Institutions* (Utrecht: H&S, 1982); Joris J. C. Voorhoeve, *Peace, Profits, and Principles: A Study of Dutch Foreign Policy* (The Hague: Nijhoff, 1979), 42–54.

[2] Alessandro Silj, *European Political Puzzle: A Study of the Fouchet Negotiations and the 1963 Veto* (Cambridge, Mass.: Harvard University Press, 1967), 41–64; J. L. Heldring, "De Nederlandse buitenlandse politiek na 1945," *Nederlands buitenlandse politiek: Heden en verleden* (Baarn, Netherlands: Uitgeverij in den Toren, 1978), 29–37.

[3] Alan D. Robinson, *Dutch Organized Agriculture in International Politics, 1945–1960* (The Hague: Nijhoff, 1961), 53–69.

Since the Dutch had a great interest in this area, they mounted an energetic campaign for a common Community external tariff, a common agricultural policy, and the supersession of bilateral agreements. Moreover, despite their disagreements with the French on a host of issues related to the institutional development of the Community and tariff policy toward third countries, a powerful Franco-Dutch coalition arose to administer and guide future thinking on agricultural issues.[4] Because of the pressures applied by the Dutch as well as the preparation they had done in laying down the technical details of a uniform agricultural policy for the Common Market, a Netherlander, Sicco Mansholt, the former Socialist minister of agriculture, was appointed the European Community's first commissioner of agriculture.

Central to the continued success of Dutch farming was the formulation of a liberal trade policy with a moderate degree of protection. The state had not sheltered its farmers from world price competition, and the specialization and technical efficiency of Dutch agriculture was comparatively advanced. There was no reason to doubt that Dutch agriculture would benefit from the liberalization of agricultural trade.

Aside from agriculture, Dutch business had never leaned on state officials for micro-intervention or tariff protection, and spokespersons for business claimed to be ready to compete freely in an enlarged market. Industry channels endorsed a wider multilateral association as a remedy against a "protectionist" Community. A business delegation requested that European foreign affairs remained under the aegis of the Ministry of Economic Affairs where the degree of politicization was substantially less than in the Ministry of Foreign Affairs. Employer associations declared that the signing of the Treaty of Rome was not a goal in itself but only a landmark on the road to total liberalization in the entire OEEC area. They urged the government to take a broad-minded view of all requests for associations and wider EEC treaties.[5]

In Belgium, the Treaty of Rome was also warmly received, and only its predecessor, the European Coal and Steel Community raised questions. In the late nineteenth century, Belgian financial groups were engaged in heavy manufacturing. The domestic market remained open, and the firms asked for low tariffs while joining international zinc, coke, and glass cartels for protection. They also created large

---

[4] P. H. Hommes, "The Agricultural Policy of the Common Market," in *The Politics of Persuasion: The Implementation of Foreign Policy in the Netherlands*, ed. Philip Everts and Guido Walraven (Brookfield, Vt: Gower, 1989), 161–74; Robinson, *Dutch Organized Agriculture*, 109–19.

[5] Voorhoeve, *Peace, Profits, and Principles*, 163; and Wichard Woyke, *Erfold durch integration: Die Europapolitik der Benelux-Staaten von 1947 bis 1969* (Bochum, Germany: Brockmeyer, 1985), 205–12.

international consortiums to take part in the construction of railways in southeastern Europe, Turkey, China, Egypt, and Mexico. After 1870, overseas investments financed tramways, and Belgian firms built the Paris metro system as well as systems in dozens of other European cities. International investment banking had generated rationalization and export growth in Belgium, and financial groups intended to replicate the domestic success story abroad. While the banking branch of the financial group provided foreigners with funding, the industrial divisions of the mixed banks won the contracts to build the projects.[6] After World War II, Belgian holding companies lost their networks in the non-Western world, but they concentrated on developing Brussels as a financial center to serve transnational corporations that desired to set up affiliates in the Community or Belgium. Financial liberalization and economic integration were therefore cherished goals after 1945.

In 1944, when the defeat of the Third Reich was imminent, the Belgian government-in-exile approached the Dutch government with a proposal to create a customs union, starting with an agreement for bilateral payments and an official rate of exchange for Belgian francs and guilders.[7] Progress toward an economic union stalled, but the Low Countries agreed on a common Benelux tariff, and regular duties on intra-Benelux trade were removed by 1948.[8]

While the Netherlands viewed the European Economic Community as a way to liberalize agricultural trade, Belgium, with its more industrial economy, was particularly interested in the establishment of the European Coal and Steel Community (ECSC). A significant part of Belgium's industrial production desperately needed more investment capital. The situation was especially acute in the Borinage coal mines, where the supply of accessible coal was practically exhausted and labor costs were extraordinarily high. The question of what to do with the exhausted mines was an extremely sensitive and potentially divisive issue for elected officials. Eventually, the political elite agreed, unless the coal mines were to receive continuous tax subsidies, they would have to be closed and regional unemployment would surge. Such an action would have strong political repercussions because most of the inefficient and outdated mines were located in Wallonia. Therefore,

---

[6] Belgian investments overseas were about BF 7 billion in 1913; see Allan Milward and S. B. Saul, *Development of the Economies of Continental Europe, 1850–1914* (Cambridge, Mass.: Harvard University Press, 1977), 173–80.

[7] Belgium and Luxembourg had already formed an economic union in 1921 under the name of BLEU. Benelux includes Luxembourg, which is not discussed in this book.

[8] James E. Meade, *Negotiations for Benelux: An Annotated Chronicle, 1943–56*, Princeton Studies in International Finance, vol. 6 (Princeton, N.J.: Princeton University Press, 1957).

politicians saw the creation of the Steel and Coal Community as a wonderful solution to a painful domestic predicament. The ECSC would be responsible for either subsidizing or closing the mines, thereby exonerating the national leadership. Fifteen years later, the former minister of economics Albert Coppé explained in a public speech that the cabinet had endorsed the ratification of the ECSC because it would solve one of Belgium's intractable problems with little risk to the incumbent coalition government.[9]

The Schumann Plan for the establishment of a Coal and Steel Community was the only proposal in the early 1950s that spurred a real debate. The proposal was controversial because it affected an industry that stood on fragile economic ground but was managed by powerful players. Coal mine owners loudly opposed the ECSC during the first parliamentary debates in 1951.[10] Accustomed to government aid and protection, mine owners feared international competition and the greater difficulties in influencing a supranational authority. Steel and coal were both central to the Belgian export economy, and the first formulation of the ECSC envisaged extensive interventionist capabilities for the High Authority, its executive council, which sparked the attention of the holding corporations that owned virtually the entire coal industry. In a similar vein, the Socialist party, while not against political federalism, worried about the cost of modernization and the erosion of the high standard of living enjoyed by the miners and steelworkers in the Socialist-affiliated confederation of trade unions. The question was how far the new ECSC would be prepared to go to fix common standards, set joint price and pay policies, and legislate Europe-wide health and safety rules. Promising to enact tax deductions and subsidies to soften the shock of open competition and modernization, the government succeeded in assuaging both financial groups and trade union cnfederations.[11] The Chamber of Deputies, Belgium's parliament, approved entry into the Coal and Steel Community by a vote of 165 to 13. Aside from the ECSC, social groups and political blocs found no further reasons to object to the multilateral clearing of intra-European trade.[12]

[9] Albert Coppé, "Herinneringen 1948–68: Van economische unie naar politieke unie?" in *Veertig Jaar Belgische Politiek* (Antwerp: Standaard Wetenschappelijke Uitgeverij, 1968), 291.

[10] Haas, *Uniting of Europe*, 199.

[11] Ibid., 147–48; R. van Eenoo, "De internationale politiek van België," *Algemene Geschiedenis der Nederlanden* 15 (Haarlem: Fibula-Van Driehoek, 1982), 374; Woyke, *Erfolg durch Integration*, 80–84.

[12] Pierre-Henri Laurent, "Beneluxer Economic Diplomacy and the Creation of Little Europe, 1945–50," *Journal of European Integration* 10 (1986): 23–37; Woyke, *Erfolg durch Integration*, 76–77.

As the Community became a fact of life after 1957, many distinguished Belgian public officials and private industrialists and financiers volunteered for official EC positions. In all likelihood, no employer federation was so deeply enmeshed in Community affairs as the Belgian Federation of Industry. A long line of Flemish and French-speaking business leaders were recruited officially or volunteered to set up Community-wide professional organizations. For example, Max Nokin, the director of the Société Générale de Belgique, organized an unofficial study group for national trade organizations of coal producers from Germany, Belgium, France, and Holland and then founded the EC Association of Coal Producers. Another Belgian, Pierre van den Rest, led the Club Siderugists in the 1950s. The former chair of the Flemish Economic Association, Leon Bekaert, founded the Association of European Industry (UNICE), which represented the largest industrial companies of the EC member states. Pol Provost, the long-term chairman of UNICE, was also from the Flemish Economic Association.[13]

## Neutrality and EC Membership

Austria and Sweden voted against joining the European Community in the 1960s. This decision is routinely interpreted as a by-product of their commitment to neutrality. For Austria, in the Moscow Memorandum of April 1955, the Republic committed itself to a policy of perpetual neutrality of the type maintained by Switzerland. The Neutrality Act, adopted by Parliament in October 1955, pledged that Austria would never enter into military alliances or permit military bases on its territory.[14] Membership in the EC was considered incompatible with neutrality.

Swedish neutrality was the product of an internal legacy and was never codified in law. Since it is self-declared, to overturn it does not depend on the formal approval of other powers. Publicly, EC membership was ruled out because the original six members were NATO allies and thus belonged unconditionally to the Western bloc. The ultimate goal of the Community's founders was to move toward a federated Europe, and this would destroy the military independence of Sweden.

[13] Baron Van Der Rest and André Sauwens, "Les milieux patronaux dans la construction européene," *Studia Diplomatica* 34 (1981): 441–56; Marcel Frerotte and Marcel Peeters, "La CECA," *Studia Diplomatica* 34 (1981): 261–91.

[14] The State Treaty signed by the Allies and Austria forbids any union with Germany. Because of West Germany's overwhelming influence in the economic structure of the EEC, membership could have been interpreted as an "Anschluss." In a separate letter, the Soviet Memorandum, Austria explicated that it would adhere to a neutrality "of a type maintained by Switzerland."

Nevertheless, when the Treaty of Rome was signed, Sweden and Austria equivocated about how to react to it. The formation of a free trade area in goods and services was irresistible to Sweden, which had a tradition of economic openness and low tariffs, and propelled a search for a magic formula that would reconcile neutrality with membership. Swedish and Austrian officials toiled for some solution, such as associate membership, which would gain them access to larger consumer markets. Frequently, the debate over neutrality and EC membership became a debate over the economic direction of each country and the safest path to stable growth. Business leaders and conservative politicians advocated an interpretation of neutrality that emphasized abstinence from military alliances or treaties but held some sort of participation in the Community to be more or less compatible with the security policy of each country. In the end, however, a second definition triumphed, an interpretation of neutrality advanced by labor leaders and the union movement as well as agriculture and small business. This definition regarded economic independence as indispensable for neutrality, and the EC was seen not only as a threat to their security policies but also to socioeconomic conditions.[15] Leftist parties and organized labor as well as selected elements in the business community perceived economic prosperity to be at odds with the opening of borders and institutionalized contacts with the Community. Socialist parties mistrusted the club of "black," or Christian Democratic, heads of governments, who were the first generation of leaders of European integration. The Left felt that the political leanings of the Council of Ministers sharply contradicted Socialist progressive and egalitarian principles. In both countries, hostile reactions toward the EC coincided neatly with party identification. Socialist voters opposed membership; conservative voters did not.[16]

The second fatal blow for integration was the isolation of the groups that supported membership. Pro-integration forces consisted of big business. When the moment came to make a decision in 1971, only a relatively small proportion of voters unequivocally endorsed the ideals of European federation and its economic benefits, whereas the major-

---

[15] Depending on one's view, some Austrian legal scholars pointed out that the neutrality policy was not necessarily in conflict with EC membership. Hans Christoph Binswanger, "Ist die Aufrechterhaltung der dauernden Neutralität mit einem Vollbeitritt zur EWG zu vereinbaren?" in *Die Neutralen in der Europäischen Integration*, ed. Hans Mayrzedt and Hans Christoph Binswanger (Vienna: Braumüller, 1970), 177–89. See also Fried Esterbauer, "Die Stellung Österreichs im europäischen Integrationsprozess und die Möglichkeit einer EG-Mitgliedschaft Österreichs," in *Die Europäische Gemeinschaft und Österreich*, ed. Fried Esterbauer and Reinhold Hinterleitner (Vienna: Braumüller, 1977), 123–35.

[16] In general, the debate in the 1960s was restricted to the political elite, leaders of the labor movement, and business. The public at large was rather uninformed.

ity was indifferent or hostile. Many politicians, voters, and interest groups expressed a desire to detach domestic economic institutions from international influences for a variety of reasons. Sweden wanted to preserve social welfare endeavors, and Austria wanted no part of the orbit of global capital.

Needless to say, the supranational features and political ambitions of the EC clashed with a policy of neutrality or nonalignment. Even industrialists and bankers accepted the conditions for continuing to inspire confidence in neutrality in Sweden. And in Austria, the legal foundation of neutrality and its geographic location in Central Europe close to the Soviet Union brought home the delicate matter of what could happen if the country abandoned its position of neutrality. Yet it is not too farfetched to speculate that the need for neutrality has occasionally been used to sidestep criticism from abroad and from the Right on a host of protectionist practices that continued to characterize the political economies of Austria and Sweden.[17]

Although the Left and trade unions in Austria and Sweden harbored many questions surrounding the status of a neutral country in an economic union led by NATO members, another aspect of their thinking can be traced to older traditions of suspiciously viewing the outside world as uncontrollable and threatening to their own ambitions. Simultaneously, the pressures from business, agriculture, and consumers to combine neutrality with membership were not sufficiently compelling to change anyone's mind. In Austria, only a few business groups (mostly from the western provinces) countenanced stronger institutional obligations. In Sweden, the transnational corporations were favorably disposed toward EC membership, but they had few supporters in the rest of society. Moreover, the SAP did not hesitate to cultivate big business through the enactment of numerous investment incentives and tax schemes. Community membership might not have been compatible with a system of investment subsidies and low interest rates that had been so beneficial to big business.

## Austria: Neutrality and the EC Debate

Austria deliberated on the issue of EC associate membership throughout the 1960s. State officials proclaimed that the country's in-

---

[17] Ulf Lindström and Lars Svåsand, "To Be or Not to Be: Austria, Finland, Norway, Sweden and the EC," paper presented at the Seventh Conference of Europeanists, Washington, D.C., March 1990. The authors claim that "non-alignment serves social democracy with an ultimate excuse for keeping the country out of the EC." Important considerations were SAP's welfare and environment policies, which it claimed were more extensive than those of the EC. And a fear that the EC would interfere with SAP's interpretation of private property, civil rights, and subsidies to peripheral problem-ridden industries.

tention to seek associate membership with the EC was fully compatible with the principles of neutrality. The official view was that security commitments and the Neutrality Act were, after all, compatible with EC association, not membership, as long as the Commission recognized Austria's constraints with regard to its constitutional law on permanent neutrality. But associate membership fell through because Brussels itself did not wish to complicate decision making and impair progress toward a united Europe by adding a member with special security requirements.

More important, a second reason for the failure to obtain an associate membership was that the Austrian establishment was hopelessly divided across party blocs. The SPÖ was genuinely anti-EC, but the ÖVP, which represented small business and agriculture, wavered. It was not eager to see a rapid dismantlement of trade barriers and an increase in foreign competition. Until the mid-1960s the Farmers' Bond opposed membership, although it changed its attitude after a new generation of more technocratic leaders assumed office.[18] White-collar unions inside the ÖVP bloc were at first pro-EC in the early 1960s and then reverted to an anti-EC stance in the late 1960s. Likewise, regional trade associations of manufacturing firms expressed conflicted opinions, and the Conservative bloc had to reconcile widely clashing views on the wisdom of joining or abstaining. Although large firms are usually the flagbearers of trade liberalization and tariff cuts, in Austria the nationalized companies did not form a cohesive bloc with a keen interest in integration.

Until 1961, EC membership was not a big issue because Austria had joined the European free trade agreement (EFTA). This step was not popular among the People's party, which felt alien in this group of Socialist-minded Scandinavian countries and Britain.[19] Nonetheless, only the Freedom party campaigned for a withdrawal from EFTA in 1961. In October 1961, when Britain and Denmark suddenly opened negotiations on EC membership with Brussels, Austria decided to go along.

In parliamentary debates, Bruno Kreisky, the minister of foreign affairs, stated in no uncertain terms that joining the Common Market contravened obligations previously entered into by the federal government. He therefore concluded that the disadvantages of not joining the Common Market were outweighed by the disadvantages that would follow a worsening of the international political climate if Austria were to join the Common Market. He also reminded his fellow citizens that

---

[18] Paul Luif, *Neutrale in die EG*, 100.

[19] Alexander Vodopivec, *Die Balkanisierung Österreichs: Folgen einer grossen Koalition* (Vienna: Molden, 1966), 274.

Austria had fought hard to regain its full sovereignty after World War II and that the Republic had accepted the idea of perpetual neutrality along the Swiss model.[20]

Yet in 1961, the coalition of Socialist and People's parties, the Grand Coalition, announced its intention to seek a stronger association with the EC under Article 238 of the Treaty of Rome, which would permit Austria to retain its special security status. Invoking this paragraph, Austria was allowed to suspend certain provisions of the association in case of a threat of war. Austria also would not cede its treaty-making powers, so that it could continue to conduct its own foreign policy and conclude commercial treaties.[21] Otherwise, the neutral countries— Sweden, Switzerland, and Austria—resolved to apply for association with the EC, claiming that neutrality was no bar to contributing to the process of European integration in an appropriate way.

In January 1963, Charles de Gaulle vetoed Britain's entry into the Community. Austria had to decide what it would do next. While the other EFTA countries withdrew their applications, the Austrians decided to continue to seek association, and it was the only neutral country to do so. Until about 1967, exploratory discussions took place to review a de facto customs union and subsequent economic union with the EC. Austria promised to harmonize its agricultural and economic policies with the EC's and to remove restrictions against free competition.[22] The Austrians also pressed the Council of Ministers to start deliberations as soon as possible so that the country's relations with the EC could be settled as early as possible. The Council of Ministers discussed Austria's application at length at the end of 1964, but a draft treaty would have taken longer to formulate, assuming that it ever got that far.

During this period, the hostility of the Soviet Union toward Austria's association with the EC was unchanged. *Pravda* published a series of articles denouncing Austria's behind-the-scenes diplomacy. In December 1961, *Pravda* argued that Austrian participation in the Common Market would be tantamount to a political and economic union with Germany and would contradict the State Treaty. As George Ball remarked in his memoirs, "To its great credit, the Austrian government shrugged all this off and applied for 'association' with the EEC."[23]

---

[20] Heinrich Siegler, *Austria: Problems and Achievements, 1945–1963* (Bonn: Verlag für Zeitarchive, 1964), 55–56.

[21] Luif, *Neutrale in die EG*, 96.

[22] Ibid., 97; Kurt Waldheim, *The Austrian Example*, trans. Ewald Osers (London: Weidenfeld and Nicolson, 1973), 107.

[23] George W. Ball, *The Past Has Another Pattern* (New York: Norton, 1982), 219. The Soviet ambassador also delivered an aide-mémoire in which EC association was seen as incompatible with permanent neutrality. Waldheim, *Austrian Example*, 104–5.

During an official state visit in 1966 by the Soviet head of state N. V. Podgorny, it was clear that the Soviet view was unchanged. According to Podgorny, a trade agreement with the EC ran counter to Austria's international position.[24] Yet when the United States suggested the less dangerous approach of tariff cuts under the auspices of GATT, the Austrian chancellor was quick to dismiss it as cumbersome and inadequate.[25]

Ironically, it was Paris, not Moscow, that killed Austria's first application for associate membership. De Gaulle did not want to disturb his country's cordial relationship with the Soviet Union. When Chancellor Klaus visited Paris in 1965 to solicit support, de Gaulle apparently told his guest that he should look southeastward, where Austria's historical role rested. "Vous êtes Danubiens."[26] Another disappointment came when Britain's second application was blocked in 1967, and the question of enlargement was shelved. A third setback involved growing tensions in Southern Tyrol (Italian since 1919 but formerly Austrian territory) caused by the terrorist activities of Austrian nationalists. Italy vetoed further talks until South Tyrol was stabilized. By the time everything had settled down, the Austrians wanted a different arrangement: a free trade agreement instead of a customs union.

The new objective to seek a free trade agreement was in part caused by a shift in power between the rival ministries of foreign affairs and trade. Each claimed foreign economic relations as its sole province and held quite different views on what was feasible and befitting. In 1963, foreign policy was in the hands of the minister of trade, and integration was actively pursued, but in the late 1960s, foreign affairs acquired this portfolio.[27] Competition among different state agencies for the right to monopolize foreign economic policy decisions did not diminish with the ascendance of the unitary People's party cabinet after 1967; the ÖVP itself was ambivalent.[28]

Through the 1960s, Austria continued to submit diverse proposals for stronger involvement in the EC through associate membership and finally succeeded in obtaining special interim arrangements for across-the-board cuts in tariffs. In 1972, tariffs were eliminated on most ex-

[24] Waldheim, *The Austrian Example*, 112.

[25] Siegler, *Austria: Problems and Achievements, 1945–1963*, 64, 72.

[26] Elisabeth Barker, *Austria 1918–1972* (New York: Macmillan, 1973), 239.

[27] Luif, *Neutrale in die EG*, 135; Robert Kriechbaumer, "Das EWG-Abkommen Österreichs 1972," *Österreichisches Jahrbuch für Politik* (1980): 319–38; Rosmarie Atzenhofer, "Österreichische Integrationspolitik seit 1948: Zwischen EG-Diktat und dem Streben nach Unabhängigkeit," in *Der Un-Heimliche Anschluss: Österreich und die EG*, ed. Margit Scherb and Inge Morawetz (Vienna: Verlag für Gesellschaftskritik, 1988), 78–83.

[28] Peter Katzenstein, "Trends and Oscillations in Austria: Integration Policy since 1955: Alternative Explanations," *Journal of Common Market Studies* 14 (1975): 171–97.

port goods, with the exception of so-called sensitive products, such as paper, paper products, raw aluminium, and certain steel products. About 15 percent of Austria's total exports to the EC were affected by the ceilings and prolonged timetable.[29]

Nobody today recalls this bizarre period in Austria's foreign relations, when it submitted numerous requests for association in the EC. Yet once the period of de Gaulle's obstructionist approach was over and after the Tyrolean question was settled, European integration was dismissed as incompatible with neutrality.

These oscillations in foreign policy do not reflect merely bureaucratic competition between the ministries of trade and foreign affairs. The debate over EC membership concealed a war of nerves between the Socialists and Conservatives for the future control of Austria. Foreign policy was one of the few issues that permitted a power contest between the Socialists and Conservatives.

For the SPÖ, neutrality represented more than military nonalignment to support socioeconomic independence. Behind the abstract formulation of principles, the Socialists supported EFTA because it was led by social democratic heads of state and had a progressive character, while they opposed the Common Market because its member states were fortresses of Christian Democracy. Participation in the EC also carried economic danger because it would bring a flood of imports that could upset the balance of payments.[30] Socialist objections also centered on the risk of increased foreign dominance and intervention, which they remembered from the interwar period. The nationalized industries were, of course, a critical source of economic influence for the Socialists, but Article 90 of the Treaty of Rome called for equal treatment of public and private firms, which might have spelled the end of the privileged existence of state-owned manufacturing. Rightly, the Socialists argued that the contribution of the state-owned sector in economic stabilization, full employment, and regional development would be menaced if Austria were forced to accept supranational direction from an authority whose mandate came from Christian Democratic governments. As time went by, their opposition increased, and the EC was dismissed as a capitalist tool.[31]

The reasons that persuaded the Socialists to reject European integration were grounds for the ÖVP to give it its full support. The ÖVP was

[29] Manfred Scheich, "The European Neutrals after the Enlargement of the Communities—The Austrian Perspective," *Journal of Common Market Studies* 12 (1974): 235–47; Barker, *Austria, 1918–1972,* 240–44.

[30] Cited in Eduard März, *Österreichs Wirtschaft zwischen Ost und West: Eine sozialistische Analyse* (Vienna: Europa, 1965), 42.

[31] Vodopivec, *Die Balkanisierung Österreichs,* 274.

not fully pro-integration but thought of the EC as a way to meet important interest groups halfway and to challenge the Socialists on their own turf—the nationalized industries. It also believed that EC membership would modernize the patronage system and strengthen political plurality and economic liberalism.

Another reason for their open support of the EC was related to the internal structure of the party, which consisted of an amalgam of associations and organizations. The party leadership lacked centralized budgetary authority and had to solicit financial contributions from interest groups. Wealthy groups such as the industrial and trade associations, therefore, exercised considerable political influence because of their financial contributions. In the 1960s, economic representatives of the western provinces became more prominent, resulting in a foreign policy orientation congruent with the more liberal and Western European orientation of that part of the business community.[32] Businesses and voters in the western provinces favored EC membership, while workers and the eastern region, with its closer commercial ties to the Eastern bloc and dependence on state-owned industries, were against membership. When the ÖVP was in government alone as a unitary cabinet in 1966–70, internal strife and bureaucratic competition surfaced to obstruct further progress.[33] But when the ÖVP governed in a coalition with the Socialists, the party adopted a more Europeanist stance; membership in the Community could dismantle the system of sharing positions in the public sector. This would liberalize the economy and dilute the grip of the SPÖ on basic manufacturing. Though the party leadership listened to the pro-EC arguments of industrialists in the Western provinces, its commitment to integration was never absolute because unions of salaried employees and ÖVP delegates in the state-owned industries opposed deregulation and liberalization. State control of the economy also benefited the careers of ÖVP party activists and complemented the economic interests of small business and agriculture. Moreover, the older guard in the People's party shared with the Socialists a deep mistrust of foreign involvement and opening the domestic market to foreign competition.

In the 1970 election, the ÖVP suffered a staggering loss of votes, and the Socialists formed a unitary government. They shelved any further discussion of integration and EC membership. Instead, the new Socialist government approached the commission in Brussels with a proposal for a preferential trade agreement. In the meantime, the Association

[32] Barker, *Austria, 1918–1972*, 257–62.
[33] Katzenstein, "Trends and Oscillations in Austria," 180; Luif, *Neutrale in die EG*, 135.

of Austrian Industry (the employers' group for big privately owned firms) had come to the conclusion that formal association with the EC was less urgent; trade with EFTA and Eastern bloc countries had notably expanded in the preceding decade.[34]

## Sweden: Neutrality and the Four Cs

Sweden also wavered on the question of association (not membership). SAP, which was in government during the entire period of the discussions on the EC in the 1950s and 1960s, rejected further institutionalized links with the EC at the last stage before legislation was drafted. The Swedish Left and Center party in their pains to explain their rejection of association, emphasized the four Cs: capitalism, conservatism, colonialism, and Catholicism, all of which threatened Swedish independence and its way of life.[35]

The formation of a free trade zone had enormous appeal for Sweden because of its tradition of economic openness and low tariffs.[36] Yet after long deliberations, preserving non-alignment was deemed more critical than reaping the fruits of economic integration.

In addition to the problem of neutrality, three developments settled the debate in favor of nonmembership in the 1960s. Inside the SAP, some party members opposed a rapprochement with the EC because of the domineering role played by Christian Democratic parties in Community institutions.[37] Community membership was supported by big business and core supporters of the Conservative party, but its share of the national vote was limited. Its message of widening Sweden's role in the EC was not well received by voters. A third factor was that the most important export markets for Swedish goods were outside the EC—the Scandinavian countries and Britain were Sweden's largest trading partners (38 percent of its exports went to EFTA and Finland in 1960). At first, therefore, Swedish officials and business reckoned that the cost of nonmembership was tolerable because Swedish firms would not suffer great harm.

In 1962, together with the other EFTA members, the SAP govern-

---

[34] Atzenhofer, "Österreichische Integrationspolitik seit 1948," in *Der Un-Heimliche Anschluss*, ed. Scherb and Morawetz, 83.

[35] Sverker Åström, "Swedish Neutrality: Credibility through Commitment and Consistency," in *The Committed Neutral*, ed. Bengt Sundelius (Boulder, Colo.: Westview Press, 1989), 33.

[36] Nils Andren, "Sweden and Europe," *Cooperation and Conflict* 10 (1975): 51–64.

[37] Luif, *Neutrale in die EG*, 117; Larry Hufford, *Sweden's Power Elite* (Washington, D.C.: University Press of America, 1977), 313–39.

ment announced its intention to seek EC association by invoking Article 238 of the Treaty of Rome. This clause provided for reciprocal rights and obligations and joint actions but separate procedural rules for states seeking "associate status." When Sweden applied for this form of membership, the EC granted several concessions in recognition of Sweden's desire to maintain its neutrality. These concessions included the right to conclude trade agreements with third countries (in practice, Eastern bloc countries), the right to stockpile certain goods to supply Sweden in wartime, and the right to terminate the association agreement in case EC policies contradicted Swedish neutrality. Gunnar Lange, Sweden's minister of trade, stated his country's desire to participate in all activities of the Common Market; Sweden wanted the range of activities to be set forth in an association agreement.[38] In the meantime, Sweden was looking forward to an "extensive, close, and durable economic relationship" with the Common Market.[39] Swedish voters and leaders were spared the difficult decision of how to proceed because de Gaulle vetoed future EC expansion in 1963. The issue of membership vanished from the political agenda.

Sweden was again interested in forming stronger institutional ties with the EC in 1966 after the Council of Ministers permitted members the right to veto any EC proposal. Because the risk of being controlled by supranational foreign policy was removed and member states retained sovereignty over critical areas of national policy-making, the official Swedish position recognized few reasons not to become more drawn into EC affairs. Confirming Sweden's desire to reopen negotiations with Brussels in 1967, Sweden attached to its application for association an open letter in which the Swedish ambassador to the EC outlined that the country would consider any form of membership status compatible with neutrality, "The Swedish government . . . does not wish to exclude any of the forms laid down in the Treaty of Rome for participation in an enlarged EEC." [40] While the details of the letter caused great confusion in Sweden, the partisans of integration claimed victory. Although it appeared as though Sweden wanted full membership, Sweden's policy of neutrality remained unchanged. The issue languished until de Gaulle's unexpected resignation in 1969, when enlargement of the EC once again became possible.

Ironically, at the very moment that de Gaulle disappeared and the road was cleared for the EC to negotiate with the waiting EFTA mem-

[38] Daniel Viklund, *Sweden and the European Community: Trade, Cooperation, and Policy Issues* (Stockholm: Swedish Institute, 1989), 15.

[39] Luif, *Neutrale in die EG*, 118.

[40] Ibid.; Viklund, *Sweden and the European Community*, 16.

ber states, the Nordic countries had completed an extensive report on the possibility of creating an internal Nordic market. But the Swedish Social Democrats ignored the NORDEK report and hastened to follow the British and Danish negotiators with the aim of ensuring Sweden's participation in the future enlargement. The exact form of this participation was left undecided and awaited informal exploratory negotiations. The proposed Nordic economic union suffered a quiet death.

What prompted this renewed effort to jump on the Community bandwagon? In the late 1960s, a number of reports from economic research institutes predicted economic woes down the road because the Nordic market was saturated with Swedish products. Discriminatory policies of the EC on paper and steel products, moreover, impeded the modernization of Swedish industry and could have led to a stagnation of Swedish export growth.[41] In addition, Britain and Denmark were both important trading partners, and their possible accession by 1973 forced a second look at the costs of remaining outside the EC. Finally, Swedish officials were sure that the idea of a federated Europe based on common defense policies and greater political coordination was not only temporarily but permanently abandoned.

In August 1970 exploratory talks were in full swing. Prime Minister Olof Palme had visited Bonn, London, and Paris in the spring of that year to plead for a careful consideration of the Swedish case. In November 1970 Sweden asked for parallel discussions between itself and the two other Scandinavian candidates—Denmark and Norway—with the argument that each faced identical problems.

Swedish government drafted a long report to demonstrate its willingness to make unilateral concessions by adopting EC trade legislation and border control regulations. Swedish officials wanted few exemptions and were willing to consider coordination in technological research, stabilization policy, and monetary issues. To foster coordination, the report suggested regular consultations between the government and the Council of Ministers, and between the Riksdag and the European Parliament.

In March 1971 the first stage in the exploratory talks was completed, but suddenly Swedish officials inexplicably reversed themselves and announced that they no longer sought associate membership. The government now wished to limit its arrangements with the EC to a free trade agreement, yet just a few months earlier Swedish negotiators had assured the Council of Ministers that Sweden was willing to conform to

---

[41] A summary of this thinking is found in Tord Ekström, Gunnar Myrdal, and Roland Pålsson, "Spezifische politische Probleme aus schwedischer Sicht," in *Die Neutralen in der Europäischen Integration*, ed. Mayrzedt and Binswanger, 300–301.

the requirements of a customs union. Swedish officials had so recently seemed willing to compromise and go to considerable lengths to prepare for candidacy. What took place between August 1970 and March 1971 to change their minds? What alarming incident had occurred to bring back the national security argument?

It was not a deterioration of international détente or a resumption of Cold War tension that changed their opinion. Rather, at the Hague conference in 1969, the member states of the EC agreed to hold regular summit meetings with heads of state to plan for further high-level coordination and charged viscount Davignon, then Belgian foreign minister, to explore the possibility of a common foreign policy. Then, later in 1969, the Werner Report reviewed, again, the possibility of an economic and monetary union. Both initiatives raised problematic questions concerning the legality of reconciling sovereignty with economic obligations.[42] To be sure, the Swedish strategy had been built on the premise that the Community would remain a free trade area with a common external tariff policy and that political integration would stall. As soon as the Swedish government realized that the movement toward political integration had a new momentum, the appeal of associate membership declined rapidly. For Sweden, broad free trade arrangements to abolish tariffs on all industrial products was a logical substitute in 1971.[43]

Apart from the unexpected EC initiative to foster greater political unity, electoral calculations also persuaded the Social Democratic party to take a harder line toward the EC. National security and neutrality were associated with the notion of economic autonomy or independence, ideas that were chiefly propagated by the Left. In public opinion polls, Socialist voters were notably more anti-EC than bourgeois voters. Thus, in 1972, two-thirds of the Socialist voters but one-fourth of the Conservative party voters rejected EC membership.[44]

Economic globalism existed alongside another tradition of cultural or social insulation. This belief was inherited by SAP activists, parts of organized labor, and the Center party (the former Agrarian party). Already in 1962, Prime Minister Tage Erlander in a now-famous

[42] Frantz Wendt, *Cooperation in the Nordic Countries* (Stockholm: Almqvist and Wiksell, 1981).

[43] Barry Turner and Gunilla Nordquist, *The Other European Community* (New York: St. Martin's, 1982), 161. The EC Commission delayed removing duties on paper, pulp, and steel.

[44] Daniel Viklund, *Spelet om frihandels avtalet: En kritisk studie i Svensk Europapolitik, 1959–72* (Stockholm: Raben and Sjögren, 1977), 137. For an argument in favor of membership, see Bo Siegbahn, "Argumente für eine Vollmitgliedschaft Schwedens in der EWG," in *Die Neutralen in der Europäischen Integration*, ed. Mayrzedt and Binswanger, 303–15.

speech to the metalworkers' union hinted at the dangers of EC membership for preserving Sweden's unique accomplishments. Among the twenty points he listed to explain why joining the Community was unpalatable, Erlander mentioned the pioneering spirit of Swedish socialism in constructing the most comprehensive social welfare state.[45]

This theme resurfaced in the later debates on the question of whether association was indeed desirable. In parliamentary debates in early 1971, Palme argued against accession on the grounds that Sweden should at all costs avoid contributing to the strengthening of monopoly capital! The same party had earlier worked for stronger bonds with the EC through association (not membership). Palme later elaborated on his remarks, saying that Sweden could not place itself outside Europe and so must arrange for technological and economic cooperation. It would not, however, subordinate its sovereignty for the sake of a supranational Europe.

Following the zigzag course of Swedish foreign economic policy pronouncements, public opinion began to perceive fewer advantages to EC membership, and support fell from 63 percent in 1967 to 31 percent in December 1970.[46] The radical view, usually advanced by articulate SAP insiders, stressed domestic policy independence and rejected the EC as an instrument for reactionary or conservative programs offensive to Swedish thinking on social solidarity. Close ties with the EC would lead to foreign domination of the nation's natural resources, industry, and finance. According to this view, Sweden could best influence European affairs by creating a progressive working-class movement. Broader Nordic cooperation was a better option because it was not based, like the EC, on monopoly capitalism and capital concentration but rather on the willingness to direct market forces for a better and more just society. Nordic union, therefore, consisted of "equal power, equal freedom, and equal welfare," whereas the EC stood for inequality, capital concentration, and regional disparities.[47]

Opponents of EC membership also referred to other aspects of Sweden's political culture, such as the notion that free trade ought to serve peace and universalism. The Common Market explicitly excluded globalism and universalism. Given Sweden's faith in global in-

[45] Olof Ruin, *Tage Erlander: Serving the Welfare State, 1946–69,* trans. Michael F. Metcalf (Pittsburgh: University of Pittsburgh Press, 1990), 280–84.
[46] Viklund, *Spelet om Frihandels Avtalet,* 136. See also Carl-Einar Stålvant, "Sweden: The Swedish Negotiations with the EEC," *Scandinavian Political Studies* 8 (1973): 244.
[47] Mats Bergquist, "Sweden and the EEC: A Study of Four Schools of Thought and Their Views on the Swedish Common Market Policy in 1961 and 1962," *Cooperation and Conflict* 6 (1971): 39–55; Donald M. Hancock, "Sweden, Scandinavia, and the EC," *International Affairs* 48 (1972): 435; Nils Andren, "Sweden and Europe," 62–64; Hufford, *Sweden's Power Elite,* 313–39.

terdependence, it should not compromise its own principles by acceding to an European experiment that by definition excluded the poorer nations.[48] Such views prevailed not only in the Social Democratic party, the Center party, with its ties to farmers, also contained many critics. In any event, the Social Democrats received 45.3 percent of the parliamentary vote in 1970, down from 50.1 percent. New developments in the EC, coupled with the troubling electoral trends, persuaded the SAP to drop further pursuit of EC association.[49]

Paradoxically, conservatives, including the Swedish military establishment, lobbied for association and sidestepped questions about neutrality (this also happened in Austria). Removing artificial barriers to trade, according to the Conservative party and the Federation of Swedish Industry, would free the movement of capital and firms across national boundaries and result in greater efficiency and rationalization. Advocates of EC membership scoffed at the implications for Swedish neutrality and argued for a flexible approach to Sweden's security demands. Moreover, membership would enable Sweden to influence EC policy directly since it was already affected by EC decisions regardless of whether it joined or not. Their grievances disappeared after the free trade arrangements of 1972 removed their greatest worries of exclusion and discrimination.

## Low Countries versus Neutral Countries

One could argue that socialist parties in Belgium and the Netherlands went along with the integration projects because they could not stop them. Undeniably, the SAP in Sweden and the SPÖ in Austria were the most vehement critics of the EC, and they were in power for long periods of time. Yet every party across the political spectrum in the Low Countries declared its unconditional support for the Treaty of Rome and accepted the subsequent erosion of national sovereignty. Apart from the minuscule Communist parties, all political groups fully endorsed the ratification of the Treaty of Rome and continued to express emphatic support for European federalism.[50]

Socialist politicians, in fact, played distinguished roles in the history of the Community. One example is Henri-Paul Spaak (one biographer

[48] Bergquist, "Sweden and the EEC," 48–54; Kjell Goldmann, "The Swedish Model of Security Policy," *West European Politics* 14 (1991): 122–42.

[49] Carl-Einar Stålvant and Carl Hamilton, "Sweden," in *The Wider Western Europe: Reshaping the EC/EFTA Relationship*, ed. Helen Wallace (London: Pinter, 1991), 211.

[50] Wichard Woyke, *Erfolg durch Integration: Die Europapolitik der Benelux-Staaten von 1947 bis 1969* (Bochum, Germany: Brockmeyer, 1985), 123–41, 249–67.

even calls him "Mr. Europe"). From 1938 to 1939, he was Belgium's first socialist prime minister, and in 1945, after the war, he served as foreign minister for many years with brief interruptions. In 1955, Spaak drafted the document that laid out the technical basis for the proposed Common Market, and the six original members of the European Community accepted this report as the starting point for further negotiations on the institutional development of the Common Market and Euratom.[51]

The two wings of the Socialist party (the francophone PS and the Flemish SP) agreed with the long-term objectives of European integration. Occasionally, in the early years, francophone Socialists questioned the ultimate impact of the European Coal and Steel Community on the national economy, and a small minority of Socialist deputies in Parliament voted against the ratification of the ECSC. The two rival trade union federations—Socialist and Catholic—supported the ECSC since they accepted Common Market justifications for improved efficiencies, higher standards of living, and better Franco-German relations. Their only reservation was the lack of joint welfare policy and labor standards.[52] Otherwise, the Socialist and Catholic federations urged the formation of a united European social and economic space that would replace the inefficiencies of national economies. This, moreover, could only happen if unified institutions were created. Whereas the Swedish and Austrian trade union federations opposed the EC because it would strengthen business interests and undermine social achievements, the Belgian union movement argued exactly the reverse: the Schumann Plan and the European Economic Community were guarantees against the dominance of capitalist alliances.

In the Netherlands, too, from 1946 on the Labor party, or Partij van de Arbeid (PvdA), backed every major initiative to enhance or quicken European integration. The PvdA believed that the Community would consolidate democracy and socialist principles, and, more important, democracy and socialism ought to be sacrificed for the sake of European unity.[53] Whenever criticism arose about the lack of a social dimension within the Community, the PvdA leadership typically proposed a supranational European solution cultivating stronger contacts

[51] Pierre-Henri Laurent, "Pierre-Henri Spaak and the Diplomatic Origins of the Common Market, 1955/56," *Political Science Quarterly* 85 (1970): 373–96.

[52] Kevin Featherstone, *Socialist Parties and European Integration: A Comparative History* (New York: St. Martin's, 1988), 21–39; Ernst B. Haas, *The Uniting of Europe* (Stanford, Calif.: Stanford University Press, 1958), 143–48, 234–40.

[53] D. F. J. Bosscher, "The Partij van de Arbeid en het buitenlands beleid," in *Wederopbouw, welvaart, en onrust*, ed. H. W. von der Dunk (Houten: De Haan, 1986), 81–82.

with other socialist parties, instead of retreating from the concept of a united Europe. In the 1980s, the PvdA looked to the Community to pull the Netherlands out of its prolonged recession and proposed a consolidation of the internal market, more financial aid for projects such as Eureka, and, ironically, the strengthening of the EMS.[54]

By comparison, the Left in Austria and Sweden was ferociously anti-EC, although it was unwilling to dismiss the Treaty of Rome outright. The economic benefits were too clear. But the leftist interpretation of what membership in the Common Market would mean prevailed because overall popular support for integration and removal of trade barriers remained modest. Elected leaders, not only from the labor movement but also from the Right, sensed that, aside from a small group of businesses and conservatives, the rest of society was ambivalent about surrendering any aspect of national sovereignty to an unaccountable supranational agency. This lack of enthusiasm was clearly fed by the harsh opposition of organized labor—both the party and the trade union movement—which felt that a loss of governing autonomy would threaten their social welfare achievements and market-steering capacity. However, the absence of financial interests striving for integration into global markets helped the labor movement establishment stave off a final affirmative response to membership. Their anti-EC rhetoric and the mood of the citizens that favored economic independence assured a firm no-vote to associate membership in the Community.

Neither Austria nor Sweden possessed the entrenched liberal traditions found in Belgium and the Netherlands. Financial interests in Austria and Sweden occupied a subordinate position in the national economy and in state agencies. Financial actors are by nature the most persistent cheerleaders of trade and capital liberalization, but in Austria and Sweden they were at the mercy of politicians or state officials. Neither was able to carve an independent niche, separate from manufacturing and with connections to international networks, to escape the restrictive climate at home.

What shapes views on foreign economic relations is an extremely complex question that must take into account many diverse factors. One influence is the economic elite, whose interest in such debates on commercial relations reflects its material and mental stakes in their outcome. The financial communities in Belgium and the Netherlands, though grown around different poles of activities, exercised considerable historical influence over the parameters of each national discourse on economic choices.

[54] Kevin Featherstone, *Socialist Parties and European Integration*, 279–83. This is ironic because the EMS with its deflationary biases is not very sympathetic to the Left. See Chapter 9 for further discussion.

CHAPTER NINE

# European Integration
# in the 1980s

With the 1987 Single European Act, the heads of governments decided at long last to introduce institutional reforms to liberalize the movement of people, goods, and capital within the European Community. Majority voting on issues related to the Internal Market (1992) project replaced the right to veto, or unanimous voting. These treaty amendments have given the Community institutions more policy competence and have brought a federal Europe closer to reality. At the December 1991 meeting in Maastricht, EC members agreed to set a firm date for completing the final stage of the Economic and Monetary Union (EMU). On 1 January 1999, the members of the Community will have established a European central bank, eliminated national currencies, and implemented a common monetary and economic policy.

The relaunching of the EMU is the European solution to sluggish growth and increased international competition in the 1980s. One major development behind the decision to create a unified, barrier-free Europe was the rising awareness among member states that the traditional instruments of macroeconomic policy-making, which were needed to halt declining economic performance, were useless in an environment of growing economic interdependence. Widening intra-European trade, and thus enlarged economic openness, diminished the effectiveness of market-steering mechanisms and compensatory policies. This process not only applied to the small European democracies but also undermined the policy independence of large nations. Undoubtedly, the two EC member states in this study, Belgium and the Netherlands, surpassed other EC members in terms of trade dependence, as measured by the ratio of exports as a percentage of the GDP. They exported almost the equivalent of 75 percent of their GDP, of

*Table 12.* Vulnerability to international pressures, 1982

| Imports and exports (% of GDP) | Geographic distribution of exports (% of trade) | | | | | |
|---|---|---|---|---|---|---|
| | OECD | | | | | |
| | EC | N. America | Other | OPEC | LDCS | COMECON |
| Belgium 130.0 | 72 | 3.5 | 9 | 4.5 | 8.5 | 1.5 |
| Netherlands 94.5 | 72 | 2.5 | 8 | 5.5 | 8.0 | 1.5 |
| Austria 52.7 | 55 | 2.5 | 14 | 5.0 | 12.5 | 3.5 |
| Sweden 55.1 | 49 | 6.5 | 23 | 5.0 | 14.0 | 8.0 |

*Source:* IMF, *Direction of Trade Statistics* (Washington, D.C.: IMF, 1983).

which approximately two-thirds went to the Community before the considerable movement forward in deregulation and integration after 1987 (Table 12).[1]

It would seem that trade dependence coupled with the economic problems of the early 1980s—high inflation, declining export markets, and faltering economic growth—hurt the small, open democracies in the Community more than similar small democracies outside the Community (Table 13).[2] Small European countries that are not members of the EC fared better in the first half of the 1980s, partly because a significant share of their import markets was outside the Community while foreign trade generally made a smaller contribution to their GDP growth (see Table 12). Austria, which is just as dependent on economic fluctuations in the Federal Republic of Germany as in the Low Countries, retained some markets in Eastern and Central Europe, while its share of foreign trade to total economic product stood at 50 percent of its GDP.[3] Austria's openness and trade dependence were undoubtedly

---

[1] David R. Cameron, "The 1992 Initiative: Causes and Consequences," in *Euro-politics: Institutions and Policymaking in the "New" European Community,* ed. Alberta M. Sbragia (Washington, D.C.: Brookings Institution, 1992), 36–39; See also Wayne Sandholtz and John Zysman, "1992: Recasting the European Bargain," *World Politics* 42 (1989): 95–128; Andrew Moravcsik, "Negotiating the Single Act: National Interests and Conventional Statecraft in the European Community," *International Organization* 45 (1991): 651–88.

[2] One possible reason for the poor record of the small countries could be that they were not able to take advantage of the recovery in the United States after 1982, though larger EMS countries could. See S. Vona and L. Bini Smaghi, "Economic Growth and Exchange Rates in the EMS: Their Trade Effects in a Changing External Environment," in *The European Monetary System,* ed. Francesco Giavazzi, Stefano Micossi, and Marcus Miller (New York: Cambridge University Press, 1988); Paul de Grauwe, "Fiscal Policies in the EMS—A Strategic Analysis," in *International and European Monetary Systems,* ed. Emil-Maria Claassen (New York: Praeger, 1990), 121–44.

[3] See the essays in Margrit Scherb and Inge Morawetz, eds., *In deutscher Hand: Österreich und sein grosser Nachbar?* (Vienna: Verlag für Gesellschaftskritik, 1990).

*Table 13.* Economic performance of small European states, 1980–85 and 1989–90 (in percentages)

|  | 1980–85 | | 1989–90 | |
|---|---|---|---|---|
|  | Real Growth | Unemployment | Real Growth | Unemployment |
| European Community | 1.4 | 9.0 | 3.0 | 8.8 |
| Small EMS members[a] | 1.0 | 10.8 | 3.5 | 9.9 |
| Small non-members[b] | 2.5 | 2.5 | 2.1 | 3.2 |

*Source:* OECD, *Historical Statistics, 1960–1990* (Paris: OECD, 1992).
[a]Belgium, Denmark, Ireland, and the Netherlands.
[b]Austria, Finland, Norway, Sweden, and Switzerland.

substantial but less than that of Belgium and the Netherlands in the early 1980s.[4]

In this chapter I discuss the impact of progress in regional integration in the 1980s and explain why Sweden and Austria were in the end unable to resist European integration and membership any longer. Most of the discussion pertains to monetary and financial integration because the effects of trade dependence pale beside the enormous force of spillover effects from financial liberalization and monetary integration. Belgium and the Netherlands were part of the European Monetary System (EMS) from the beginning, whose establishment is one of the most important milestones in the brief history of European integration.[5]

As participants in the exchange rate mechanism of the European Monetary System (a separate agreement to manage intra-Community exchange rates and to finance exchange rate market intervention), the Dutch and the Belgians have agreed to keep the exchange rate of their currency within the permissible margins of the central rate between two currencies. Following this agreement on exchange rate management and financing, central banks are obliged to intervene as soon as the currencies threaten to go below or above the permissible margins (a total of 4.5 percent fluctuation is permitted). The participating currencies are allowed to adjust their exchange rates occasionally; the EMS is a fixed but adjustable exchange rate regime. Since its founding in March

[4] The marked increase in export trade and the concentration of trade of EC members in the Community is mentioned by others as one of the contributing causes for the Single European Act. Cameron, "The 1992 Initiative," in *Euro-politics*, ed. Sbragia, 38–40.

[5] On the history of the EMS, see Marcello de Cecco, *International Economic Adjustment: Small Countries and the European Monetary System* (Oxford: Blackwell, 1983); and Peter Ludlow, *The Making of the European Monetary System: A Case Study of the Politics of the European Community* (London: Butterworth, 1982).

1979, the number of realignments has declined, with most of the exchange rate adjustments having occurred in the first four years of its existence. The real impact of the EMS exchange rate agreement is in terms of domestic adjustments and macroeconomic policy convergence. The procedures of the EMS, which were less onerous for low-inflation countries than for high-inflation countries, have not been kind to leftist coalitions or governments. Four broad consequences flowed from the obligations contained in the exchange rate mechanism of the EMS to manage the exchange rate of the currency: (1) macroeconomic measures contrary to the main trend in the EMS area are fraught with risks and undesirable side effects; (2) central banks command greater voice, respect, and influence in domestic policy deliberations; (3) financial groups gain in economic strength; (4) global diversification and capital mobility of firms increased. All four points have one thing in common: they make it more difficult for participating governments to pursue Keynesian-style demand management with its emphasis on reflation and redistributive incomes policy.

Institutions of the EMS were designed to bring monetary stability to Europe. With the failure of the Bretton Woods regime in mind, the founders of the EMS spoke of creating a system containing a large degree of symmetry and flexibility. It had to be sufficiently flexible to tolerate different levels of inflation in the participating countries also sufficiently symmetric to permit an equal sharing of the burden of adjustment.[6] But most analysts agree that the technical workings of the EMS impose asymmetric costs on its participating countries. The EMS is dominated by the German Bundesbank, which limits the policy choices available to other counties and functions as a disciplinary device on high-inflation countries. According to this view, EMS membership means surrendering national monetary policy autonomy to the Bundesbank, with the DM playing a central, hegemonic role.[7] Because the DM is the anchor currency, weaker economies with higher price instability must bring inflation down through coercive incomes policies and fiscal spending retrenchments. But the leading country does not provide the others with a growth stimulus.[8]

[6] Paul de Grauwe, *The Economics of Monetary Integration* (New York: Oxford University Press, 1992), 93–129.

[7] For example, see Francesco Giavazzi and Alberto Giovannini, "Models of the EMS: Is Europe a Greater Deutschmark Area? in *Global Macroeconomics*, ed. Ralph C. Bryant and Richard Portes (New York: St. Martin's, 1987), 237–65; Massimo Russo and Giuseppe Tullio, "Monetary Policy Coordination within the EMS: Is There a Rule?" in *The European Monetary System*, ed. Giavazzi, Micossi, and Miller, 41–82. For a counter view, see Michele Fratianni and Jürgen von Hagen, "Asymmetries and realignments in the EMS," in *The European Monetary System in the 1990s*, ed. Paul de Grauwe and Lucas Papademos (New York: Longman, 1990), 86–116.

[8] Frank McDonald and George Zis, "The European Monetary System: Towards 1991 and Beyond," *Journal of Common Market Studies* 27 (1989): 183–202; Michael J. Artis and

During the 1978 negotiations for creating an island of monetary stability in Europe, the Germans were adamant that the intervention mechanism should be based on a bilateral parity grid rather than on ECU parities. Such an arrangement ensures that the pressure to adjust would be on the weak currencies. Central banks in the countries with weak currencies would have to draw down foreign currency reserves to defend the central exchange rate. Since their reserves are finite, after a while weak currency countries would request an exchange rate realignment to devalue their currency. But the Bundesbank stipulated that when a country requested a devaluation it must also present a companion package of deflationary measures to ensure that the exchange rate realignment would not simply translate into higher inflation.

Devaluation can be avoided, but countries with inflationary economic policies have to fight off speculation against their currency by raising interest rates. High interest rates defeat the purpose of stimulating investments and creating jobs.[9] In the long run, a sounder alternative is to bring down inflation. We see therefore a large measure of inflation convergence in the EMS area.

The EMS has eliminated instruments of traditional Keynesian economic policies and can no longer be used to buttress class compromises. Low interest rates to stimulate business activities prompt large capital outflows, while deficit spending to reflate the economy leads to large current account deficits that cannot be financed through higher interest rates because they are determined abroad. Since countries can no longer monetize public expenditures, they go into debt. To induce savers to hold government bonds, there will be a strong urge to maintain interest rates aligned to German rates. Setting one's interest rates according to German levels will force governments to control public spending as much as possible to guard against sudden unexpected interest rate increases. Debt payments will grow or shrink with the interest rates set by the German Bundesbank, and any prudent government will want to be careful about spending programs.[10]

Not even expansionary budgetary policies in Germany are a solution

Mark P. Taylor, "Exchange Rates, Interest Rates, Capital Controls and the EMS: Assessing the Track Record," in *European Monetary System*, ed. Giavazzi, Micossi, and Miller, 185. Horst Ungerer, "The EMS and the International Monetary System," *Journal of Common Market Studies* 27 (1989): 238.

[9] C. Mastropasqua, Stefano Micossi, and R. Rinaldi, "Interventions, Sterilization, and Monetary Policy in the EMS Countries, 1979–1987," in *European Monetary System*, ed. Giavazzi, Micossi, and Miller, 283.

[10] Marcello de Cecco, "The EMS and National Interests," in *The Political Economy of European Integration*, ed. Paolo Guerrieri and Pier Carlo Padoan (Savage, Md.: Barnes and Noble Books, 1989), 85–99; Loukas Tsoukalis, "The Political Economy of the EMS," in *Political Economy of European Integration*, ed. Guerrieri and Padoan, 58–84; Rudiger Dornbush, "Problems of European Monetary Integration," in *European Financial Integration* (New York: Cambridge University Press, 1991), 305–28.

to the deflationary biases in the design of the EMS. After German unification in 1991, the budget deficit of the federal government widened considerably and was equal to about 6 percent of the GDP. It forced the Bundesbank, Europe's most independent central bank, to raise interest rates to their highest level since 1945. Other countries followed, and German high interest rates needlessly depressed economic growth in the rest of Europe. Discontent with German leadership provoked the British establishment to blame the Germans for turbulence in financial markets caused by currency speculators fleeing the British pound.

Monetary integration and financial instability undermine the autonomy of central banks, yet their weight at home in national policy deliberations rises because of the ongoing requirement to manage the exchange rate and the concern about price stability. Central bank governors are in constant touch with each other through the Committee of Central Bank Governors of the EC, and they can use their supranational connections to reiterate the centrality of price stability, a message that resonates well in financial circles. Converging movements toward price stability endow central bankers with the means to define the parameters of a healthy economic performance. Surprisingly, central banks in countries with weak currencies and high inflation did not necessarily resist the dominance of the Bundesbank; they accepted the asymmetry in order to import credibility for their own anti-inflation program and to persuade governments to pay attention to the consequences of spending programs on price stability.[11]

Finally, the reduction of exchange rate variability and convergence of national economic policies toward an emphasis on price stability abet the growth of international financial transactions and capital mobility. High capital mobility and deepening financial integration, as shown in preceding chapters, are damaging to the intervention tools of leftist administrations.

The extent to which the binding constraints of the EMS restrict macroeconomic management varies with the existing degree of central bank independence and the partisan composition of government. Right-wing governments were more likely to embrace the discipline imposed by the EMS on spending habits than left-wing governments. In both the Netherlands and Belgium, elections in the early 1980s

---

[11] For a description of the various consultative committees composing the EMS, see John T. Woolley, "1992, Capital, and the EMS: Political Institutions and Monetary Union," in *Euro-politics*, ed. Sbragia, 188–90; Jacques Melitz, "Monetary Discipline, Germany and the European Monetary System: A Synthesis," in *European Monetary System*, ed. Giavazzi, Micossi, and Miller, 51–79; John Goodman, *Monetary Sovereignty: The Politics of Central Banking in Western Europe* (Ithaca: Cornell University Press, 1992), 195–97.

brought to power center-right coalition cabinets, which had run electoral campaigns on the promise of slimming down the public sector, bolstering the profits of private enterprises, and slowing down labor costs and inflation. In addition, the philosophical inclination of the central bank also determined the extent to which a country accepted the rules of the EMS. Thus, in the Netherlands, where a strong and stable guilder was fully integrated into macroeconomic management, the exchange rate mechanism of the EMS was compatible with prevailing principles on monetary policy. But in Belgium, where the central bank was less dogmatic about a strong and stable currency and the economic activities of financial actors ranged from steel and domestic banking to international investments, entry into the EMS and requirements to harmonize the monetary side of macroeconomic policymaking to the new European order justified new banking legislation that introduced stricter monetary policies.

## Monetary Discipline in Belgium

As country with a weak currency, Belgium had installed exchange controls to ward off recurrent attacks on the Belgian franc.[12] In the late 1970s, Belgium's unemployment surged and current account deficits widened. The Belgian central bank had pegged the franc to the German mark, but the lack of confidence in government policy produced a continuous outflow of capital and downward pressure of the currency. The monetary authorities raised the interest rates to shore up the currency, and real long-term interest rates were 4.2 percent in 1978, 5.2 percent in 1979, and 7.6 percent in 1980.[13] Exchange controls were of little help in arresting speculation, and capital outflows continued to destabilize the exchange rate.

The outflow of capital and the prolonged run on the Belgian franc sparked a lengthy political stalemate as the Belgian central bank insisted on the removal of cost-of-living indexation and drastic spending cuts to deal with a ballooning budget and current account deficits. The continuous outflow of capital and turmoil in the foreign exchange markets eventually required an exchange rate realignment, which could only be implemented after the Council of Economic and Finance Ministers and the Monetary Committee of the European Community considered its effect on participating currencies in the EMS. During

[12] Alfred Steinherr and Geoffroy de Schrevel, "Liberalization of Financial Transactions in the Community with particular reference to Belgium, Denmark, and Netherlands," *European Economy* 36 (1988): 130.
[13] Göran Therborn, *Why Some Peoples Are More Unemployed than Others* (London: Verso, 1986), 150.

the meeting, the Belgian delegation requested a 12 percent devaluation and defended the size of the adjustment by pointing to the multiple financial and economic imbalances in Belgium and the enormous outflow of capital. Neither the Germans nor the French wished to grant such a large devaluation and countered that such a sizable realignment would cause an unforeseeable ripple effect on the parity grid. They suggested that the Belgians accept a 9 percent devaluation. At the next session, when the Belgian delegation announced its agreement with the lower rate, the Germans had changed their minds and suggested an 8.5 percent devaluation. That was final. Belgium was also asked to rein in domestic spending, although the reform package outlining domestic measures was not instrumental in the decision and was discounted by the others in judging the possibility for an exchange rate realignment.[14]

In retrospect, the devaluation was insufficient to give Belgian producers a real competitive price advantage, aside from drastic changes in in the political economy, and recurrent central bank intervention was required as the Belgian franc frequently sank to the bottom of the exchange rate band between June 1983 and March 1985.[15] Real interest rates were also relatively high. But the welfare gains that labor had won were gradually rolled back under the banner of reforms. In February 1982, the government declared a general price freeze through the end of March and a selective freeze thereafter, and wage restraints were renewed until the end of 1984. The Catholic trade union confederation accepted the cuts and eliminations after the Social Christian party emphasized the lack of alternatives. The trade union confederation's position caused a rift with the socialist confederation, whose main political ally (the Socialist party) was in opposition. The socialist confederation therefore felt no obligation to support the antiunion policies of the government.

Belgium's devaluation highlights novel features of the European Community in an era of intensified regional integration that will probably be even more pronounced in the near future. Important steps by national governments concerning alterations in monetary or exchange rate policy now require the intervention and approval of bureaucrats in other countries, who do not hesitate to modify or reject a proposal for substantial exchange rate realignments. EMS members frequently seek to modify a country's request for a devaluation by demanding deep

[14] The story of the 8.5 percent devaluation was recounted during an interview with the author. See also Jozef Smits, "Less Democracy for a Better Economy," *Res Publica* 25 (1983): 141.

[15] Francesco Giavazzazi and Alberto Giovannini, *Limiting Exchange Rate Flexibility: The EMS* (Cambridge, Mass.: MIT Press, 1989), 64–66.

budget cuts and other domestic adjustments. For these countries, the purpose of such demands is to avoid bearing the burden of another country's economic misfortune or mismanagement. Normally, governments respond to the requests by the participating countries of the EMS by pushing through spending ceilings, budget cuts, and mandatory pay freezes, which were in any event already planned.[16] But elected officials, remembering election time, do not always feel courageous enough to go ahead with unpopular programs. The procedures of the EMS enable national governments to ignore the pleas and threats of their own electorate and shift the blame for painful adjustments to some vague reference to prior commitments.

Although some Belgian politicians, considering the potential electoral backlash, may have hesitated to take the advice of other governments seriously and might have planned to undo the austerity measures at the earliest opportunity, new legislation passed by Parliament redefined the statutory power of the central bank in 1990. Because of the ongoing need to coordinate and consult on monetary decisions, the central bank needed more latitude to determine domestic credit and financial objectives. The new legislation allowed the Belgian National Bank to engage in spot sales and purchases of foreign currencies (currency swaps), so it can now sell its gold reserves without seeking the government's permission. Similarly, the Banking Commission, once a fairly weak body, has been renamed the Banking and Finance Commission and has been given broader responsibilities to break stock exchange monopolies, renegotiate commissions for brokerage firms, and issue new rules on capital adequacy and market structure.[17] While in the past private financial groups undermined the authority of the Belgian Banking Commission, the new rules enable the monetary officials to clamp down on financial abuses or shady deals and to monitor the performance of financial institutions more closely. Other financial reforms have been geared to easing the financial burdens of the Treasury, which now permits both foreign and nonfinancial companies to bid on treasury papers during regular auctions. The new subscription rules, inviting more competitive bidding, are primarily meant to lower

---

[16] Smits, "Less Democracy for a Better Economy," 141. See also Artis and Taylor, "Exchange Rates, Interest Rates, Capital Controls and the EMS: Assessing the Track Record," in *European Monetary System*, ed. Giavazzi, Micossi, and Miller, 185–202; McDonald and Zis, "The European Monetary System: Towards 1991 and Beyond," 183–202.

[17] OECD, *Economic Surveys. BLEU 1988/89* (Paris: OECD, 1989), 74–78. Kredietbank, *Monthly Bulletin of the Kredietbank* 45 (1990): 1–15. *Financial Times*, 4 January 1991, p. 9.

the cost of government borrowing. The restructuring of the capital market will break the monopoly of Belgian banks on state financing.[18]

Central bankers transferred their constitutional powers to an inter-governmental institution and suffered a loss of economic autonomy. Yet their political standing rose. The central bank's newly gained prestige and reputation supplied advocates of sound finance with extra ammunition to impel recalcitrant politicians to curb budget expenditures and deal forcefully with combative unions. Belgium achieved better price performance at the expense of investments and jobs; employment was traded for monetary stability.[19]

## Shadowing the German Mark for a Strong Guilder in the Netherlands

During the preliminary negotiations on the creation of a European exchange rate system, the Dutch, the Germans, and the Danes insisted on a parity grid between each combination of two currencies instead of pegging the exchange rate to some other unit such as the ECU (a basket currency composed of the all EC currencies, weighted according to the size of their economies). Germany and the Netherlands wanted an exchange rate system based on a bilateral parity grid between currencies because it would impose an obligation on countries of any two currencies that reach their limits inside the bilateral band to intervene. For an appreciating currency (the guilder, for example), the Dutch central bank (DNB) would have to sell more guilders. For a depreciating currency (such as the Belgian franc), the Belgian central bank has to buy francs on the foreign exchange markets to arrest its fall. But central banks have limited reserves and cannot indefinitely support a depreciating currency. Hence, a country with a weak currency would have to make domestic policy adjustments first. A strong currency would not have to do much. In contrast, a system based on the ECU would single out the divergent currency whether it would be an appreciating or depreciating one, as opposed to a pair of divergent currencies. The Dutch reasoned that their own domestic objective of price stability would be vulnerable to such rules because the DM was prone to move upward, and a system based on a single unit would more often push Germany to the front line of intervention with unfortunate conse-

[18] The Economist Intelligence Unit, *Country Profile. Belgium, 1991/92* (London: The Economist Intelligence Unit, 1991), 21.

[19] Not everyone thinks that the EMS resulted in a convergence in inflation rate, brought down to the German level. This seems to be a minority view. Susan M. Collings, "PPP and the Peso Problem: Exchange Rates in the EMS," in *International and European Monetary Systems*, ed. Claassen, 99–121.

quences for monetary stability in countries that desired to import policy credibility by pegging their currencies to the German mark.[20]

Once the idea of a single currency area was revived, the discussions among the EC member states centered on how to interpret the provisions and stages outlined by the much earlier 1970 Werner Report on monetary and economic union. The question rose whether a common currency policy was at all feasible without wide-ranging harmonization of fiscal and economic policy. For the Germans and the Dutch, representing the economist view, the answer was that strict economic and budgetary guidelines and binding stabilization programs should precede monetary integration. If not, they claimed, countries with a strong currency like the Federal Republic and the Netherlands would be in danger of importing the inflationary tendencies of the weaker economies or currencies. Weak currency countries like Belgium and France, for identical reasons, argued for a quick monetary union because that would automatically spur policy coordination and economic harmonization. The costs of adjustments would then be shared among weak and strong currency countries. The Germans and the Dutch won this debate.

In general, the Netherlands has not allowed itself any monetary autonomy and voluntarily sets its short- and long-term interest rates according to rates in Germany.[21] This policy is not always unanimously supported. For example, in the fall of 1989, the central bank raised the interest rate by 1 percent following a similar increase by the Bundesbank. The Dutch finance minister criticized the decision because of persistently high unemployment in the Netherlands; a more expansionary budget policy would likely have led to job creation.[22] In response to such criticism, the monetary authorities need only remind governments of the Netherlands' dependence on Germany—27 percent of its trade is with the Federal Republic—and that deviation from German monetary policy leads to inflation, loss of faith in the guilder, higher interest rates, and a deteriorating balance of payments. Al-

---

[20] Giavazzazi and Giovannini, *Limiting Exchange Rate Flexibility: The EMS*, 63. Not everybody agrees. Germany seems to influence short-term but not long-term interest rates, which are more important determinants for consumers and investors. Heinz-Dieter Smeets, "Does Germany Dominate the EMS?" *Journal of Common Market Studies* 29 (1990): 37–52.

[21] Smeets, "Does Germany Dominate the EMS?" 46. Denmark relied on capital controls until 1983 to minimize German influence via interest rates. But since 1983, its short-term rates are set by Germany, and the EMS is a DM zone for Denmark and Holland.

[22] Frederick van der Ploeg, "Towards Monetary Integration in Europe," in *De Europese Monetaire Integratie: Vier visies*, ed. P. de Grauwe et al. (The Hague: Wetenschappelijke Raad voor het Regeringsbeleid, 1989), 91–93.

though central banks admit that a slight depreciation of the guilder vis-a-vis the German mark stimulates exports, the long-term effects include rising import prices and overall worsening export competitiveness. Shadowing the German mark also allows the monetary authorities to keep interest rates as low as possible to stimulate economic growth and diminish the burden of interest payments on the budget deficit.[23] The Netherlands retains some economic autonomy with regard to government spending. As long as the budget deficit is financed through internal means and the domestic capital market, the external balance is unharmed (see Chapter 6).

Dutch monetary diplomacy after the demise of the Bretton Woods system aimed to maintain the internal and external value of the guilder by suppressing inflationary tendencies. It also aimed for a system of fixed exchange rates to promote international trade. Such an exchange rate regime would compel other countries to restore their internal equilibrium. Since the Dutch have encouraged the global spread of economic activities through international investments, it made perfect sense for them to follow the path of the German mark. Since the Netherlands does not believe in capital or exchange controls, crippling capital flows must be prevented through other instruments. The only alternative is to reassure international investors over and over again that the Netherlands will continue to strive for a balanced monetary framework.[24]

The EMS emphasis on disinflation and stable exchange rates conforms with some of the most deeply held convictions of Dutch officials. In fact, during the interwar period, Dutch economists and state officials published academic tracts on the monetary theory of moderate monetarism, which was later implemented by Marinus Holtrop the first postwar president of the central bank.[25] The theory was fully congruent with the aims of the EMS, and the main policy tool was infrequent and microscopic external adjustments and stable internal prices and costs. The DNB never attempted to issue money growth targets and has always argued that in addition to money creation, other aspects of the economic process, such as wage formation and budgetary deficits, are of equal importance for the realization of a balanced and effective

[23] Jan Q. T. Rood, "The Position of the Netherlands: A Lesson in Monetary Union," in *Monetary Implications of the 1992 Process*, ed. Heidemarie Sherman et al. (London: Pinter, 1990), 131.
[24] Folkert de Roos, "De gave Gulden," in *Lessen uit het verleden: 125 jaar vereniging voor de staathuishoudkunde*, ed. A. Knoester (Leiden: Stenfert Kroese, 1987), 128–30; G. A. Kessler, "Wisselkoersbeleid en monetair beleid," in *Lessen uit het verleden*, ed. Knoester, 439–61.
[25] M. M. G. Fase, "Het voorportaal van het Nederlandse monetarisme, 1914–1945," in *Lessen uit het verleden*, ed. Knoester, 133–55.

policy. Exchange rates themselves have never been utilized to strengthen or recover cost competitiveness before or after Bretton Woods. Nonetheless, according to official Dutch statements, it is extremely advantageous for the Netherlands to revoke any pretense of monetary policy independence.[26]

Ironically, the strong guilder ought to have harmed the Netherlands' efficient farming. But for agriculture, the Dutch have access to the expensive Monetary Compensation Amounts (MCA) that have effectively shielded Dutch farmers against lower-cost producers. Agricultural exports, which accounted for 22 percent of total exports in 1989, have been net beneficiaries of the Common Agricultural Policy, a costly program which subsidizes products from high-exchange-rate countries while those from low-exchange-rate countries, such as France and Italy, are penalized.[27]

*Competitive Devaluations and the Credibility Gap in Sweden*

Conventional analysis of trade shares would suggest considerable economic integration between EFTA and the EC in the 1980s. This is not true. Trade barriers other than tariffs and discriminatory policies are much higher in EFTA countries than in the original six members of the EC. Indicative of less integration are the differences between prices in Sweden—where average consumer prices are high for household products, clothing, food, and various services—and average EC prices. Firms sheltered by policies or oligopolistic power have been able to avoid the ramifications of the free trade agreements in different market segments. But the founding members of the Community exhibit very little variation around the sectorial average EC price. In Sweden, the combination of nontariff barriers and a small domestic market enables monopolistic and inefficient practices to go unchecked.[28] This is not surprising; the Social Democrats have selectively protected different parts of the market, often to the benefit of the most viable companies.

Sweden was, of course, not an EMS participant. It did join the

---

[26] G. A. Kessler, "Wisselkoersbeleid en monetair beleid," in *Lessen uit het verleden*, ed. Knoester, 458. The author was the director of the DNB from 1963 to 1981.

[27] Peter M. Hommes, "The Common Agricultural Policy," in *The Netherlands and EC Membership Evaluated*, ed. Menno Wolters and Peter Coffey (London: Pinter, 1990), 41–48.

[28] Thomas Wieser, "European Economic Integration: Concepts, Measurement, and Degree of Nordic Integration," in *The Nordic Countries and the Internal Market of the EEC*, ed. Lise Lyck (Copenhague: Handelshojskolens, 1990), 87–106; Harry Flam and Henrik Horn, "Ekonomiska konsekvenser för Sverige av EGs inre marknad," in *Svensk Ekonomi och Europaintegration*, ed. Peter Englund (Stockholm: Ekonomiska Radet, 1990), 13–101.

"snake," the short-lived precursor of the EMS. Following the loss of confidence in the U.S. dollar in 1972, EC leaders created the snake, in which EC currencies would move up and down within a narrow band. Sweden joined and then left the snake in 1977 after it had become a system for pegging the currency to the German mark. Sweden's departure reflected two different calculations. Although an externally strong currency yielded lower inflation, it also made it very difficult to achieve high employment. Second, the DM parity undermined the competitiveness of Swedish exports and drove up interest rates. After August 1977, the Swedish krona was fixed to a group of fifteen currencies weighted by their respective share in trade with Sweden.[29] One unintended advantage of the pegging to a mixed composite of currencies was that the appreciations of the DM in the mid-1980s were canceled by the fall of the dollar.

Nonparticipation in the EMS gave Sweden a small measure of monetary independence. Deviant fiscal and monetary policies, which were in conflict with the direction of policies in the main European countries, maintained full employment though sharp rises in domestic cost pressures led to inevitable devaluations a few years later. The bourgeois government that ruled from 1976 to 1982 faced an increasingly large cost gap and announced a devaluation in three installments. The first came in October 1976 and was not accompanied by new economic measures. The next two, in April and August 1977, were part of economic packages that marked a major policy shift. Brakes were put on domestic consumption, and prices were temporarily frozen. Lower export prices and lower domestic demand were expected to improve export performance. The wage determination system accommodated the devaluation. Contractual increases in industrial workers' hourly earnings rose by about 12 percent, to which wage drift added under 10 percent, bringing the total increase to about 22 percent from 1977 through 1979. Since consumer prices rose 30 percent in that period, industrial workers took a cut in real, pretax income of more than 8 percent. Wage settlements permitted the devaluation to take effect, and cost improvements were used to reduce relative export prices and to restore profit margins.[30]

When the Social Democrats regained power in 1982, they repeated the devaluation strategy of the previous coalition with impressive re-

[29] OECD, *Exchange Rate Management and the Conduct of Monetary Policy* (Paris: OECD, 1985), 106–11; Niels Thygesen, "Exchange Rate Experiences and Policies of Small Countries: Some European Example of 1970s," *Essays in International Finance* 136 (1979).
[30] Andrew Martin, "Wages, Profits, and Investment in Sweden," in *Politics of Inflation and Economic Stagnation*, ed. Leon Lindberg and Charles S. Maier (Washington, D.C.: Brookings Institution, 1985), 455.

sults. Six years of bourgeois rule had led to a cumulative fall in industrial investment of 38 percent. The 1982 devaluation, coinciding with global trade recovery, replaced this depressing statistic with a surge in investments that canceled the sharp deterioration of previous years. Of course, the timing of the last devaluation was particularly auspicious. With the economic recovery in the United States, demand for merchandise exports rose. The decline in the prices of dollars and oil also occurred at a critical moment, when the positive effect of the devaluation had more or less exhausted itself. Recall that the Swedish krona is fixed to the dollar, whose weight inside the currency group is disproportionate to the size of Sweden's trade with the United States. The drop of the dollar also meant a fall of the krona relative to the European currencies of its main trading partners.

Competitive devaluations, which are only possible with a flexible exchange rate stance, may occasionally work wonders. Of course, Sweden succeeded precisely because other countries clung to their pegged or fixed exchange rates. Sweden, in effect, may have pursued an extremely short-term strategy by choosing an optimal trade-off for which the bill must be paid at some later date. If Sweden is required to sustain repeated currency devaluations to balance its external account, real income will eventually suffer. However, the SAP government has kept its word; it did not devalue the currency in 1985 when capital outflow and new current account deficits put pressure on the exchange rate. Instead, it raised domestic interest rates until the exchange rate had stabilized. Domestic interest rates reached 8 percent over the Eurodollar rate before the current account improved.[31] By 1989, however, Sweden's inflation rate because of an overheated economy and tight labor market had risen to over 7 percent. By comparison, inflation in the Netherlands for that same year was 1.6 percent.

In the past, Swedish Social Democrats tried to stabilize domestic activities by regulating interest rates and by rationing credit. But the deregulation of financial markets in 1986, which had spurred a credit boom and added to spiraling inflation, was soon followed by the final liberalization of foreign exchange movements. In 1989, Sweden removed all foreign exchange controls, making it possible for nonresidents to purchase Swedish interest-bearing securities; the concomitant increased financial flows entailed a further loss of monetary independence. Accordingly, interest rates, which were formerly geared to promoting domestic investment spending, are now used to stabilize currency flows and are market-determined. The growth of foreign

[31] Erik Åsbrink and Lars Heikensten, "Currency Flows in 1985 and Swedish Economic Policy," *Skandinaviska Enskilda Banken Quarterly Review*, no. 1 (1986): 22.

financial commitments has increased Sweden's sensitivity to interest rate differentials and exchange rate expectations, and has thus increased both the openness and dependency of Swedish financial markets and monetary policy on international developments.[32]

In the fall of 1990, foreign speculation against the krona gathered steam as a result of persistently high inflation and a sharp deterioration in the current account. Rumors of an impending devaluation prompted a record currency outflow of Skr 12 billion.[33] In reaction to the lack of confidence in the Swedish economy, in the spring the SAP cut total public expenditures. With the help of the Liberal party, the SAP shepherded through Parliament a plan to raise indirect taxation to 25 percent and to delay the implementation of an annual holiday entitlement of six weeks.[34] Despite these measures, the economic situation deteriorated and forced more stringent cutbacks. The biggest and most symbolic step was the formal abandonment, after six decades, of the policy of full employment. The measure was expected to stimulate market forces and bring down wage drift.

Then, in a long-anticipated statement, former Prime Minister Ingvar Carlsson announced that it was "Sweden's ambition to become a member of the European Community."[35] This declaration reflected the change in the Left's thinking since the 1960s and 1970s.

The foreign affairs committee of the Riksdag had already issued a new position in 1988. The newer view was that Sweden had a vital interest in participating fully in the realization of all the Community's goals except those related to foreign and defense policy. In 1990, Carlsson remarked that the rationale of neutrality had disappeared. These new utterances of the SAP convinced the Liberal and Conservative parties to propose in 1991 that Sweden apply for membership. Social Democrats proclaimed that this would give a "new dimension to an old social democratic aspiration" and that there was "no future for social democracy in isolation".[36]

---

[32] OECD, *Economic Surveys. Sweden 1986/87* (OECD, Paris, 1987), 47. Sveriges Riksbank, "Introduction," *Sveriges Riksbank Quarterly Review*, no. 1 (1990): 5–11.

[33] Robert Taylor, "Sweden's Climate Becomes More Austere," *Financial Times*, 22 October 1990, p. 4.

[34] Robert Taylor, "Welcome for Swedish Austerity," *Financial Times*, 7 April 1990, p. 2.

[35] The cuts are modest and would amount to less than 2 percent of total public expenditures of Skr 892 billion. Some of the measures involve reducing the size of the state bureaucracy by 10 percent and a cut in the level of sickness benefits for the first three days of illness to 75 percent of earnings and 90 percent thereafter. In addition, reducing the school starting age from seven to six years would save about Skr 3 billion on expensive preschool child care programs. The state will also save on a partial privatizaion of the Swedish state sector, such as telecommunications and electricity. Reported by Robert Taylor, "Sweden Unveils Crisis Package," *Financial Times*, 27 October 1990, p. 1, and his "Social Democrats Aim to Cut Public Sector," *Financial Times*, 27 October 1990, p. 2.

[36] Quotations from Kjell Goldmann, "The Swedish Model of Security Policy," *West European Politics* 14 (1991): 138.

The seeds of the Left's turnabout on EC membership were planted already in the mid-1980s and were to some extent unrelated to developments in the Community and the breakdown of Sweden's economic policy machinery. The U.S. embargo on technology transfers to the East also restricted exports to Sweden. This raised the question whether advanced Swedish engineering firms could in fact be internationally competitive if barred from the U.S. market of technology. It also spread doubts about the viability of neutrality. Could Sweden preserve its policy of nonalignment if it were so dependent on imported technology? These questions were extensively discussed in the media.[37] The worried response of the government and business was to call for closer cooperation with European technology programs such as EURAKA. Fears of marginalization prompted Swedish firms to become articulate participants in the European roundtable and to seek regular connections with Brussels.[38]

A different consideration, and of greater consequence for the shift in thinking, involved the widening economic links with the Community. Export markets had shifted from EFTA, where more than half of Sweden's import markets were in 1970, to the Community, where 52 percent of the exports went in 1988. And in 1988, Sweden's net investment in the Community was Skr 22 billion or 70 percent of total net direct investment abroad in 1988.[39] More important, the tools of the past no longer proved effective in curing persistent monetary, economic, or financial imbalances. The strongest evidence of this was Sweden's inflation rate, which was persistently higher than that of its trading partners. In May 1991, the SAP government made the big step of pegging the krona to the ECU.

To combat inflation after the wage determination system had broken down required a credible monetary policy and a strong message to market actors that Swedish authorities would no longer accommodate inflation with devaluations. This was a challenge because Swedish and foreign speculators, financial agents, and investors anticipated an accommodating stance by government. Expectations of accommodation by the monetary authorities impelled holders of Swedish currency to convert to other currencies against which they believed the krona would devalue. With pressures on the krona becoming relentless be-

[37] For example, Sweden's largest daily newspaper, *Svenska Dagbladet*, published several long articles on this topic: for example, Eva Adauktsson, "Svårare exportera teknik," *Svenska Dagbladet*, 28 April, 1986; Johan Myrsten, "Eureka kan minska beroende," *Svenska Dagbladet*, 16 July 1986; Sune Olofson, "Teknikexperter varnar för USA-beroendet," *Svenska Dagbladet*, 13 May 1986.

[38] Daniel Viklund, *Sweden and the European Community: Trade, Cooperation, and Policy Issues* (Stockholm: Swedish Institute, 1989), 28–29.

[39] Ibid., 38.

cause everybody believed that the monetary authorities would soon seek an exchange rate adjustment, a devaluation became nearly inevitable. Central bank officials tried to resist a devaluation by drawing on their reserves and raising interest rates to offset the risks perceived by the financial community of holding Swedish money. Both these options worked temporarily, but the Swedish authorities had to counter expectations about the conduct of monetary policy in a more systemic fashion.

One legislative initiative to break the common perception of accommodating monetary policy was to increase the independence of the central bank by lengthening the term of each governor to five years, from the previous three-year term that coincided with general elections.[40] Then the krona was pegged to the ECU to import credibility. Pegging to the ECU did not allay the doubts of financial asset holders, and the outflow of capital in the fall of 1991 was only arrested after interest rates climbed to an astonishing 24 percent. In the long run, pseudomembership in the EMS requires drastic budgetary, fiscal, and labor market alterations.[41]

Reforms were finally discussed during the third week of September 1992. The currency was again under attack in September, and Sweden was in the midst of yet another battle to stave off an unwanted devaluation. The first line of defense was to increase overnight interest rates to an extraordinary 500 percent to deter speculators from borrowing kronor from the central bank in order to sell them, provoke a devaluation, and buy them back at a tidy profit. A few days later, on September 20, the government introduced its second weapon to fight off the money markets. Realizing that the welfare state is too expensive, the Social Democrats agreed to sign a pact with the government coalition to slash the budget deficit by reducing housing subsidies, workers' sickness benefits, and foreign aid, and by asking employers and unions to pay more for health benefits and sickness insurance. Total spending cuts amounted to $7.6 billion a year to reduce the budget deficit. At the same time, Swedish officials reiterated their belief that Sweden was ready for membership and should be part of the monetary union with EC's stronger economies.

To conclude, the new enthusiasm for joining the EC cannot conceal the end of an era of Social Democratic hegemony. As more financial barriers came down, the steering mechanisms and market intervention methods of the SAP became useless and cumbersome. Financial liberal-

[40] This was decided in 1989; see OECD, *Economic Surveys. Sweden 1990/91*, 50–52.
[41] Gunnar Wetterberg, "Vad kan EMU betyda för Sverige?" *Tiden* 3 (1991): 173–78. *Tiden* is the official organ of the Social Democratic party. Sveriges Riksbank, *Sveriges Riksbank Quarterly Review*, no. 1 (1991): 3–10. Cf. Woolley, "1992, Capital and the EMS," in *Euro-politics*, ed. Sbragia.

ization, however, was itself a response to mounting internal contradictions and global changes in financial markets and instruments.[42] One symptom of these domestic and international changes was the outflow of investment capital by domestic transnational corporations, which rose by 200 percent between 1983 and 1988, and the trend picked up after 1986. Evidently, the rise in capital outflow is directly related to the launching of the internal market project, which more or less coincided with financial liberalization in Sweden.[43]

What might be the gains of membership? The abolition of trade barriers against Sweden would mean that firms located on Swedish soil would be guaranteed full and equal access to the Community market. Foreign investors would be more likely to invest in Sweden if trade barriers were totally eliminated. Otherwise, Sweden would have to promise a very high rate of return to foreign investors by offering lower wages, cheaper land, or more favorable taxes. Swedish companies invested eight times more in the EC than EC firms invested in Sweden—there is clearly room for a better symmetry.[44] In addition, a number of studies seem to suggest that EFTA countries will benefit much more from Project 1992 than longer-standing members in terms of efficiency, lower prices, and the break of monopolistic practices.[45] What might be the costs? Unemployment rose to 7 percent in 1992, the highest rate since the 1930s. This is not to say that EC membership is correlated to high unemployment. Rather, the Community does not care about full employment and does not put any resources behind labor market programs or policies.

*Pseudo-EMS Participation and the Social Partnership in Austria*

It is widely assumed that Austria's conduct of monetary policy follows the EMS stabilization regime because it pegs its currency to the

[42] For a more general treatment of the converging trend toward deregulation and liberalization of financial markets, see Louis W. Pauly, *Opening Financial Markets: Banking Politics on the Pacific Rim* (Ithaca: Cornell University Press, 1988); and the essays in Turig Banuri and Juliet B. Schor, eds., *Financial Openness and National Autonomy: Opportunities and Constraints* (Oxford: Clarendon Press, 1992).

[43] Jan Karl Karlsen, "Economic Integration between the Nordic Countries and the EC—Indications from Data on Direct Investments," in *Nordic Countries and the Internal Market of the EEC*, ed. Lyck 63–73.

[44] Håkan Arnelid, "Vad förlorar och vad vinner vi?" *Tiden* 4 (1991): 246–51; Carl-Einar Stålvant and Carl Hamilton, "Sweden," in *The Wider Western Europe: Reshaping the EC/EFTA Relationship*, ed. Helen Wallace (London: Pinter, 1991), 199–200.

[45] See, for example, Clive Church, "The Politics of Change: EFTA and the Nordic Countries' Responses to the EC in the early 1990s," *Journal of Common Market Studies* 33 (1990): 401–30; Gunnel Gustafsson, "Challenges confronting Swedish decision-makers: Political and Policy Responses, 1974–1987," in *The Politics of Economic Crisis: Lessons from Western Europe*, ed. Erik Damgaard, Peter Gerlich, and J. J. Richardson (Aldershot, U.K.: Avebury, 1989), 146–63.

German mark. It has lost, for all practical purposes, its monetary autonomy. But Austria's pegging to the DM is different from EMS participation because the membership in the Community also involves economic and capital market integration. Austria, as was argued earlier, has been very cautious about opening its financial and capital markets to external influences. A plausible explanation for the strong economic performance of Austria, despite an exchange rate that ties the schilling to the DM, is therefore precisely that Austria's connection with international markets is relatively shallow. A study on real interest deviation and capital mobility indeed concluded that the variation between Austrian rates and the Eurodollar rate was larger than in most developed countries.[46]

Austria is also different from other EMS members in that nothing stands in the way of an exchange rate realignment. In the late 1970s, the Austrian authorities decided that the rate should not change, and it has not. They offset the disadvantages of a hard currency by supplying tax concessions and subsidized interest rates for productive investments and by accelerating the timing of public-sector investments. The Austrians were able to do this precisely because their market is less exposed to international fluctuations and currency movements than those of Belgium or the Netherlands. The economic openness of Austria is qualitatively different because its foreign trade ratio and degree of financial integration are lower. Austria's financial links to the outside world are modest. Austrian holding companies were told not to invest abroad, and small business is more oriented toward the home market.[47] The total share of Austrian direct investments abroad reached 1.62 percent of the GDP in 1985. Austria's large corporation in terms of foreign assets ranked 173rd among the world's three hundred largest corporations in 1978. Ten years later, only 6 percent of the main state holding company (ÖIAG) work force of 96,500 was employed abroad.[48] In Belgium, where foreign direct investments by local firms are also modest, the outstanding share of direct foreign investment was 3.2 percent of the GDP.[49]

As in Sweden, though, many subtle and not so subtle changes point

[46] Jeffrey A. Frankel and Alan T. MacArthur, "Political versus Currency Premia in International Real Interest Differentials: A Study of Forward Rates for 24 Countries," *National Bureau for Economic Research Working Paper*, no. 2309 (1987).

[47] Jean-Pierre Anastassopoulos, Georges Blanc, and Pierre Dussange, *State-Owned Multinationals* (New York: Wiley, 1987), 52.

[48] Hans Hinterhuber, Karl Obernosterer, and Andreas Unterweger, "ÖIAG und IRI—zwei Unternehmen auf dem Weg zu einer neuen Identität," *Wirtschaft und Gesellschaft* 4 (1988): 488.

[49] Claudia Pichl, *Internationale Investionen: Verflechtung der österreichischen Wirtschaft*, WIFO Working Papers, no. 32 (Vienna, 1989), 164.

to painful choices for the future. Germany has always invested heavily in Austria, and its share in foreign direct investments rose by 16 percent in 1988 to double the previous years' flows, as the partially privatized possessions of the state banks and the cast-off divisions of ÖIAG were bought by German private firms.[50] This development ought to worry the Austrian establishment for several reasons. First, the state firms created a buffer between domestic and foreign capital, which enabled government officials and labor representatives to influence investment behavior and business cycles. Reducing the size of the entire state-owned sector would inevitably diminish the steering capacity of Austrian coalition governments. Second, concurrent with the selling off of state-owned property, the ever-larger penetration of German and other foreign investors will eventually augment Austria's sensitivity to the capricious decisions of foreign chief executives and management teams. Already, some industry branches such as electronics and chemicals are practically owned by German transnational corporations.[51] Since affiliates of foreign transnational corporations tend to form global enclaves, there is no guarantee that they would still consider Austria a low-cost country ten years from 1992. As seen from the Belgium case, it is risky to depend upon foreigners for research and development and advanced technology. So it is unfortunate that the subsidiaries of foreign transnational firms in Austria are clustered in the most advanced ranks of manufacturing.[52]

Privatization of the state-owned enterprises gained momentum in 1986, as many public officials and voters recognized that nationalized firms were deprived of critical opportunities if they operated only within the national borders. To privatization and deregulation, a third motto was added: internationalization. Two-thirds of the country's exports were destined for the Community in the late 1980s, and its dependence on the external tariff policy and internal developments of the EC was considerable.[53] But besides trade, Austria has no other economic linkages to the Community because its connections to the global economy are largely passive; it does not actively seek involve-

[50] This is more than ironic since many state-owned companies had initially been reappropriated from Nazi-German possession.

[51] Inge Morawetz, "Schwellenland Österreich? Aktuelle Veränderungen der österreichischen Eigentumsstruktur im Sog der Internationalisierungsstrategien der Bundesrepublik Deutschland," in *In deutscher Hand: Österreich und sein grosser Nachbar?* (Vienna: Verlag für Gesellschaftskritik, 1990), 89; Hans Glatz and Hans Moser, *Ausländische Direktinvestitionen in Österreich: Auswirkungen auf Beschaftigung, Wachstum und Wettbewerbsfähigkeit der Industrie* (Frankfurt: Campus, 1989), 84–90.

[52] Glatz and Moser, *Ausländische Direktinvestitionen in Österreich*, 191–92.

[53] T. Wieser and E. Kitzmantel, "Austria and the European Community," *Journal of Common Market Studies* 33 (1990): 431–50.

ment but rather creates a receptive environment at home for transnational corporations from neighboring countries. While Sweden's companies are safely ensconced inside Community frontiers, Austria's firms are fundamentally uninational and have no foothold in the EC. This delayed internationalization is now viewed as a major threat to Austria's competitiveness and future. Government-sponsored reports have published alarming figures about the small number of jobs abroad controlled by Austrian firms and the minuscule contribution of Austrian foreign investments to gross domestic production. In the late 1980s, Austrian firms had only 23,500 employees abroad, and their foreign activities equalled 1.3 percent of the GDP. Public officials believe that underdeveloped international corporate networks will slow the modernization and capacity utilization of Austrian business and undermine its long-term competitiveness. On top of the lagging industrial rationalization and restructuring in the 1980s, foreign ownership of Austrian assets shifts the impulse for domestic growth to agents beyond the orbit of business-labor exchanges.

The social partnership is therefore poised for change. The selling of state companies implies a shrinking of the buffer that protected the private sector and trade union confederation from external shocks. But at the same time, the acquisition of Austrian firms by foreigners widens Austria's connections with world markets and increases its sensitivity to international disturbances. Changes in the economic structure of Austria and greater international interpenetration catapulted the Association of Austrian Industry into new prominence at the expense of the slightly protectionist and worried voices of small business.[54]

Yet the decision to apply for membership, like the earlier choice not to join, was a typical product of power squabbles between the two main parties. EC membership is treated on a par with the lowering of taxation, eliminating bureaucratic interference, and more privatization of public monopolies and state-owned companies. Many proponents of EC membership freely bring up the metaphor of cleaning Austria of its remaining imperial vestiges and raising the political and economic standards to that of the ostensibly more advanced states of Western Europe.[55]

[54] Margit Scherb, "Die Europäische Gemeinschaft—Objekt österreichischer Begierden: Zum Character der Europäischen Gemeinschaft und des österreichischen Beitrittswünsche," in Der un-heimliche Anschluss: Österreich und die EG, ed. Margit Scherb and Inge Morawetz (Vienna: Verlag für Gesellschaftskritik, 1988), 41–43.

[55] Heinrich Schneider, Alleingang nach Brüssel: Österreichs EG-Politik (Bonn: Europa Union, 1990), provides a detailed account of the events leading up to the application for membership. René Schwok, "The European Free Trade Association: Revival or Collapse?" in The External Relations of the EC: The International Response to 1992, ed. John Redmond (London: Macmillan, 1992), 55–76.

Setting off the membership debate was Alois Mock, the leader of the ÖVP and foreign minister and vice-chancellor after the 1987 election, who was disheartened by the popularity of the SPÖ chancellor Franz Vranitsky, who had a surprising number of admirers in the ÖVP. To revive his own fortunes, Mock, as foreign minister, introduced a new concept: Europe. Under his prodding, the ÖVP adopted the first of its many statements on the new relations between Austria and the EC in 1988.[56] The coalition cabinet appointed several study groups and called in more than two hundred experts to assess the consequences of adopting EC rules and joining the Community. In 1987, neutrality was still a legal obstacle, but the Austrians decided that the Soviet Union had no legitimate grounds for interfering.[57] The ÖVP was especially adamant that Austria should preserve its permanent neutrality as an EC member. The Federation of Austrian Industry and the western provinces were the most insistent that Austria apply sooner rather than later.

In 1988, the simmering feud between the SPÖ and ÖVP became comic as Vranitsy and Mock bickered for several months about who would draft the letter of application for membership and send it to Brussels. Vranitsky felt that the honor should not go to Mock, while the Conservatives strongly believed that membership was their idea and the credit should go to them.[58] After the summer recess of 1989, they reached the solution of a joint approach. But as soon as that was settled, younger Socialists in Parliament exerted pressure on the SPÖ cabinet members not to rush ahead. Opinion polls in early 1989 showed that 44 percent of SPÖ voters were against membership, compared with only 29 percent of ÖVP voters.[59] In the end, the SPÖ agreed on EC membership with the provision that neutrality was nonnegotiable. In late 1989, the application reached Brussels.

The stage was set for reconceptualization of EC-Austrian relations even before the appearance of Gorbachev's perestroika and glasnost. For example, the technology embargo frightened Austria, and senior political leaders spoke of the possible "Albanization" of Austria. The country was at risk of becoming stranded and isolated from its main markets; since 1971 trade with the Eastern bloc had dropped from 12 to 7 percent while that with the EC had risen from 39 to 63 percent of total exports.[60]

This reorientation in trade corresponded with a shift in the balance of influence between enterprises from the eastern and western pro-

---

[56] Melanie A. Sully, *A Contemporary History of Austria* (New York: Routledge, 1990), 58.
[57] Ibid., 121–23.
[58] Paul Luif, "Austria," in *The Wider Western Europe*, ed. Wallace, 128–29.
[59] Sully, *Contemporary History of Austria*, 129.
[60] Alois Mock "A View from Vienna," *International Affairs* (Moscow) 2 (1989): 15–19.

vinces. Small- and medium-size firms from eastern Austria dominated the federal Chamber of Commerce, and the governing body had been very reluctant to press for integration. The regions bordering Eastern bloc countries experienced a cumulation of economic and industrial problems with the turmoil in Eastern Europe, which strangled foreign trade, and with the precarious state of many nationalized firms. But businesses in the western regions fared much better in the 1980s precisely because of their location and chance to take advantage of the fruits of accelerating regional integration in the EC. The prosperous firms from the western regions gained in influence and demanded a quick decision on membership.[61] In late 1987, the federal Chamber of Commerce finally endorsed full participation in the EC.

### EMU and Enlargement

The addition of Austria and Sweden to the European Community, coupled with the reemergence of Social Democratic parties in the Belgian and the Dutch cabinets, might alter the tenor of deliberations in the European Council or the Commission. Rather than stressing market deregulation and competition, a Council of Ministers under Social Democratic leadership would naturally be concerned with social reforms and democratization of Community institutions. If voters in Germany reelect leftist governments after their long absences, social welfare or a social dimension would be even more likely to head the EC's list of priorities. The coming to power of conservative or center-right coalitions in the early 1980s undoubtedly lent extra weight to the internal market initiative. The rightward shifts in Britain, Belgium, Denmark, and the Netherlands, to name a few prominent examples, were accompanied by an offensive against government interventionism and market intrusions and brought government legislation to free market forces and strengthen corporate profitability. A simultaneous leftward shift in several countries might bring a renewed emphasis on collective goods and egalitarianism at the Community level.

Any movement at the EC level on behalf of social concertation or progressive social policy programs seems highly unlikely. Although the EMS has become more symmetric in that the number of realignments has declined since 1987 as a consequence of convergent inflation rates and a less pronounced differential between the inflation rates of weak currency and strong currency countries,[62] financial liberalization and

---

[61] Luif, "Austria," in *The Wider Western Europe*, ed. Wallace, 135.

[62] Francesco Giavazzi and Luigi Spaventa, "The 'New' EMS," in *European Monetary System in the 1990s*, ed. de Grauwe and Papademos, 63–84.

monetary coordination continues to constrain independent economic policy-making and restricts Keynesian-style demand management. The establishment of the Economic and Monetary Union (EMU) also offers no reason to assume that the Community will have a stronger social democratic profile.

In the Treaty of Maastricht, negotiated in December 1991, the heads of states of the EC are committed to adopting a single currency by 1996 and to reach the stage of the EMU no later than January 1999. EC leaders have set a series of tough criteria for countries to meet before they could move to a single currency. In fact, the criteria are so rigid that few countries would have qualified in 1992. For example, a successful candidate should have an inflation rate of no more than 1.5 percent above the average of the three EC countries with lowest price rises. National budget deficits must be less than 3 percent of the GDP, and public debt ratio must not exceed 60 percent of the GDP.

Until the arrival of the single currency in 1997, central bankers will be the prime movers behind a country's preparations for the big decision in 1999. After the EMU comes into being, central banks will turn into national offices of the European Central Bank (ECB) and lose all their independence. The management of EMU would entail a high degree of centralization of monetary authority in the European Central Bank whose constitution strikingly aproximates the structure, mandate, and independence of the German Bundesbank. The ECB's central objective is to maintain price stability and, "without prejudice to the objective of price stability," support the general economic policies of the Community. Both the ECB and the national central banks are not to seek or take instructions from the Community or member states and are to be as independent of political interference as the German Bundesbank. Justifiably, Chancellor Kohl could proudly declare that the conditions of the EMU "matched anything we have in Germany."[63]

For the economic elite in Belgium and the Netherlands, the establishment of the EMU and the creation of a European central bank are seen as major and long overdue accomplishments. Both countries see no reason to object to submitting their monetary policy decisions to ex ante coordination within the Committee of Central Bank Governors.[64] In the rounds of debates on the final phase in monetary integration, the Dutch position, like the German, was to await the parallel economic development of member countries before moving ahead. The tough requirements for EMU entry are therefore considered not more than

[63] *The Economist*, 14 December 1991, p. 52.
[64] Niels Thygesen, "Institutional Developments in the Evolution from EMS towards EMU," in *European Monetary System in the 1990s*, ed. de Gauwe and Papademos, 5.

normal.[65] Neither Belgium nor the Netherlands meets the standards for economic and monetary convergence. Belgium had a budget deficit of 6 percent and public debt of 129 percent of the GDP in 1991. The Netherlands' budget deficit was 4.4 percent of the GDP, and its public debt was 78 percent of the GDP in 1991. The center-left coalition governments in both countries must therefore start to think again about drastic savings and reductions in the future budgets. The room for social democratic Keynesianism is simply not there.

Ironically, Sweden satisfied the economic-convergence conditions for European monetary union because its general government budget was no more than 3 percent of the GDP, and its outstanding public debt was less than 60 percent of the GDP in late 1991. Inflation is likely to fall to 3 percent in 1992.

Carl Bildt, the new prime minister, and his partners in the Conservative-Liberal-Center coalition learned a lesson from their earlier experience in power (1976–82). Three years is not much time to turn things around, and the cabinet has decided to push ahead as quickly as possible with the membership application. The coalition has promised to hold a national referendum in 1994 to decide on EC accession. If everything goes as planned, Sweden will enter the EC in 1995. Whether Brussels is prepared to act on such short notice is doubtful. Enlargement is not a burning issue for the Community, although Austria and Sweden are first in line to be accepted as new members.

In preparation for accession, the Austrian central bank is busily strengthening its cooperative mechanism with the Community and the governors of EC central banks. Since 1990, regulations concerning foreign exchange, foreign banks, and short-term currency flows have been brought into conformity with EC guidelines. Domestic banks will now face greater competition from foreign banks, and domestic banks are asked to apply EC capital reserve ratios. Moreover, in the words of Hellmuth Klauhs, the former president of the Austrian central bank, there is no trepidation in Austria about transferring a part of monetary sovereignty to an independent European central bank.[66] Austria, too, unlike Belgium and the Netherlands, meets the criteria for membership in the EMU. In 1991, its budget deficit was less than 3 percent of the GDP, and the federal government debt was less than 50 percent of the GDP. This is to say that both Austria and Sweden have already

---

[65] Jan Q. T. Rood, "The Position of the Netherlands: A Lesson in Monetary Union," in *Monetary Implications of the 1992 Process*, ed. Sherman et al., 140.

[66] Hellmuth Klauhs, "Europäische Währung und Europäische Zentralbank aus österreichischer Sicht," in *Die Europäische Zentralbank*, ed. Otmar Franz (Bonn: Europa Union, 1990), 83–89.

laid the foundations for participating in Europe's most ambitious project of creating a new European political entity. They accomplished this only by abandoning the core tenets of social democratic Keynesianism and by allowing unemployment to rise according to fluctuations in the demand and supply of labor. Their accession will not give the Community a stronger leftist character.

# CHAPTER TEN

# The Future of
# Social Democracy

Is the erosion of social concertation unavoidable? Could social democratic politics and class arrangements be revived? The answers, I believe, must be given with care and must differentiate between domestic/national and European/transnational politics. At the national level, social concertation is no longer feasible; at the European level, some elements could be revived. Whether this revival will happen hinges on how class politics unfold in the new regulatory space created by the leaders of the European Community.

At the national level, social concertation crumbled first in Belgium and the Netherlands, although it lasted through the 1980s in Austria and Sweden. Because the Low Countries had stronger and wider links with international markets, they were more sensitive, perhaps overly so, to shifts in international competition. Heightened economic vulnerability challenged strategies previously formulated to cope with external exposure to international market forces. Rather than attributing the decline of social concertation to exhausted labor power resources, the factor most often mentioned in the comparative political economy literature, my analysis centers on the growth of transnationalism of business and finance and its effect on social protection or compensation.

It is worth repeating that the Left in Belgium and the Netherlands was not as marginal or inferior as cross-national behavioral studies on the role of socioeconomic institutions in policy outcomes often assume. Undoubtedly, the political elite in each of the four countries created venues to foster social exchanges between labor and business after 1945. In the 1960s, collective wage bargaining and centralized pay agreements characterized the industrial relations system in Austria and Sweden as well as in Belgium and the Netherlands. Governments legislated a plethora of social programs to strengthen the economic security of wage earners and to better the standard of living of the disadvantaged. Social solidarity also characterized many centralized settlements because pay leveling and income redistribution dominated wage bargaining from the 1960s until the end of the 1970s. The only exception to this trend was in Austria where the trade union confederation exchanged egalitarian pay scales for full employment and control over nationalized industries.

Considering that each of the four countries developed institutions specifically to foster social concertation and that governments in each of the four countries created large welfare states to protect society from external fluctuations, the declining fortunes of social concertation in the 1980s call for further investigations.

My explanation for the decline of social concertation in small European countries accepts the view that industrial relation systems, financial markets, and economic policy-making had to adjust to the changing nature of international economic competition. For example, reforms of financial markets were instituted to stay ahead of competing foreign markets and new financial instruments. Alternatively, government cabinets redefined policy agendas to stimulate the supply side of the economy and impose greater wage and price discipline, while centralized wage bargaining underwent decentralization to permit greater flexibility in setting wages and regulating working conditions. In each instance, external pressures forced restructuring of domestic institutions until they corresponded to parallel trends taking place in neighboring countries. The converging movement toward greater market-determined social relations and economic decisions underscores the extent to which national jurisdiction or sovereignty has been eclipsed by the transnational growth of capital. Moreover, high capital mobility, which is among the most visible driving forces behind market liberalization, not only influenced the policy agenda of governments and various institutionalized market relations but also shifted the burden of economic and social adjustment onto labor.[1]

High capital mobility and deepening financial integration prompt governments to remove or alter institutions and practices objectionable to business and finance. In a world of free capital markets, national governments compete against each other to offer the environment most conducive to transnational business and international finance. This competition usually implies the removal of so-called labor market and social-welfare rigidities.

[1] Juliet B. Schor, Introduction to *Financial Openness and National Autonomy*, ed. Tariq Banuri and Juliet B. Schor (Oxford: Clarendon Press, 1992), 1–14.

Remarkably, the processes of adjustment, although moving along parallel paths, began more swiftly and earlier in some small European countries than others. Social arrangements in Belgium and the Netherlands were more vulnerable to external shocks because financial integration and business internationalization had made considerably more progress by the early 1980s than in Austria and Sweden. An obvious mediating factor is EC membership and subsequent participation in the European Monetary System. The EMS was supposed to undercut monetary autonomy, and it did. The removal of exchange controls and financial liberalization coupled with a semifixed exchange rate led governments to rein in spending programs and curb policy initiatives deemed inflationary.[2] Community membership and EMS participation also hold a country hostage to sudden capital flows, preventing governments from taking the steps needed to conserve corporatist interest mediation.

An example of how EMS membership interferes with the sort of macroeconomic management compatible with redistributive politics is the pressure on participating governments to maintain low inflation and monetary stability. Unemployment or growing pay discrepancies are tolerated in order to obtain price stability and a stable exchange rate. Such monetarist norms are slowly assimilated by policy officials as central banks demand and receive more bureaucratic leeway to ensure that price stability and a stable exchange rate are indeed procured. In general, financial integration within the framework of the EMS has meant following the monetary and economic decisions of Europe's currency, the German mark. In the summer of 1992, the preoccupation of the German central bank with the currency's stability and its function as the guarantor of German economic well-being produced extraordinarily high interest rates, resulting in rising unemployment and slower economic growth in the rest of the Community. Nothing else elucidates so well the decline of national autonomy and the resulting constraints on social concertation. The latter cannot exist unless governments intervene by bridging the opposing interests of business and labor by ensuring an overall healthy climate for job creation and investments. But the Keynesian route of full employment no longer exists in a world of free capital markets and monetary integration.

In addition to the EC and the EMS, domestic structural factors also contributed to the qualitatively different degrees of economic vulnerability in the two pairs of countries I have examined. In the Nether-

---

[2] John Grahl and Paul Teague, "A New Deal for Europe?" in *Towards a New Europe? Structural Change in the European Economy*, ed. Ash Amin and Michael Dietrich (Aldershot: Edward Elgar, 1992), 166–90; John N. Smithin, "European Monetary Arrangements and National Economic Sovereignty," in *Towards a New Europe?* 191–212.

lands and Belgium, business developed strong preferences for transnational linkages well before the acceleration in European integration in the early 1980s. The stronger international orientation of business and the multiple connections of the financial community with international markets also shaped monetary and central bank decisions in that a stable currency and capital market liberalization preoccupied state officials before the founding of the EMS. Membership in the EC complemented and reinforced the general predilection for liberalization and integration.

By comparison, finance and business in Austria and Sweden acquired somewhat different interests or preferences. Neither became as internationally oriented as similar economic actors in Belgium and the Netherlands. In Sweden, finance was homebound, while in Austria both finance and business possessed strong and extensive ties to the home market. Accordingly, monetary policy in both Austria and Sweden was more integrated into domestic arrangements, and central bankers were more attuned to the social priorities and electoral considerations of political leaders while simultaneously less dedicated to opening the domestic market to external forces.

Whether neutrality was compatible with European Community membership was widely questioned. In addition, political leaders and the economic establishment in both Austria and Sweden felt ambivalent about the integration process and believed that the EC framework would irrevocably harm their most cherished accomplishments: in Sweden, organized labor and some sections of business feared the impact of EC membership on social welfare statism; in Austria, policy officials and interest groups feared losing political control over heavy manufacturing. In short, a mixture of factors associated with a country's relationship to the EC and the prior preferences of business and finance determined the degree of economic vulnerability to external shocks in the two sets of countries. Subsequently, a higher or lower degree of economic vulnerability determined the fate of social concertation in the 1980s.

In the end, social partnerships in Austria and Sweden have not escaped unharmed. Internal tensions, together with the diminishing effectiveness of instruments used to foster class compromises, pushed elected and state officials into designing solutions that often entailed the dismantlements of precisely those mechanisms that had shielded the domestic market from international disturbances. Two examples, one from Austria and the other from Sweden, will illustrate this point. Let us first take a look at Sweden.

I have argued that the opening of the financial market in Sweden in the mid-1980s was the product of a gradual reassessment of the costs and effectiveness of credit restrictions and banking prohibitions. Increased monetary volatility of the previous years and the precarious health of the commercial banks in the late 1970s, which were burdened by credit restrictions and other rules, gave the authorities no choice other than to reevaluate the numerous banking and credit regulations in existence since the 1950s. Private commercial banks lost customers and earnings because alternative finance houses, unencumbered by banking restrictions, could offer a wider variety of services at lower costs. Since this situation was unacceptable in the long run, officials had the option of extending credit regulations to the new finance companies or of abolishing restrictions on commercial banks. Re-regulating the credit market was impossible as the costs and complexity had risen with the surge in inflation and exchange rate variability. The authorities therefore decided to abolish credit restrictions and compulsory credit allocations.

On the one hand, the removal of restrictions gave the commercial banks more freedom to compete at home and abroad. On the other, it questioned the legitimacy of barring international banks or international financial institutions from the Swedish market. These prohibitions had been enacted to protect the private banks from unfair competition from foreign banks exempt from domestic credit rules. After several years of deliberation, the monetary authorities and the Social Democratic government removed restrictions on foreign banks and permitted them to open branches in Sweden. The removal of barriers against capital and financial flows after the mid-1980s drew the country closer into the orbit of international markets. Policy officials subsequently discovered that budget programs and economic policy trends fed into capital outflows and currency speculation. Currency crises and falling confidence in the krona required a reversal of policy intentions and greater attention to price stability. The Swedish central bank, which had previously conducted an accommodating monetary regime, was unable to arrest the speculation against the krona because financial asset holders acted as though the central bank would accommodate the fall of the krona in foreign exchange markets through a devaluation. General apprehension among investors about Swedish monetary conditions coincided with the passing of the Single European Act by EC leaders in 1986. Financial uncertainty at home and increased opportunities abroad spurred Swedish companies to divest, and capital outflows rose significantly after 1986.

In response to capital and financial outflows, the political establishment decided to increase the authority of the central bank and to peg the krona to the ECU (the composite currency of the EC). Both measures constituted a major departure from traditional Social Democratic intervention, using an array of monetary and fiscal instruments to minimize social and economic dislocation. The emphasis of first Social Democratic then bourgeois cabinets shifted away from full employment and economic growth to price stability and a stable exchange rate.

A similar mixture of domestic and international factors increased the international openness of the Austrian economy to challenge the government's steering capacity. The state holding companies were a critical link between trade union federation, government strategy, and tripartite bargaining. They brought labor and business together in a common concern for the well-being of the state-owned companies and legitimized recurrent wage concessions in the eyes of the trade union federation and rank and file. Labor acceded to wage moderation because full employment was guaranteed by a policy of not laying off workers in the state holding companies during periods of economic downturn. However, fraud, inefficiencies, and declining productivity turned public opinion against the holding companies and prompted politicians to consider privatization. Privatization in Austria's small capital market and the need to modernize the state-owned companies that remain in the public sector could only be done by extending Austria's relations with international markets. Austria has always had a one-way relationship with transnational capital: the latter invested in Austria. In the near future, the web of interaction will be more complex in that banking liberalization and greater foreign direct investment activities will pull Austria further into the international political economy. In a situation analogous to that in Sweden, external pressures on domestic institutions or routines were relived by seeking wider involvement in international markets. Moreover, the piecemeal adoption of neoliberal prescriptions to bolster productivity and profitability moves Austria and Sweden closer to Belgium and the Netherlands.

In the light of the troubles with tripartite redistributive arrangements in the four European democracies discussed here, our assumptions about the ability of small states to withstand international pressures must be reconsidered. If anything, it appears that small states are less capable of protecting their citizens from the vicissitudes of world markets despite long acquaintance with foreign trade dependence. At best, we can say that small states fared as well as larger countries. But it would be difficult to argue that the adjustment programs of small countries show greater adaptability, are more responsive to social dislocation, or are more likely to spread the burden of adjustments among different sectors of society.[3] In the preceding chapters I have

[3] Cf. Peter Katzenstein, *Small States in World Markets* (Ithaca: Cornell University Press, 1985).

pointed out that the macroeconomic performances of Belgium and the Netherlands were among the worst in the OECD and that the adjustment costs fell disproportionately on organized labor and the welfare state.

Nor is it very helpful to view class compromises as arrangements that reduce the costs of economic fluctuations emanating from external shocks.[4] Although economic vulnerability may be deeply embedded in the institutional foundation of a small country's policy strategies, this practice has not prepared them for the shifts and costs of new competition during the 1980s. Class compromises, tripartite redistributive arrangements, and corporatist interest mediation cannot cope with capital mobility and deepening financial integration. While Austria and Sweden seem to have weathered the 1980s in relatively good shape, this achievement must be traced to their limited exposure to international disturbances or, paradoxically, to decreased openness. Their economic openness and vulnerability were moderate because capital mobility and financial integration were held at bay through administrative rulings until the late 1980s. Class compromises survived in Austria and Sweden longer than in Belgium or the Netherlands not because they were meant to diffuse exogenous pressures but rather because these two countries were not part of the EC or the EMS. Moreover, they turned down EC membership partly because their business and finance sectors did not depend on transnational activities to the same extent as those in Belgium and the Netherlands.

This conclusion is confirmed by the real and growing threats to the vaunted Swedish Social Democratic model. Not only are central wage bargaining and solidaristic pay strategies at risk but the total social welfare system faces serious restructuring. Nonetheless, Swedish business, regardless of tax reductions and smaller public-sector expenditures, plans to focus on further cross-national expansion and globalization. Business is firmly committed to dismantling centralized wage bargaining and to further public-sector cuts. The defeat of the Swedish model is unexplainable in the theoretical frameworks built on the concept of labor power and social democratic hegemony.

Nor do these theories adequately account for the surprising durability of the Austrian social partnership. After all, Austrian organized labor faces an equally organized conservative bloc. Ranking countries along a scale of social democratic achievements, as measured by public spending, social legislation, and commitment to egalitarianism, puts

---

[4] Cf. David R. Cameron, "The Expansion of the Public Economy," *American Political Science Review* 72 (1978): 1243–61; Francis G. Castles, *Australian Public Policy and Economic Vulnerability: A Comparative and Historical Perspective* (Boston: Allen and Unwin, 1988).

Austria behind Belgium and the Netherlands, and far behind Sweden. Despite years of Socialist party rule, social democratic values and ideas do not permeate Austrian society. Yet the Austrian Social Democratic party (it jettisoned "Socialist" for "Social Democratic" in 1990) preserved centralized wage bargaining and the broad outlines of the social partnership into the 1980s. One plausible explanation for the remarkable resilience of the Austrian domestic arrangement is the dominance of banks and firms with undeniable home-market orientations and Austria's relatively one-dimensional connection to world markets. Not that Austria has remained unchanged; the public sector is trimmer; public budget deficits have been slashed; and various components of economic life have been liberalized. Nonetheless, of the four countries discussed, Austria has experienced the mildest economic tremors during the 1980s.

The findings of this book therefore raise a second question about the putative relation between historical patterns of policy making and small European countries. There might very well be some association between sensitivity to external fluctuations and consensual compensation policies. However, a causal relation between a country's position in the world economy and the evolution of its institutions and policy outcomes is far from obvious. Only in small countries, where protectionist attitudes among business and state officials prevail and barriers against international capital or financial markets exist, do class compromises have a chance to resist and absorb external shocks. Truly open, integrated small economies cannot sustain a politics of redistribution and consensual deliberation. Thus, in small countries that carefully filter their involvements and linkages with international markets, domestic compensation schemes function in the way in which they are supposed to operate. But in small countries with numerous international and cross-national linkages, social arrangements are pointless endeavors, unable to protect society against the repercussions of economic vulnerability.

## Social Concertation and Social Democracy in the Future

Class politics as we once knew it will not return any time soon. This form of political contest was premised on a precarious balance of power between labor and capital, an accommodation in which business promised to reinvest profits to sustain full employment and future economic growth while labor promised to moderate wage demands and to settle conflicts amiably. This understanding has broken down because business and capital have outgrown the institutional boundaries of the nation-state and national working-class organizations. Nonetheless, national trajectories of the collapse of domestic arrangements vary just as national histories of the emergence of social concertation differ. Which factors determine how labor parties and movements respond to the shifts in international competitiveness and production are more often than not a function of how business and finance connect with international markets. The more internationalized business and finance are, the more likely that social concertation will fail.

Because the trend in the advanced industrialized world is toward ever-increasing financial integration and business internationalization, national accords between labor, government, and capital are unlikely to reemerge. The evidence in this book does not hold great promise for social democracy. Core ideas regarding Keynesian economic management and social democratic ideology have ceased to be a source of alternative ideas and electoral appeal. This is not to say that social democratic parties will fade away. On the contrary, left-wing parties will continue to seek election and occasionally win power. However, these parties have little in common with their predecessors in terms of articulating progressive options and pursuing programs different from the conservative, or establishment, view.

In its attempt to achieve greater economic justice, redistribution, and solidarity, the Left needs the tacit cooperation of business or capital because only through sustained economic growth and continuous reinvestment can a country increase prosperity. In the past decade, growth has been sluggish, and investments have stagnated. Unemployment and declining wages marked the 1980s. Governments could combat such situations by spending money on public programs, increasing public employment, or raising social transfer payments, but no government can afford to do this today. Budget deficits from past spending programs hamper further expansion of public programs. More important, monetary integration and liberalization have made every high-spending government vulnerable to financial asset holders. Expectations of increased inflation, reflecting proposals to increase budget spending or to lower interest rates, motivate financial asset holders to invest in other, more stable currencies. Central bankers have access to foreign exchange reserves to bolster the currency in international markets. But once reserves are depleted, the monetary authorities must consider a devaluation. If a country participates in the EMS, other member states will request an austerity program to prevent another run on the currency and to enhance the credibility of the reform package of the devaluating country.

Increased capital mobility constrains expansionary policy action, which hurts social democratic governments more than conservative ones. Financial deregulation and monetary integration mesh well with the neoliberal reforms aimed at shrinking the roles of the state and the public sector. Deregulation and liberalization reinforce the political platform of right-wing governments to trim social programs, privatize state-owned companies, and reduce public employment. The opposite is true for left-wing governments, which base their appeal on redistribution, egalitarianism, full employment, and expensive social welfare programs.

Is there then no future at all for progressive political movements? Left-wing parties could find a future in supporting and influencing the form of European integration. With the new contours and competences of the institutions of the Community still undecided, the Left has the opportunity to influence the future of Europe itself. If social democratic parties and their allies miss this critical opportunity, they will fail to counter the influence of capital at the European level and will fail to inject a progressive element into the supranational European regulatory space. Possibly, the launching of a European campaign could also invigorate worn-out social democratic parties and labor movements.

National leaders have not done much to explain to their electorates how the European Monetary Union will come about and what it implies for national politics. Left-wing parties should seize this omission to educate voters on the various deficiencies of the ambitious program of a united internal market. Pointing out the lack of accountability in the proposed structure is one obvious way the Left can become involved in the European project. What cannot be changed is the way in which various domestic institutions are forced to come to terms with the changes in the structure of international competition, production, and financial mediation. A consolidation of social concertation at the European level seems therefore highly implausible. Therefore, the Left should focus instead on the procedures of intergovernmental bargaining and elitist decision making to steer the Community into the direction of implementing a social dimension or charter. Market mechanisms on their own will not result in an equitable distribution of gains from the establishment of the internal market. With unemployment already high, the internal market will continue to burden disadvantaged sectors or groups.

Another convincing argument for taking the European project seriously is that the structural power of international capital owes much of its strength to the division of the world in competing states and labor movements. Only a Europe-wide labor movement and a united social democratic bloc can obstruct a further accumulation of power in the hands of big business and international capital. Representatives of Europe's largest corporations have numerous connections with Brussels and the Commission. The national confederations of trade unions of the member states have not developed an equally sophisticated network of contacts and organizational bodies to deal with the Community bureaucracy. Organized labor in general has played a very limited role in the process of European integration. We can only hope that the European social democratic parties will soon wake up and realize that they are the only organized interests truly committed to a European social space, one that encompasses not only a social charter but also guarantees for industrial democracy, codetermination, and European social solidarity. There is a future for social democratic parties and labor movements, although it is linked to progress in transnational governance structures and European politics.

# Index

Agrarian party (Sweden), 25, 212, 214
Agriculture: in Austria, 205; in the
 Netherlands, 197, 229
Alpine-VÖEST, 101
AMRO-ABN, 141, 145
Anschluss, 37, 201n
AP-fund, 182–84
Article 90, 207
Article 238, 205, 210
ASEA, 126, 129, 130
Association of Austrian Industry (VÖI),
 34, 106, 173, 238; and European
 Community, 203, 209, 240
Association of Dutch Enterprises (VNO),
 27, 46–47, 109–10; and central bank
 policy, 142; and corporatism, 48, 64–
 65; and the EC, 198; and financial reforms, 148; and incomes policy, 64–
 65, 110; and neoliberalism, 68; politicization of, 111–12
Association of European Industry (UNI-
 CE), 201
Austerity measures: in Belgium, 62–64,
 223; and EMS exchange rate realignment, 225; in the Netherlands, 68–69,
 223; in Sweden, 74, 134, 189, 232,
 234
Austrian People's party (ÖVP), 33; and
 the central bank, 166, 168; divisions
 within, 204, 206; and the EC, 204,
 206–8, 239; and small business, 109;
 and state holding companies, 34, 99,
 102–3

Austrian Socialist party (SPÖ): and the
 central bank, 166–68; and the EC,
 204, 207–8, 239; and the nationalized
 sector, 34–35, 38n, 77, 99, 103, 107;
 and neutrality, 207; and policy-
 making, 74–76; in the 1990 election,
 77
Austrian Trade Union Confederation
 (ÖGB): and the central bank, 162;
 and hard currency policy, 172, 174;
 and nationalized industries, 35–36,
 105–6; and the People's party, 33; and
 price stability, 165
Austro-Keynesianism, 75

Ball, George, 205
Bank Act of 1935, 45, 153–54
Banking Commission, 152–53; and increased regulatory impact, 225; and
 weakened authority, 155
Bekaert, Leon, 201
Belgian public debt, 63, 153, 157, 159,
 223, 226, 242
Belgian Socialist party (PS/SP): and the
 crisis of the franc, 161; during the
 economic crisis of the 1970s, 160; and
 the ECSC, 200, 215; and foreign companies, 93; and holding companies,
 93, 155; return to office of, 55; and
 the steel crisis, 88; and the 1982 devaluation, 161
Belgian trade union confederation: and
 austerity, 64; and centralized wage de-

Merchant houses, 31
Mitterrand, François, 8
Mixed banks: in Austria, 36–38; in Belgium, 43, 45, 129, 153–55, 199
Mock, Alois, 239
Monetary Compensation Amounts (MCA), 229
Monetary credibility, 222
Monetary policy, 21; of Austria, 169–70, 172, 175; of Belgium, 158–61; comparison of, 189–90; of the Netherlands, 51, 115, 118, 144, 151; of Sweden, 33, 176, 178–82
Monetary Policy Act (1980), 180
Monetary Policy Measures Act (1974), 179
Monetary restrictiveness: in Austria, 169, 171–72; in Belgium, 159–60; in the Netherlands, 51, 144, 149, 151, 227

National Bank of Austria (OeNB), 39, 164; and anti-inflation policy, 138; and commercial banks, 166; compared to DNB, 168; and the EMU, 242; and hard currency policy, 170–72; interest rate policy of, 171–72; and pegging to DM, 236, 238; political dependence of, 137, 167–69, 175; and protectionism, 174; and social partnership, 138
National Bank of Belgium (NBB/BNB), 138, 139, 152; autonomy of, 156–57; and crisis of the franc, 160–61, 163, 223; and the EMU, 241; and increased regulatory power, 225; and parliament, 153, 155; and views on exchange rate stability, 159–60
Nationale Bank van België/Banque Nationale de Belgique. *See* National Bank of Belgium
National Pension Insurance Fund, 177
Nationalized sector: comparison of, in Austria and Belgium, 40; politics in, 34, 100; and private business, 35; size of, 38
NATO, 203, 210
Nazi Germany, 45, 47, 95, 237n
Neutrality: of Austria, 201–5, 210; and business, 203, 209, 214; of the Netherlands, 50, 197; of Sweden, 129–31, 201–2; and technological embargo, 233
Neutrality Act, 204, 210
Nokin, Max, 201
NORDEK, 211
Norway, 211

Oesterreichische Nationalbank. *See* National Bank of Austria
ÖIAG. *See* State holding companies
Österreichischer Gewerkschaftsbund. *See* Austrian Trade Union Confederation
Österreichische Volkspartei. *See* Austrian People's party

Palme, Olof, 211, 213
Parliament: in Austria, 99, 201, 239; in Belgium, 63, 155, 215, 225; in the Netherlands, 111; in Sweden, 30, 211
Partij van de Arbeid. *See* Labor party, Dutch
Pay disparity: in Austria, 35, 105–6; in Sweden, 31
Peace settlement of 1918, 37
Pension funds. *See* Institutional investors
Petrocurrency effect, 149
Philips, 110–11, 114
Planned economy, 131
Power resources: failures of, of Dutch and Belgian labor, 57; theory of, 9, 16, 17, 20, 77, 244
Protectionism: in Austria, 169, 172–73; in the Netherlands, 198; in Sweden, 129, 186–87, 229
Provost, Pol, 201
Przeworski, Adam, 9–11
Public spending, 4, 10, 21; in Belgium and the Netherlands, 69; in the Netherlands, 18, 46, 67

RABO, 145
Research and development: in the Netherlands, 113; in Sweden, 125
Rest, van den Pierre, 210
Riksdag, 211

Saab-Scania, 123, 130
Saltsjöbaden, 40
Savings banks, 154, 156
Schumann Plan, 200, 215
Shell, 110–12, 114, 124
Siemens, 97n
Single European Act, 195
Skandinaviska Enskilda Banken (SEB), 32, 183
SKF, 126, 129, 133
Small business, 109–10, 113, 126–27
Small state argument, 12–14, 77–78, 250–51
Social Christian party (CVP/PSC): actions of, in the 1980s, 223; and austerity in the 1980s, 55, 62–63, 80; and business associations, 40; and crisis of the franc, 161, 224; and prominence

*Cornell Studies in Political Economy*

EDITED BY PETER J. KATZENSTEIN

Library of Congress Cataloging-in-Publication Data

Kurzer, Paulette.
  Business and banking : political change and economic integration in Western Eu-
rope / Paulette Kurzer.
      p.   cm. — (Cornell studies in political economy)
  Includes bibliographical references and index.
  ISBN 0-8014-2798-3 (alk. paper)
      1. European Economic Community countries—Economic policy—Case studies.   2.
  Banks and banking, Central—European Economic Community countries.   3.
  Europe—Economic integration.   4. Austria—Economic policy.   5. Sweden—
  Economic policy.   I. Title.   II. Series.
HC240.K797   1993
332.1'1'094—dc20                                                92-56780